The Florida Keys Paddling Guide

The Florida Keys Paddling Guide

From Key Largo to Key West

Bill Keogh

BACK COUNTRY

BACKCOUNTRY GUIDES
WOODSTOCK, VERMONT

ISBN 0-88150-544-7
ISSN 1547-2191

Cover and interior design by Faith Hague
Composition by Chelsea Cloeter
Cover and interior photographs by the author
Line drawings © Sali Binard
Maps by Paul Woodward, © 2003 The Countryman Press

Published by Backcountry Guides,
a division of The Countryman Press,
P.O. Box 748, Woodstock, Vermont 05091

Distributed by W.W. Norton & Company, Inc.,
500 Fifth Avenue, New York, NY 10110

Printed in the United States of America

10 9 8 7 6 5 4 3 2 1

*T*his book is dedicated to my Mom and Dad—Dad for instilling in me my love and respect for the wilderness and wildlife, and Mom for her 100% encouragement in all my endeavors.

Contents

PART I
Starting Out

Preface

This book started out as a simple guide to some of my favorite paddling routes in these ocean islands. The natural history aspect just kept growing and growing as I researched and looked back on my 20 years of outdoor experiences in the Keys. The guide to the critters is by no means complete, but it will give you a good idea of just how many tropical and temperate creatures make their home here. The guide to the routes should be considered only as basic directions for travel, as some of the best trips are the ones with unplanned detours and unexpected discoveries.

My hope is that you will use this book as a reference to introduce yourself to some out-of-the-way places in the Keys inhabited by some out-of-this-world creatures. My enthusiasm for this watery wilderness has not diminished, and after 20 years of exploration I am still discovering new wonders. I hope you do as well.

A project of this size is never really the product of just one person. My name is the only one on the cover, but that is only because there is not enough room for the hundreds of friends who inspired me and helped me along the way. Thanks to my friends who typed, researched, answered questions, cooked meals, made me take time off, opened my mind to new questions, edited my writing, created nautical charts, illustrated my ideas, modeled for photos, lent me an iMac during deadline, took me flying, and all the other thousands of things that it takes to live a life with a book as a goal. Many thanks to Mark, Julie, Darya, Ann, and all the rest who helped me along the way. Special thanks to Sali for the line illustrations.

Orientation

Many say that the Overseas Highway is one of the longest dead-end roads on the continent. But with over 43 bridges and miles of ocean, this "dead-end road" offers unlimited opportunities for instant ocean access. The highway that stretches through the Keys is marked with little green signs that denote the distance from the end of the road in Key West. These mile markers start at 0 in Key West and go to 127, just 1 mile south of Florida City. Many of the directions you receive, in this book and elsewhere, will rely on these mile marker numbers for orientation. There is another way into and out of the Keys, on Card Sound Road. This traverses the upper reaches of Key Largo and then cruises over the graceful arc of the Card Sound Bridge to continue on toward the mainland. It connects with US 1 (the Overseas Highway) at the southern end of Florida City. There is a $1 toll for this bridge but the view, and the road-less-traveled appeal, is worth the buck.

Everyone seems to get confused with his or her compass orientation in relation to the Overseas Highway. This is because the road actually starts out going south until you reach Key Largo. Then it takes a southwesterly tack as it brings you to Marathon. Finally it will head west for the last 50 miles to Key West. As you head toward Key West, anything located on the right side of the highway is considered "bayside," and all locations on your left will be considered "oceanside."

Tides and Currents

The tides are sometimes quite confusing in the Keys. As you can imagine, when you mix hundreds of islands, two oceans, shallow protected bays a foot deep, deep channels, and wind from all directions, it can all get a little complicated. Some Keys guides maintain that to accurately tell the tide in a specific area, you have to go there and see for yourself. I have put together some guidelines in the Appendices that will get you close to the actual time and stage of the tide for most any area.

Most areas of the Keys experience 2 low and 2 high tides per day, about 6 hours apart. The differences in when they occur, relative to Key West's tides, vary. It seems that the tidal surge washes down the Atlantic side of the Keys from Key Largo to Key West and then flows into the Gulf to affect the backcountry islands nearly 3 to 8 hours later than Key West. Strong winds can keep water from entering or leaving some shallow bay areas, thereby slowing some tidal waters.

Evaporation can account for low water levels in some of the interior salt ponds that don't experience a lot of tidal flow. Some of the shallows always seem to be low or dry during the winter lunar cycles. Heavy summer rains can fill interior salt ponds and cause a continuous outflow of water, even through the incoming tides. These factors and more can affect water levels in these shallow seas and should be considered when planning a trip.

Weather

Many visitors to the Florida Keys seem to think that we have warm, balmy, 80-degree weather every day of the year, but there are many seasonal changes that take years of observation to be aware of. In general, though, the weather can be divided into hurricane season (June through October) and cold front season (November through April). For simplicity I will refer to these as summer and winter.

Summer generally brings an east to south breeze averaging 10 to 15 knots. These warm winds are great for sailing and downwind tours by kayak. As the day progresses the warming of the earth causes a warm updraft that eventually coalesces into cumulus clouds. These clouds can carry tremendous rain and lightning potential. In general, these storms move east to west, but they can also generate their own direction of travel. It is always wise to keep your eyes on nearby storms and determine a safe course of travel or an island to hide near as a storm blows by. Some storms will blow in with a fury in their frontal edge, with winds up to 25 knots and visibility reduced to near zero.

During the rainy season approximately 40 inches of rain will fall, with individual storms dumping as much as 6 inches. This can actually change the water's salinity and temperature considerably in the shallows, as well as fill up the cockpit of a kayak in a hurry. Although you can get pretty chilly in these summer rains, the real danger is lightning. Lightning strikes occur in weird and unusual ways, and it is best to take cover and lay down the paddle when a storm approaches. Water will conduct electricity so the best thing to do is get close to some cover and hunker down in the kayak.

Keep well insulated by using your life jacket and any other cushioning and keep all metal objects away from you and the boat. Some people go so far as to tether the aluminum paddles so they are some distance from themselves and the boat and will have no possibility of conducting electricity toward them.

In the wintertime, cold fronts alternate with balmy breezes. During the peak of winter it seems that every 5 to 7 days, masses of cold, arctic air make their way down from the Midwest and charge down the Florida peninsula. Not very many of them make it all the way to the Keys, but the ones that do come in with a bone-chilling vengeance.

Advancing cold fronts are usually marked by a series of wind shifts. As the cold air approaches south Florida, our east winds will clock around to the south, then west, and sometimes flatten out altogether as the front comes closer. With the severest storms, a black edge of clouds will peek above the northern horizon and slowly grow as the cold air mass rolls our way. National Oceanic and Atmospheric Administration (NOAA) weather forecasting has a better track record nowadays than formerly, and can predict these rain-laden cold air masses well in advance. If you are on the southern edges of our islands, be sure to hug the shoreline and stay protected. Consider the wind effect when planning a route during the approach of a cold front.

One thing that seems really hard to predict is the severity and longevity of the front. Sometimes they can be over within a matter of 10 to 30 hours, but the effects on nearshore water temperatures and turbidity can last longer. In these shallow seas temperatures can plummet 20 degrees overnight, shocking fish and stunning other creatures. If the sun is strong enough, that same water can heat up 10 degrees in a day. The winds can create a suspension of bottom sediments that looks like a vanilla and coffee milkshake. This recycling and redistributing of nutrients usually settles out in a matter of days, and the shallow seas return to our more typical "aquarium" viewing conditions.

Charts and Navigation

The early Spanish explorers made some of the oldest charts of the Florida Keys. They referred to these islands as *Los Martyrs* because they were stunted scrubby islands whose salt-washed shores seemed to suffer so from the tropical heat. Anyone who was washed ashore during a shipwreck also became a martyr, as there were unfriendly Native Americans, few sources of fresh water, and numerous insects to stress the castaways. These old charts gave only a simple glance and only hinted slightly at how complicated navigation can be in these shallow waters. Today, with excellent high-altitude photos and satellite mapping, we have a thorough and accurate representation of the Keys' shallow waters and rocky reefs.

The maps in this book are meant to indicate the locations of the launch sites and routes. They should not be used for navigational purposes. When you go out on the water, please bring a full-size map or chart with you. There are several available for this region.

The official government survey charts available for this area are produced by NOAA and are accurate, but there are several others available and each has its own merits. Websites and contact information for each are in the Appendices.

NOAA charts are printed on paper and just don't stand up to use on wet watercraft like kayaks and skinny-water skiffs. They make great wall hangings, and are perfect to keep on an office wall so you can daydream and reminisce about your backcountry journeys.

The waterproof charts are printed on a type of Tyvek material and hold up well to the elements. I have found these charts washed up on shore and covered with marine growth, and was able to clean them up and put them back in service.

Two different companies supply them; the first is called Waterproof Charts. Their charts are basically replicas of the NOAA charts, and you can roll them up in a tube. They come in several different types, with specialized fishing and diving versions available.

The other type is folded to a 7-by-12-inch size and is called the TOPSPOT. This one is a specialized fishing, diving, and recreation map, and includes tons of information on fishing, diving, boat ramps, refuge and park boundaries, and more. TOPSPOT charts also delineate designated special-use areas, closed areas, research areas, and lot of other useful information. The most beautiful maps are made by Standard Mapping and feature a NOAA chart on one side with a wonderfully produced color aerial photomap on the other side. The resolution is such that I can stare at these for hours trying to interpret information about specific areas. Individual coral heads, bomb holes, undercut island edges, and sneaky deeper channels are all shown in full color. When used in combination with NOAA nautical charts, the charts from Standard Mapping will provide the user with inspiring views of the Keys' backcountry waters. The visitor center at the Great White Heron National Wildlife Refuge headquarters displays 4-by-4-foot enlargements hanging on the walls that are from the High Altitude Aerial Photography Program. These full-color images are incredibly detailed and can give you a great idea of the complex nature of the shallow backcountry waters in the Keys. The visitor center is located in the Winn-Dixie plaza on Big Pine Key.

All of the above charts are great starting points for the skinny-water navigation skills needed for backcountry exploring, but there is nothing that compares to *local knowledge*. Most of the "local knowledge" routes in Keys waters are highlighted with markers made of white PVC pipe, some adorned with reflective tape, plastic reflectors, stop signs, and the like. I know of one that has a toilet seat attached to it! The trick is to know what these particular markers denote. Some may mark hazards to navigation, while others will mark the outside of a channel or a turning point in a route. Fortunately, as you move along in a kayak, things don't happen too fast, and you have time to figure out exactly what these markers might denote. But if you're in a motorboat and unsure, it is best to slow down and figure out what these marks are telling you about the surrounding shallows.

From a sitting position in a kayak it can be a little difficult to see landmarks and island masses. If you have the balance and ability to stand in your kayak, this will allow you to double the distance of your *viewable horizon*. The earth's surface curves downward about 6 inches per mile. This means that a person sitting in a kayak, whose point of view averages 3 feet above sea level, should be able to see 3 miles of ocean out to the apparent horizon. The average person standing on the water can see about 6 miles of ocean. This is a simple, basic gauge for traveling open waters based on flat, calm sea conditions.

If you are a little more technically oriented you may want to invest in a Global Positioning System (GPS) unit. These electronic wonders utilize satellite signals to triangulate and confirm precise positioning. Many units also offer charts, tide information, navigational aids, and electronic compasses, and some can even calculate speed. One of the best is the Garmin GPSMAP 76. I have used it to track almost all of the routes in this book, and have found that it performs well unless there is too much foliage overhead. The tide information is as good as it gets, considering all the factors that influence the tides here in the Keys.

One final note about navigation and finding your way: This quote is heard often from visitors and residents alike: "All these islands look the same." Indeed they do, and all these islands look different as you retrace your route on the return trip. This is true of the creeks and their entrances, as well as the islands on the horizon. This is why you will want to turn around at key points in your route to see what the route will look like during your paddle back. It is also wise to use surveyor's tape or a clothespin to mark some of the more hidden creek entrances or turns. Characteristics like bottom type and depth, broken or dead branches, and unique root formations all give you clues to remember your way home. If you happen to have a digital camera you can photograph these key points in a route to refer to on your return. The most important thing, though, is to remain constantly aware of your surroundings.

Here is some more local knowledge you may find helpful for navigation:

- Seaplanes and ultralights prefer to land and taxi in marked channels.
- Operators of Jet Skis and other motorized personal watercraft are sometime unknowledgeable novices or tourists renting machines they may be not be too familiar with. Give them a wide berth.
- Commercial fishing boats will usually travel in a straight line, pulling one trap after another. Yield the right of way to them.
- When coming home from the sea, keep the red triangular markers on your right and the green on your left. This keeps boats in the deepest parts of the channels. Remember: "Red, right, returning" (from the sea).
- You may see a low, flat motorboat with an angler on the bow and the captain high up on a poling platform in the rear, pushing the boat

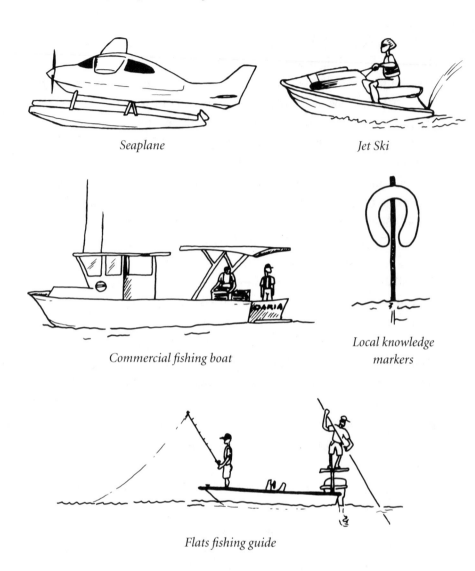

Seaplane

Jet Ski

Commercial fishing boat

Local knowledge
markers

Flats fishing guide

along with a long pole. This is a flats fishing guide with his client.
Give them a wide berth and try not to cut in front of them, because
they are stalking fish that are wary of humans and loud noise.

Equipment and Paddling Techniques
With the wide range of ocean environments in the Keys, it seems that one
should have a wide range of boats to handle specific waters. That is how I

justify having so many different boats in my fleet. At last count there were two motorboats, a shallow-water sailing vessel, and close to 30 kayaks. These are all part and parcel of my kayak business on Big Pine Key, and each vessel has a wonderfully unique suitability to the surrounding waters.

It is difficult to speak in generalities today about kayaks because there are hundreds of different models that are specialized in their applications. In general, though, the kayak world can easily be divided into sit-on-top and sit-inside models. Usually the sit-on-top kind is a wet recreational boat with not much protection between you and the water surrounding you. These boats are perfect for shallow-water exploring in wind-protected areas and quite functional when combining kayaking with a swim or snorkel adventure. But many of the sit-on-top kayaks have through-hull holes. These "scuppers" are drainage holes for water that washes into the cockpit, and will fill with an inch of water at equilibrium as you sit in the vessel. This is great when you are in the big waves and plowing into a headwind and your cockpit is full of water. It slowly drains as you push forward and gives you a real "at-one-with-the-outdoors" experience. When paddling in protected waters, you can easily use rubber plugs to stop all water from moving through the scuppers and have an enjoyable, completely dry experience.

Sit-inside vessels are of numerous varieties as well. They are usually very dry boats and have adequate dry storage. All of the multiday touring vessels are based upon this design and offer speed, rudders, and beautiful lines.

When considering the use of a kayak there are many factors to take into account, including how you intend to use the boat and what types of waters and winds you are likely to encounter. For fishing and photography adventures, I prefer a boat that is stable enough to stand in, and it should have enough cargo carrying capacity so I am not cramped or overweighted. I also like a very dry boat when using camera gear and fishing tackle.

If you're snorkeling for lobster, exploring the reef, or photographing in the mangroves in the summer, a sit-on-top kayak with an ankle leash and a dive flag would be preferable. Most kayaks are relatively easy to tow slowly as you snorkel along and make great platforms to carry underwater camera gear. A small anchor and a paddle leash come in handy when exploring in this manner.

On multiday backcountry excursions where camping overnight and covering miles are part of the plan, a sit-inside boat with a long waterline, rudder, and storage capacity would be ideal. The long waterline helps the boat maintain top-end speed, and the rudder enables you to hold a course without the wind becoming a big factor in that process. Usually these boats are built with great dry storage spaces fore and aft, as well as a narrow hull width and sharp entry to maintain the top speed.

The basic paddling techniques necessary for flatwater kayaking are fairly simple. The first choice is whether or not you will use a feathered kayak blade. Feathered means that as you hold the kayak shaft in your hands—which are about shoulder width apart—the blades will be slightly offset from one another. Find the home position by aligning your right hand with the first-joint knuckles pointing up at the sky. Your right-hand paddle blade should be perpendicular to the water's surface. This gives the right-hand paddle blade the best entry and purchase in the water. As it exits the water, you twist your right-hand palm toward the sky and let the paddle shaft pivot in your left hand, and this should make the left blade dig into the water correctly. You may notice that all this twisting places the paddle blade that is in the air at a more efficient angle to cut through a headwind, rather than acting like a sail and causing resistance.

The backpaddle is used as a brake and for avoidance steering, in case you are about to hit something or run aground. If you backpaddle on your left, you reverse and your bow slides to the left. If you backpaddle on the right, you slow down and your bow will slide to the right. These are the basics, and are only an overview of what could easily take up an entire chapter.

There are just a couple of other strokes that bear mentioning. In a stable craft and after some experience, it is possible to stand in and pole many different types of kayaks. You must have a great sense of balance and be willing to fall in a lot at first! This can be dangerous and is not for everyone, but if you can walk on a balance beam, this trick may work for you. Standing affords a better view of the surrounding waters and enables you to spot fish before they see or feel you coming. To stand I try to start out with my feet under the center of the bulk of my body weight and rise slowly, using the paddle as a balancing stick. Once up, I attempt to pole the boat using the paddle grasped with one hand on the shaft and the other on the blade's edge.

This is similar to what the flats fishing guides do to propel their boats over the flats in search of various sport fish. I also use this pushpole method to move slowly over soft or muddy bottoms, since it doesn't sweep along the bottom and stir up lots of sediments. As you slide forward, you can trail the blade in the water as a rudder to correct for your desired course. When you get comfortable with this maneuver you will feel as if you are on a magic carpet ride as you glide silently over glassy calm waters.

The final stroke I want to cover in this primer is the "sun stroke." This one is the relaxed, laid-back form that should be expected from paddling in the tropics. If you are in a closed-deck kayak it is mandatory to lean back and put your legs up on the deck for maximum sun exposure. This, along with a casual dip of each blade in the water, will propel you slowly. It is really helpful if a 12-knot breeze is assisting you in your direction of travel. The name and refined technique of the "sun stroke" were coined by Sunny Pitcher of Potomac Paddle Sports, who brings groups from the Washington, D.C. area every winter to experience the Keys paddling environment. I hope you can perfect this stroke.

Tropical Safety, Clothing, and Gear

At night in these island tropics it is possible to count, with the unaided eye, up to 3,000 stars. During the day we can see only one, our sun. Its powerful rays can burn us, dehydrate us, and generally wear us out. Fortunately, there are lots of things we can do to protect ourselves from the intensity of the sun.

Dehydration can cause many problems. There are many stories of SCUBA divers who dove within the limits of safe diving and wound up getting bent because of dehydration. It can cause headaches, nausea, and disorientation while on the water paddling as well as afterward. Personally I drink a lot of watered-down sports drinks for the electrolytes and minerals they contain. A physical therapist once told me, and I experienced myself, the fact that those electrolytes will ward off any possibility of a dehydration headache and enable your body to utilize the water you drink in a more efficient manner. Everybody has different needs, and you should be aware of what works best for you, but always bring plenty of water and drink it frequently.

During the summer, heat cramps, heat stroke, and heat exhaustion are all heat-related illnesses to be aware of. All these conditions are brought on by overexposure to heat and other environmental factors such as wind and humidity. Personal factors such as poor circulation, heavy clothing, and certain medications can aggravate the effects. Heat cramps are the first warning signs and usually manifest themselves as muscle spasms in the legs and abdominal area. Shade, rest, stretching affected muscle groups, and plenty of fluids are the antidote to these conditions. Heat exhaustion will cause cool, moist, pale, or flushed skin in addition to headache, dizziness, nausea, and general weakness. This serious condition must be dealt with immediately or it may progress into heat stroke. Heat stroke manifests as red, hot, dry skin and a rapid but weak pulse. Changes in consciousness and rapid, shallow breathing are also signs that you should seek prompt medical attention. Early treatment for these conditions is the best first aid. If the victim exhibits exhaustion or more the best course of action is to get the victim to rest in the shade and cool down. Administer water in small amounts (6 ounces every 15 minutes) and place wet towels or bandanas on the exposed skin to cool the exterior by evaporation. The victim should not resume normal activities that day. If heat stroke symptoms are apparent, keep the victim lying down on their side and try to cool with cold packs or ice wraps while waiting for medical attention. Always keep an eye on the victim's consciousness, breathing, and pulse. All of these heat-related illnesses have early warning signs that allow us to detect problems before they become dangerous.

One of the most common problems caused by solar radiation is sunburn. In attempting to get that enviable vacation tan, it seems that everyone maximizes sun exposure on the first day and regrets it that first night. Sunscreens with a sun protection factor (SPF) of 30+ and water-resistant characteristics are the best. Lip balm with aloe and a large-brimmed hat make life pleasant while on the water. Be sure to apply sunscreen evenly and don't neglect your nose, ears, neck, and shins.

Eye protection and glare reduction are the two biggest factors to consider in the selection of sunglasses. Polarized glasses are best for cutting through the reflections on the water's surface, and will allow you to see more underwater wildlife. Sharks, rays, barracuda, and other flats creatures can be spotted more easily without the glare off the water's surface. To check if your glasses are polarized, test them by looking through two pair at one time. The first pair should be on your face in the normal manner. Hold the other pair out in front of you in a vertical orientation. If the glasses completely "black out" the light, both pairs are polarized glasses. Polarization essentially reduces the scattered light rays that are allowed to enter, allowing in only parallel light rays, which produce the most colorful and glare-free image. There are also some color choices that can be made to enhance contrast in low-light conditions, blue water, and bright shallow waters. Many paddlers find that yellow lenses are best for low light, gray lenses are best for seeing into deep, blue water, and brown lenses offer the best views of the shallows.

The gear you bring can make or break the trip. Review this list and find the items that are most suitable for you and your specific adventure.

Comprehensive Gear List

- Extra drinking water, more than a gallon per person per day.
- Life jacket, worn not stowed per Coast Guard regulations. No matter how well you swim, it is difficult to swim while unconscious. Buy the best life jacket you can afford. Lotus Life Jackets by Patagonia are recommended for quality, fit, and function.
- Flashlight, flares, and glow sticks.
- Compass and charts.
- Hand pump or large sponge for bailing.
- Whistles, on jacket and boat.
- Anchor and 50 feet of line.
- Ten-foot bowline.
- Sunscreen, lip balm, and insect repellent.
- Simple first aid kit in a waterproof baggie: Band-Aids, moleskin, antibacterial ointment, meat tenderizer (for jellyfish stings), aspirin, Ziploc bags, wire ties, and duct tape.

- Weather radio or handheld VHF.
- Cell phone in dry bag.
- Poncho or tarp for extended rainstorms.
- Spare breakdown paddle.
- Leave a float plan with someone on shore.

Clothing

- Zip-off, quick-dry pants.
- Quick-dry, loose, ventilated shirt with SPF factor of 20+.
- Hat with wide brim.
- Hat with large bill and flap of cloth to protect ears and neck.
- Quick-dry swimsuit.
- Soft gloves if prone to blisters.
- Bandana to wear wet for its cooling effect.
- Wading shoes, sports sandals, or water mocs.
- Dry bag with a towel.
- Raingear in the summer.
- Windbreaker or polypropylene jacket for warmth in winter.
- Polypropylene neck gaiter for head or neck warmth.
- Polarized glasses with strap.
- Mosquito headnet.
- Clothespins.

Dive Kit

- Mask, fins, and snorkel.
- Dive skin.
- Dive flag and pole.
- Gloves.
- Paddle leash.
- Mesh carry bag.

PART II

Natural History

Ecosystems and Habitat Types

The Coral Reef

Although coral communities are found in almost all areas of the Keys, the substantial portion of the coral reef community is found offshore, a bit farther than most kayakers will want to paddle. Throughout most of the Keys, the true fringing coral reef is approximately 4 miles out from U.S. Highway 1, with lots of open water between you and the reef. If you really want to venture to those fringing reefs, I highly recommend a dive charter boat excursion so you can explore the reef safely. The nearshore patch reefs are well within paddling distance and can offer some excellent snorkeling. The easiest access to some of these nearshore patch reefs is found in the Upper and Lower Keys (see trips #1, #19, and #26). An anchor with 50 feet or more of line and a dive flag are necessary items for snorkeling these areas. The sit-on-top variety of kayak makes getting in and out of the boat a lot safer and more efficient for this type of exploring.

The coral boulders of varying green and gold hues are actually living colonies of animals. The individuals that make up this colony all have a thin veneer of tissue upon a calcium carbonate base. This tissue is spread like a sheet of skin over a rocklike skeleton, which grows about 2.5 centimeters per year. The individual animals, called polyps, have stinging tentacles, which extend at night and on cloudy days to capture planktonic prey. They also receive nutrients and oxygen from symbiotic algae that live in their tissue. Brushing up against the coral with hands, fins, or other body parts easily damages this thin veneer of tissue, so please use extreme caution when exploring these areas.

The competition for living space in the ocean is an ongoing battle, and the coral skeleton provides a home for many creatures. Oftentimes the coral boulders exhibit great caverns, nooks, and crannies that are inhabited by creatures as large as a 300-pound goliath grouper and as small as the diminutive, ½-inch squat anemone shrimp. The real beauty of the reef is that all these creatures live in balance, inextricably tied to one another for a variety of reasons. Some provide homes; others serve as food; and still others provide grooming and cleaning services, such as cleaner fish and shrimp. While exploring the coral areas, if you come across some small, blue-striped fish known as neon gobies, or the thin, white, whiplike antennae of the banded coral shrimp, hover in that spot for awhile. This is most likely a cleaning station, and if you wait patiently and without too much movement you will no doubt see a variety of fish come in for a cleaning. Large and small fish will slowly maneuver into the cleaning zone. The fish open their mouths and flex their gill covers to signal the cleaners to get to work and peck off dead skin, parasites, and other unwanted de-

Coral reef

bris from their bodies. Snorkeling slowly and observing the bottom, you might find a pile of freshly cleaned mollusks. A small shell collection like this on the bottom usually signals that an octopus's abode is quite close. Check carefully and try to find the intelligent eye or a line of suction cups hiding in crevices nearby. These are just a few examples of how to look closely and truly appreciate the complex web of life on the coral reef.

The Sponge Flats

From the vantage point of the kayak it will appear to be a sandy bottom with many dark shadows pockmarking the bottom; these are the sponge flats. These shallow, sparkling seas bewilder the eye with colorful shapes and forms that turn quickly into a Monet painting from the ripples upon the surface.

Often no more than 5 or 6 feet deep, this habitat is grounded on a solid layer of calcium carbonate stone, which makes it easy for the sponges and other creatures to hang on tight to the substrate. Although they may look like dark rocks strewn on the bottom, the sponges and soft corals that comprise this ecosystem are actually colonies of animals. The fish in these areas are usually small and considered prey by many of the groupers, snappers, and other predatory fish that hunt the area. Between the sponges and soft corals taking up almost all the available substrate will be marine algae of all colors and forms. Since this area receives intense sunlight, it is an excellent habitat for a forest of diverse algae.

The Sea Grass Flats

If you think of their forms as spaghetti you will always remember the three major types of marine grass. First and most abundant is **turtle grass** (*Thalassia testudinum*), which is like linguini. It is about the width of your pinky nail and can grow to lengths of 3 feet, but is usually about 1 to 2 feet in length. Turtle grass is named after the green turtle, which establishes grazing plots in these rich beds.

Manatee grass (*Syringodium filiforme*), is round in cross section (as a manatee is round) and reminds me of thin spaghetti #9. Manatee grass is most common in Florida Bay and is the dominant species in brackish waters. When it breaks free from the substrate it will form dense, floating mats that usually wash up in red mangrove roots or upon shorelines. This material decomposes quickly and is a great addition to the compost pile effect of the red mangroves' prop root system.

The other grass is known as **shoal grass** *(Halodule beaudettei)*, and is flat like turtle grass but considerably thinner (one-quarter to one-third as wide as turtle grass) and usually grows no more than 4 inches tall. Shoal grass has a unique feature in that it has three teeth at the tip of the blade. Shoal grass is the species usually found in the shallows that are awash during low tides and is usually outcompeted in the deeper waters by the other grasses and algae. An interesting growth phenomenon occurs when a parasitic fungus actually causes the swelling of sections of the blade to resemble a string of green pearls. All these grasses have flowers and seeds, although those of the shoal grass have never been observed. I have observed the flowers of the turtle grass in the summer and they resemble a waxy, flattened sea star.

A sweeping vista of rich green meadows will greet you in the backcountry areas of the Florida Keys. As these grasses get longer they are colonized by animals and plants living on the surfaces and amongst the blades of grass. Look close and you can see anemones, crustaceans, sponges, flatworms, mollusks, and many other creatures. It is like a miniature rainforest in a shallow sea. Scores of creatures live both in the mud below the grass roots and up high in the canopy of blade tips that sometimes arch at the ocean's surface, absorbing sunlight.

As you cruise over many of the grass flats you will sometimes come across small mounds of sand in the shape of a volcano. These can be from any of several burrowing creatures. The two most common are the burrowing shrimp—which usually has a defined circular hole as an entrance—and the burrowing sea cucumber, whose mounds have a small depression at the top filled with fine sediments and fecal casts. These grass flats are a favorite of foraging fish like shark, bonefish, and permit.

Sandy and Muddy Substrates

Soft mud, sometimes a meter deep, comprises some of the lee shores of many backcountry islands where the currents are not so swift. Storms, the prevailing winds, and decomposing sea grass contribute to the buildup of these sediments. If you have to take a stretch or want to get out of the kayak and wade, this is not the place to do it. This wonderful ooze can swallow you and your footwear right up to your thigh. I have seen more than one flip-flop lose its mate in this wonderful, slippery soup.

Usually these substrates are out of the wind and have dozens if not hundreds of **upside-down jellyfish** soaking up the sunshine in the shallows. Many other creatures are hard at work breaking down all those organic nutrients and recycling the energy for the rest of the creatures in the food chain.

All the Keys' sand is biogenic in origin, meaning that at some point in time it was part of a living plant or animal. If you look close at the grainy constituents you may be able to identify calcareous algae, bits of broken coral, shells and spines of urchins, and other calcareous remnants of living creatures. There are not many sandy beaches in the Keys, as most of the shorelines are comprised of fossilized coral or mangrove forest.

Sandy areas near the mangrove shorelines usually indicate that a strong tidal current sweeps by the area. These places usually have more wildlife traffic and the potential for hidden mangrove creeks. Any time you see a big sandy wash on the shore of a mangrove island, be on the lookout for some possible little currents that may feed into some rich creeks. Wildlife viewing is also enhanced on these sunlit sand patches, because of the contrast they provide between the bottom and the creatures. Many times the shadow of a fish will be more easily visible on the sandy bottom than the fish itself, which tends to blend it with its surroundings.

The Rocky Intertidal

The fossilized coral limestone shoreline can provide some great tide pool viewing. As the tide falls and leaves the rock exposed, many creatures get caught up in the nooks and crannies of the shoreline.

The fossilized coral skeletons are quite prominent and can be great places to search for crabs, fish, and mollusks in the shallow, warm waters. This substrate is particularly rough on any type of kayak or unprotected feet, but this environment is also stressful for the creatures that live here. Some small pools reach over 100 degrees in the summer's heat and drop to 60 degrees after a few cold nights in winter.

The Mangroves

Mangroves are complex trees in a simply magical place. Anywhere in the world near the equator, at the sea's edge, you can find several of the 50 or more mangrove species. Mangroves are a group of plants that can tolerate a salty environment. Their ability to deal with the excess salts and minerals manifests itself in several ways, but the two main processes are exclusion and extrusion. Red mangroves can actually exclude the salts from entering their root tips by a process similar to reverse osmosis. A filtering or ultra-screening mechanism excludes such a high volume of salt and minerals that the mangrove's sap is only about 1/70 as saline as the surrounding seawater.

The other method is extrusion, and the black mangrove exhibits that process on the backsides of its leaves. Its sap is one-seventh as salty as the surrounding waters, and it offloads the salt throughout the day through pores on the backsides of the leaves. Early settlers used black mangrove leaves to add seasoning to their meals. In the heat of the summer it is fascinating to turn over a leaf and see large, chunky salt crystals adhering to the backside. It will be the finest, freshest sea salt you will ever lick.

The **red mangrove** *(Rhizophora mangle)* is most easily identified by its arching prop roots. These are shoreline stabilizers and also provide excellent habitat for all sorts of land and sea creatures. The roots can be alive with invertebrates, marine plants, and an amazing diversity of fish life. Almost all the ocean's fish depend on the mangroves for some portion of their life, as a food source, habitat, or a place for the juveniles to grow up. The root system has inspired artists, poets, painters, and nature lovers with its intricate and seemingly impenetrable tangle of arcs. Spend some time in a small, quiet, mangrove-lined creek, and you will be surrounded by an array of creatures that bend the rules. Working the sky and the sea are the mangrove tree crabs. They pause and freeze when you enter and there may be hundreds on the backsides of the tree limbs or right in plain sight. Half-dollar-sized, dark, and constantly moving claw to mouth, they conjure up visions of a dark and primitive forest ecosystem. Sitting and watching for only 20 or 30 minutes, you can spot an array of bird life moving through. White ibis and green herons stalk through the roots in search of fish and crustaceans, while red-bellied woodpeckers and warblers work the

The prop-and-drop roots of the red mangrove–fringed creeks create an enticing visual feast.

branches for insect life. The white ibis, with its pink, curved drinking straw of a bill, can probe in the mud for crustaceans and suck them out from depths of 6 inches. Their honking can usually be heard in the roots. The adults are all white except for their black wing tips. The green heron can sit and wait for extended times without moving a feather and when a small fish comes within striking distance it will lunge out and impale the small, unsuspecting meal.

Red mangrove forests flower in the summer, and their smallish yellow flowers give way to an almond-shaped seed. The seed actually germinates right on the host tree. These string bean-shaped propagules can reach 8 to 12 inches and are ready to grow as soon as they fall off the tree. Although they are most productive during the summer, you can find seedlings on the trees at any time of year. Once they hit the water they can root on the spot or drift away to new territory and still be viable for up to 9 months. In this way they are able to colonize seashores throughout the tropics as tropical storms, hurricanes, and currents disperse them far and wide. During the summers when they are at their most productive, you can find floating weed lines thick with red mangrove seedlings. Many creatures eat the seedlings, but the most spectacular I have seen was the smallish manatee that I watched eat several mouthfuls of weed line and finally end up with a huge seedling, which it nibbled into its mouth like a rabbit eating a carrot. The manatee was using its front flipper to ease the seedling slowly into its choppers.

The unique pencil roots, or pneumatophores of the **black mangrove** *(Avicennia germinans)* distinguish it from all the other mangrove species. Usually found at slightly higher elevations than the red mangrove, the black mangrove has adapted to tidal flooding by utilizing its snorkel-like roots to provide gaseous exchange during flood tides. Their netlike lateral root structure also provides for shoreline stabilization and erosion control.

Flowering occurs during the summer, and the small whitish flowers were a great resource for beekeepers in the past. They benefited from the dark, molasses-like honey that the bees conjured from the flowers, and you could usually find some at the flea market on Big Pine Key. Another commercial use for the black mangrove was the charcoal that was left after smoldering a pile of it. In the early 1900s this was one of the main ways to cook a meal at home, and kilns as big as 25 feet in diameter and 12 feet tall could yield more than 200 bags of charcoal.

The **white mangrove** *(Laguncularia racemosa)* and the **buttonwood** *(Conocarpus erectus)* are the most treelike members of the mangrove family. They live in the highest, driest zones and have no strikingly pronounced adaptations except for their ability to thrive in the saline, flood-prone environment of the Florida Keys.

Seaside Shrubbery

The war on exotic vegetation includes as a casualty the **Australian pine** *(Casuarina* species). This common tree was introduced to Florida in the early 1900s and has literally taken over some areas. Its habit of rendering the ground below unsuitable for other native species, along with its tendency to fall over in high winds because of its shallow root system are the reasons for its removal. In mature stands, like the forest at Fort Zachary

Taylor State Park, it provides wonderful shade, and the sounds of the wind whooshing through its needles puts me in a trance. This large, whippy, pinelike tree can be seen everywhere.

The **sea grape** *(Coccoloba uvifera)* has big, 6- to 9-inch, oval, leathery leaves that turn colors in February and March. The rich reds, oranges, and yellows remind me of my many autumns spent in New England. In early summer they sprout large clusters of grapes that are an important food for wildlife. A few enterprising humans make jam and jelly from this abundant, prolific tree.

The tall, thin stalk that holds the seeds of **sea oats** *(Uniola paniculata)* can be found on many Florida beaches. This important plant is a dune stabilizer and a good food resource for seed-eating birds. The beach on the ocean side of U.S. 1 at Mile Marker 74 on Lower Matecumbe Key offers a beautiful view of large stands of sea oats. The flats just off the highway are a great spot to watch for bonefish and wading fishermen.

Like a sharp stick, the **sandbur** *(Cenchrus tribuloides)* can cause a shiver of pain emanating from your foot. These dune stabilizers are armed and ready to penetrate the unshod foot. It is the seedpods that have these sharp spines with recurved hooks, and a cluster of seeds can number in the dozens. The long, thin, green leaves splay out on the ground with a scattering of bristly seedpods lying in wait to hitch a ride.

The yellow flowers of the **sea ox-eye daisy** *(Borrichia arborescens)* are a brilliant contrast to the green-leafed bush. This salt-tolerant species brightens up the dunes and adjacent shorelines with its solitary blooms in spring and summer.

Mangrove fern *(Acrosticum aureum)* have deeply notched fern leaves and grow in the root structures of red mangroves and other coastal salt forests. It is the only species of fern found in this area.

Saltwort *(Batis maritime)* shrubbery has a fernlike appearance from a distance, but upon closer inspection you can see the woody stems that hold the small succulent green leaves, which are only about an inch long.

Glasswort *(Salicornia bigelovii)* is ground cover on the salt flats. Its jointed, 3- to 5-inch segments stand erect, and the lateral root system crisscrosses the ground. It can exhibit colors that are a mixture of pastel reds, yellows, and greens.

Sea purslane *(Sesuvium portulacastrum)* is a fleshy herb that creeps along the shorelines. The linear, succulent leaves are edible and were utilized as a staple in the diet of the prisoners and staff at Fort Jefferson in the 1800s. The salty, juicy leaves make a fine addition to salads.

Prickly pear cactus *(Opuntia* species) exhibit brilliant yellow flowers in the spring, which give way to a pear-shaped fruit. This is edible, but has small clusters of spines that must be scraped off as you peel the fruit.

The Creatures

The following is a brief compilation of the diversity of creatures one can run across in these tropical islands. I have tried to give a broad overview of the range of creatures that inhabit this melting pot of temperate and tropical environments and the more I researched the more that was added. It is by no means comprehensive so there is a great bibliography section in the appendix to assist you further in identifying the things you see and the lifestyle they live.

Fish

Wakes, tails, shadows, and splashes all denote the presence of creatures that live in the seas. More often than not the disturbances on the water's surface will be caused by some kind of fish. Depending on the disturbance, you can sometimes actually identify the fish by its signature on the surface. The stingray will produce a distinctive double boil as its huge, flat pectorals thrust the water for propulsion. Most other fish will leave a single boil of water as they speed away using their tailfins. Some will tail slowly as they search the skinny waters for food, and others will rip over the shallow water, exposing their backs and dorsal fins as they chase prey.

The fishes can be divided into two categories, cartilaginous and bony. The cartilaginous fishes include the sharks, rays, and skates, which have skeletons that are composed of cartilage, the same stuff that gives your nose and ears their flexibility. Of the two groups, the sharks exhibit the most dramatic response.

The waters were at a June full moon, dead low tide, and as calm as a reflecting pool. A large, triangular fin as big as a Frisbee at the base was sitting still in the tropical shallows. It seemed to sway slowly and rise and fall with the shark's respiration. Slowly wading in the shin-deep waters, my kayak anchored behind me, I approached the 11-foot giant. Her scarred pectoral fins proved that she had recently been in an amorous interlude with one or several of the males hovering nearby.

Watching a large **nurse shark** *(Ginglymostoma cirratum)* rise and fall with each breath as a remora slowly slid over her back was an intense moment that was made even more exciting by her sliding into motion and heading right for me. She swam by slowly and actually brushed me with her pectoral fin, did a circle behind me, and then brushed me with her other pectoral before lying down in the turtle grass bed. It was nurse shark mating season, and there were lots of the big animals in the shallows awaiting the proper moment. Nurse sharks reach sexual maturity at 15 years and live to be more than 25 years old. When the females give birth, 20 to 30 live pups can pop out, and over the previous weeks many of the black-spotted nurse shark pups had been seen on the sponge flats. Secluded bays and backwater coves all over the Keys have been privy to this annual event, and now with so many skinny-water paddlers out there,

A nurse shark can grow to be up to 200 pounds and can be found in all habitats in the Keys.

more and more of these unique behaviors are being documented.

Nurse sharks are usually implicated in most of the relatively few shark interactions that occur in the Keys. This has much more to do with curious human behavior rather than with aggressive shark behavior. Because the nurse shark is one of the few sharks that can lie on the bottom and still breathe, many think the shark to be injured or possibly dead and tend to investigate to the fullest. Most other sharks have to swim continuously to force water through the mouth and gills to oxygenate their blood, but the nurse shark has a mouth and muscles that are made for vacuuming things off the bottom, and this allows for volumes of water to be sucked through the gills as they lie on the bottom. Sucking lobsters out of crevices and conchs right out if their shells are the trademark of the eating habits of this catfish-like shark. If a casual observer tugs at the shark's tail, it can circle around and give a great sucking

Nurse shark

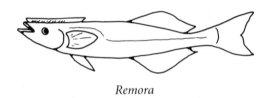

Remora

bite at whatever appendage is nearby. Luckily its teeth are relatively small, so tissue damage is not too severe, but it can hang on for some time as it sucks in a mouthful.

A teenager off Marathon learned this a few years back when he had a smallish nurse shark attach itself to his chest. It had a good mouthful, so the captain decided to have the Coast Guard transport the boy to the local hospital for surgical removal. This was an unusual occurrence, and it is unclear what prompted the shark, but the lesson learned is to give these creatures a little breathing room and respect while you're in their environment. Nurse sharks are fished commercially in the Caribbean and are highly regarded as the source of an excellent tanned hide for sharkskin products.

The closest I have come to a shark attack in all of my water time in the Keys was an encounter with a **shark sucker,** *Echeneis naucrates.* This small, bony fish has a head like a sneaker sole that it uses as a suction cup to attach itself to larger fish for a free ride. It can also let go at opportune times to take advantage of a free meal of falling morsels from its feeding host. I suppose that it will also nibble on small ectoparasites that are on its host fish, and that must have been the reason for its attack on me. Snorkeling in the tropical water, I suddenly felt a wispy brush on my leg and thigh and found it to be a small shark sucker that hovered nearby for ten minutes or so. When it was up around my chest area trying to get a grip, it came across my nipple and must have thought that it was some type of parasite. As it bit me my immediate reaction sent the fish swimming off into the distance and all I could think was "What was it attached to before it met me?" Many adult nurse sharks have **remoras** on or around them, and other sharks, rays, and whales commonly carry this freeloader as well.

A smallish member of the hammerhead family is also found frequently on the flats. A tall, sharp, triangular dorsal fin and a wagging tailfin cutting the surface in 6 inches of water usually can be attributed to the **bonnethead** or **shovelnose shark**, *Sphyrna tiburo.* The distinctive spade-shaped head, tall, skinny dorsal fin, and white-edged pectorals are good field identification marks. These sharks usually grow no larger than 3 to 5 feet long and average 10 pounds, although the world record is 23 pounds.

Most all the sharks in this area are livebearers, and when the cobia move through in the spring we frequently find baby bonnetheads in the stomachs of the cobia. Cobia are one of the few fishes that consume sharks, and somehow they know where to find those little 12-inch bonnetheads. The bonnethead can live up to 7 years or more, and reaches sexual maturity at 2 years of age. The 12-inch pups are birthed in a litter size of 4 to 16 individuals. Crabs are never safe from patrolling bonnetheads, which rarely travel alone, and they take their share of small fish and various invertebrates as well.

The **lemon shark** *(Negaprion brevirostris)* is another common shark in the skinny waters. The young, which pop out with 4 to 17 siblings, are the most beautiful, inquisitive, and approachable creatures in the backcountry lagoons in spring. They have slowly snaked by our kayaks and given us such an encounter that you hold your breath as they pass. Two dorsal fins about the same size and a yellowish belly are good field-identification traits, and the young have black edging on their triangular pectoral fins. These sharks will slowly swim by to reveal sun-sparkled dermal denticles in their skin, and the striations in their muscle tissue will be apparent as the twin dorsals cut the surface. This species can reach a maximum size of 11 feet, although 6- to 7-foot individuals are more common. In the larger sizes and with chum or speared fish in the water, lemon sharks are considered unpredictable and potentially dangerous.

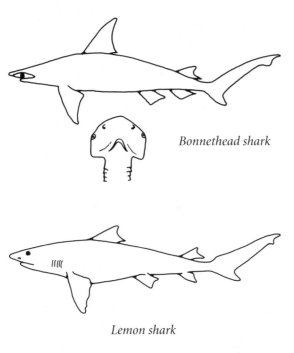

Bonnethead shark

Lemon shark

The **spinner shark** *(Carcharhinus brevipinna)* and the **blacktip shark** *(Carcharhinus limbatus)* are also found in our waters, but usually in the deeper channels or on the ocean side of the Keys. Both these shark have a distinctive whitish stripe on the flank and a black tip on the dorsal, pectoral, and anal fins, and on the bottom of the tailfin. They also have a black coloration on the insides of the pectorals. The spectacular acrobatics of spinners and blacktips when hooked make for a sporting light-tackle adventure. They reach 150 pounds, but are more common in the 50-pound range.

The **bull shark** *(Carcharhinus leucas)*, the **scalloped hammerhead** *(Sphyrna lewini)*, the **smooth hammerhead** *(Sphyrna zygaena)*, and the **great hammerhead** *(Sphyrna mokarran)* are usually migratory and follow the large schools of tarpon in the spring. Averaging 6 to 9 feet but reaching more than 12 feet long, they feed on the silver kings wherever they are schooled. Ask any tarpon fisherman for a hammerhead story, and I am sure he has one. For many years "Big Mo," probably a great hammerhead close to 20 feet in length, was sighted at Bahia Honda Bridge during the

Baby lemon shark are common in the shallow sponge flats. This one is being released after a light tackle-fishing experience.

spring as it tore into weak, tired, or hooked tarpon. This entire group of sharks is a rare sighting, and you should consider yourself fortunate to view these top predators in their natural habitat.

Every year there is a sighting of an albino **spotted eagle ray** *(Aetobatus narinari)* at the No Name Key Bridge. Schools of up to 15 or more are spotted in the spring, and it seems that they are most active with their jumping antics during the first few weeks after arrival. Many theories have been put forth about the reasons for the jumps, but the one I like best is "because they can." Some believe that the rays are able to define territory, shake loose external parasites, or even assist in the birthing process by doing these belly flops. I have seen the young in small groups in the same locations several months later, and I do believe that all the above theories have validity.

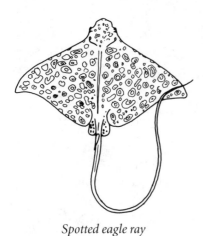

Spotted eagle ray

With wingspans ranging from 4 to 8 feet, these beautifully spotted rays dig about in the bottom searching for mollusks and other edibles. The white markings on the dorsal side of the spotted eagle ray are unique to each individual and can range from large dots to miniature doughnuts, and the base color can range from black to gray.

The **southern stingray** *(Dasyatis americana)* is the most commonly seen ray on the flats. The dorsal side varies from brown to gray to black, but the underside is distinctly white. At low tide it is possible to see

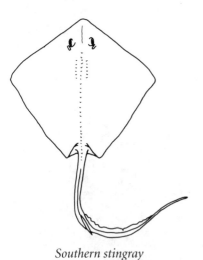

Southern stingray

both fins break the surface as the animal is cruising along, and you can easily judge the size of this fish, which reaches 5 feet in width. There is a stinger at the base of the tail, but it is easily seen and usually quite wary, so you would have to be not paying attention to step on one. Stingrays feed by either ramming a jet of water into the substrate to uncover prey or by sucking water up through the mouth and jetting it out through the spiracles on the dorsal side. These mudding monsters can leave a thick trail of mud, silt, and debris as they uncover food. This mud trail makes it easy to spot them, and attracts many other fish that feed on one another, as well as on other creatures in the debris plume. A common hunting technique of flats guides is to search behind a mudding ray for bonefish, jacks, and cobia.

Another, smaller ray is the **yellow stingray** (*Urolophus jamaicensis*), which camouflages itself well on the flats and reaches a width of 15 inches. The yellow stingray has little yellow spots and blotches that can change color dramatically. It will sometimes raise its front edge to trick prey into thinking there is a good hiding place in the shadows beneath its lifted body. All of the rays mentioned give birth to live young, and in the spring it is possible to see a yellow stingray bulging with young in its womb on both the left and right sides of its back.

The bony fish that live here are one of the reasons the Florida Keys are so famous. Recreational and commercial fishing are integral to most any lifestyle in the Keys, and the variety of species is enormous. What follows is really only a thin slice of the most common finfish found in the Keys. If you really want to know the full extent of the diversity of the fishes, a great reference is *Atlantic Coast Fishes* by Robins, Ray, and Douglass in the Peterson Field Guides series, which lists over a thousand species.

It's springtime in the Keys and finally the mangrove salt creeks are getting some big full-moon tides, which energize all the creek creatures with large flushes of clean ocean waters. This is when the killifish and livebearers seem to light up with brilliant colors and aggressive displays to attract mates. There are about nine species of these fish found in the mangroves and nearshore habitats. These killifish range from 1.5 to 7 inches in length and comprise the bottom of the fish food chain. The most common of this group is the **longnose killifish** (*Fundulus similes*), which has the appearance of a tiny 4.5-inch snook because of its sloped head and long body. These fish are usually abundant in the creeks or around the mangrove roots and exhibit different colorations or patterns for the males and females.

The livebearers also exhibit different coloration between the sexes, with the grand prize going to the **sailfin molly** *(Poecilia latipinna)*. The dorsal on the 5-inch male can be as big as its body when erect and the wonderful red, orange, and cobalt colors are enchanting. Sit tight and watch closely as he shakes, corrals, and shimmies his way into the female's heart. The female carries the 20 to 80 eggs for 8 to 10 weeks, whereupon the young are born live into the rich organic forest of the red mangrove root system.

The 1.5-inch **mangrove gambusia** *(Gambusia rhizophorae)* is small but has quite a positive effect on our lives, because it consumes mosquito larvae by the millions and produces up to 1,500 young during its lifetime. In 1905 thousands of mangrove gambusia were shipped to Hawaii, and the fish virtually eliminated the mosquitoes there. The upward-turned mouth is proficient at gulping mosquito larvae as they rise to the surface to breathe, and it also enables the fish to make use of the oxygen-rich layer of water near the surface. This enables it to survive in stagnant, polluted habitats, or in the warm waters of the tropics.

Also at the edges of mangrove islands, you will encounter hundreds of 2- to 4-inch schooling fish that move in unison as you glide by them. Sometimes the underwater bow wake will trigger a domino effect and the **hardhead silverside** *(Atherinomorus stipes)* or **Key silverside** *(Menidia conchorum)* will arc from the water in unison, looking like so many short

Key silverside

pieces of tinsel electrified by the sun. This aerial display is meant to fool predators with a disappearing act, but you can usually see some needlefish or barracuda slam into the school and slice a fish or two. It is quite a visual feast to don a mask and snorkel to watch the schools of silversides dance around the mangrove roots and part company to make room for a marauding mangrove snapper. The **bay anchovy** or **glass minnow** *(Anchoa mitchilli)* is another common baitfish that forms dense schools in this habitat. They usually don't provide the aerial acrobatics of the silversides and can be distinguished by having a single dorsal fin versus two dorsals on the silversides. Glass minnows are commonly found at Keys bait and tackle shops, often sold frozen in blocks.

Other slightly larger baitfish that are found in large schools near the channels include various **herrings, sardines, and pilchards.**

Imagine it is so dark out as you wait for the moonrise that you can
barely make out the other paddlers nearby. The million-candlepower
flashlight you hold scans the horizon and captures many jumping fish in
its beam; suddenly one careens with a thump off your bow. You have probably just encountered a ballyhoo or needlefish.

Ballyhoo *(Hemiramphus brasiliensis)* and **halfbeak** *(Hyporhamphus
unifasciatus)* are schooling baitfish that are 12 to 18 inches long and shoal
up near the surface in schools. These two are relatively common baitfishes
that have a narrow, paddle-shaped lower jaw and a relatively small upper
jaw. Ballyhoo tend to stay near the oceanside reefs, while the halfbeak can
be found in the coastal shallow waters. Both escape predators by jumping
out of the water and propelling themselves with the bottom of the tailfin.
Although the ballyhoo's
lower bill is stout, it does
not even come close to
the size and structure of
the largest of needlefish,

Needlefish have top and bottom jaws of the same size.

the **houndfish,** *Tylosurus crocodilus.* Houndfish can reach 10 pounds and 5
feet in length and have been known to cause serious wounds as they jump
toward bright lights held by fishermen at night. Usually found on the
ocean side of the Keys, the houndfish is not too commonly seen because
of the its ability to blend in with surface reflections. There are three other
species of **needlefish** *(Strongylura* species) that are found in the nearshore
waters, and all are slender, less than 2 feet long, and have a mouthful of
short, needlelike teeth in their tapered beaks. Wherever you can find
schooling silversides, around the perimeter you will always find needlefish
waiting to ambush the smaller prey. Because they spend so much time
near the brightly lighted surface, they have evolved the adaptation of a
fleshy sunshade at the top of each eye.

Needlefish are lightning fast and scurry away under cover of the light
refractions on the wave tops. They are perfectly camouflaged predators,
but occasionally will fall prey to the **barracuda** *(Sphyraena barracuda),*
which can be found on the flats and near the shorelines in small, medium,

and jumbo sizes. This large-eyed predator can reach 6 to 7 feet in length, and the world record is 85 pounds, but the most common size near the mangroves is 2 or 3 feet long. Barracuda have been given a bad rap and really pose no danger to humans in or on the water. There are a series of

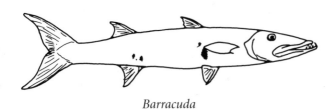

Barracuda

documented freak accidents that show just how savage an interaction with a barracuda's jaws can be. Razor sharp and able to rip off great slabs of flesh in one bite, these triangular teeth are fearsome indeed, but barracuda never intentionally attack humans. An "attack" is usually a case of mistaken identity, or due to someone spearfishing in the fish's hunting territory. Some people eat barracuda up to 5 pounds or so, but the bigger ones can sometimes carry ciguatera, a serious type of fish poisoning that unfortunately is neither detectable nor rendered inert after cooking.

Many fish can use a structure in the skin known as a chromatophore to change colors for communication and camouflage. If you happen upon an emerald and electric blue scrawling pattern on a boxlike fish, you have discovered the **scrawled cowfish** *(Lactophrys quadricornus),* whose trunklike structure does not allow for high speeds. The exoskeleton is perfect body armor composed of hexagonal plates over most of its soft tissue. The skin that covers this armor is able to change colors to blend in with the

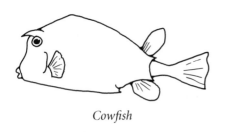

Cowfish

fish's environment. They are also able to protect themselves with a secreted toxin and can shoot jets of water to uncover crustaceans in their turtle grass habitat. Locals tell me that the large individuals (18 inches or so) are quite tasty if roasted over an open fire, but all the literature I have read states that scrawled cowfish may be toxic. I believe this may be due to the difficulty in properly filleting this fish, and during cooking some of the internal organs taint the flesh.

Darting along the bottom in the shallows in small schools of 20 to 50 individuals, the mojarras seem to produce the best "nervous water" and occasionally several V wakes. Nervous water is a term used to describe the isolated, choppy, rippling effect on the surface seen on bay waters just above a school of fish. These waters seem to shimmer and jiggle with an energy all their own The deeply forked tails of the mojarras are the best field mark for these 3- to 16-inch-long fish. There are about nine species found in the Keys, the largest being the **yellowfin mojarra,** *Gerres cinereus,* whose vertical bars and large size make it the most visible. All the mojarras have an extendable, low-slung mouth that is used for mudding about on the bottom for invertebrates. They are also occasionally seen tailing as they feed in

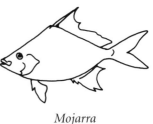

Mojarra

the shallows. One of the smallest is the **silver jenny** *(Eucinostomus gula)*, which can be found in the sandy shallows holding perfectly still. Since it is silvery white it camouflages really well on the substrate, but can be seen shoveling in mouthfuls of detritus in search of the critters it eats.

While driving through the Saddlebunch Keys, you may see on the flats what appears to be a huge wash of water the color of a vanilla milkshake. Look closely and you will probably spot the fish responsible for the mess jumping out of the water in a short attempt at flight. There are about six species of **mullet** *(Mugil* species) found in the Keys, the most common being the **white mullet** *(Mugil curema)*, which can reach 1 to 3 feet in length. The schools can each number in the thousands of individuals, and all those little mouths chewing up the bottom in search of detritus and plant material can cause quite a flurry of mud in the water. Many of the smallest young mullet are oceanic and when they reach adult size they can be found near shore and become a sought-after food for ospreys, pelicans, predatory fish, and humans. Eaten fresh, canned, or smoked, they have a delicious white flesh.

During the off seasons for lobster and crab harvest, you still might run across some traps attached to buoys. These buoys will probably have a name or boat numbers on them, and if you peer closely you might see that that the trap is full of small finfish. (Do everyone a favor—please respect private property, and don't tamper with any buoys or traps in the ocean;

this is a finable offense.) A majority of these fish will be **pinfish,** *Lagodon rhomboids,* which are mollusk-grinding bottom feeders that make the most excellent live bait. Pinfish belong to the porgy family, of which about a dozen species are found in the Keys. This group of fish is an important

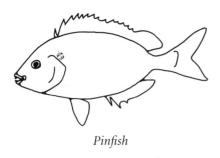

food and baitfish found in the warmer oceans of our world. Pinfish can usually be found at most bait and tackle stores and provide kids, who catch and sell them, a great little hobby business.

Look on any menu in a Keys restaurant and you will encounter in the seafood section grouper and snapper.

Pinfish

Anywhere you travel in the Keys, you are likely to run into one of these two groups of fish. The grouper or sea bass family has about 15 large, 15 medium, and 15 small members, but the three usually found on the menus are the red, black, and gag grouper. As the name suggests they look like bass, and sometimes individuals can be seen in shadowy roots or rocky crevices on the bottom. They can lie in wait without moving much and slowly stare you down. The **goliath grouper** or **jewfish** *(Epinephelus itajara)* can reach a weight of 600

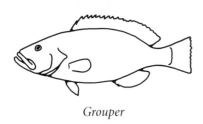

pounds, and many old photos of them can be found at bait and tackle shops. They have been a totally protected species since the 1980s and are now quite common in the nearshore waters. They especially like the cover of mangrove-lined creeks, where

Grouper

there is protection and food. There is a little creek in Cudjoe where I have seen five individuals sitting in the outgoing tide waiting for snacks to float by.

Snapper usually travel and live in large schools. Among the nine or so common species, the **mangrove** or **gray snapper** *(Lutjanus griseus)* is almost always encountered on a kayak trip. They school by the score in hidden mangrove roots and crash into baits with their fanglike teeth snapping. Large individuals of 20 inches are sometimes well hidden in the dark shadows, but the average size of 10 to 14 inches will make up the bulk of

the school. Shrimp, pin-
fish, and the occasional
mangrove tree crab that
falls from its perch com-
prise its diet. When caught
and iced immediately,
snappers turn a lovely
mango-red color, and an-
other of their common

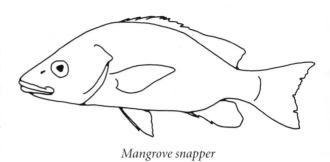

Mangrove snapper

names, mango snapper, is thought to derive from this phenomenon.

The big three fish that are highly sought after on the flats include the **bonefish** *(Albula vulpes)*, the **permit** *(Trachinotus falcatus)*, and the **tarpon** *(Megalops atlanticus)*.

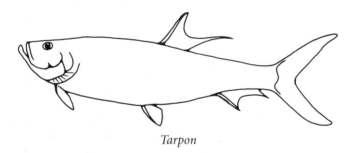

Tarpon

Baby tarpon are year-round Keys residents and can almost always be encountered somewhere near a backcountry mangrove island. Feeding most actively at dawn and dusk, they will readily take a plug, spinner, or live bait. Their acrobatic leaps are wonderful, and they tend to porpoise as they loll around at the surface. These fish have a remnant lung that can be utilized for oxygen absorption when in stagnant waters, and you can see them burp bubbles to the surface on flat calm seas. Their bigger brethren, which migrate through the area in the spring, can reach to 100 to 150 pounds and easily eat a foot-long mullet in one swallow. They migrate by the thousands through the channels and passes in the Keys.

Bonefish are the silent ghosts on the flats. On the highest flood tides we sometimes come across them sitting still in the sunshine in the furthest backwaters. They are quite approachable at this time, and we can get quite

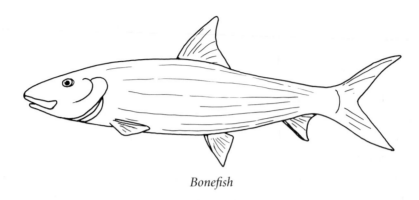

Bonefish

close to them in the foot-deep water. Other times it is spellbinding to watch the tailfin flop and wag at the surface as the bonefish noses in the mud for invertebrates. If startled they quickly jet off, leaving a streamlined V wake and usually alerting others. Although good eating, they do live up to their name and provide a number of false rib bones that are impossible to fillet out of the flesh. Most Bahamians who eat bonefish poach or steam them and pick the flesh off the skeleton.

Permit are large members of the jack family and can grow to 50 pounds. Its deep body and long, knifelike dorsal and tailfins make this flats

Permit

predator hard to miss. Permit have been seen charging through 6 inches of water chasing bait, with 5 inches of their back above the surface. Aggressive, fast, and great fighters, they are probably the hardest fish to land on the flats. They feed mainly on crabs and migrate offshore to the deepwater wrecks and reefs during midwinter and midsummer.

Redfish (*Sciaenops ocellatus*) and **common snook** (*Centropomus undecimalis*) are a rare sight in the backcountry of the Lower Keys, but there are healthy populations in the Upper Keys.

The redfish keeps quiet on the flats and can lie in the turtle grass beds and never be seen. One of the first ones I encountered in a kayak gave itself away only because of the unusual scarring on its back. I noticed several scratch marks on a dark field as if someone were keeping score at a dart game. As I looked closer, it became apparent that this was the dorsal side of a big redfish that had an osprey or eagle had used for target practice. The bird had probably hooked up with the fish but couldn't fly off with its 2-foot-long prize. Redfish will tail on the flats while feeding, and add a flopping, popping kind of noise to their antics. Overfished almost to a population collapse in the 1980s—because of the "blackened redfish" craze that began in Louisiana—it is now on the rebound because of sound fishery management techniques.

Snook

Sometimes a large, lone fish will be hiding in the shadows of the mangroves, and when you can make out the heavy black lateral line you can be sure that a snook is in view. This fish spawns in passes leading to large bays or open seas during the full-moon phases of June to August. Large specimens can be seen at the coral reefs weighing in at over 30 pounds, and the state record is 44 pounds. Snook are more common in the Upper Keys and Florida Bay areas.

Turtles

There are eight currently recognized species of sea turtles in the oceans today and we have five of the eight here in the Keys. The largest and least common is the **leatherback turtle** *(Dermochelys coriacea),* which can reach weights of 600 pounds and dive to more than 3,300 feet. There was one instance of a nesting female in the Marquesas in past years, but overall only 20 to 30 nests annually occur outside the tropics. Hatchlings can consume twice their body weight in jellyfish every day, and the adults will migrate 3,100 miles annually from their nesting beaches to their feeding grounds.

Sometimes as you paddle over the channels and flats you will see a gnarled trap buoy with yellow lines that takes a breath of air and then submerges. This will probably be a **loggerhead turtle** *(Caretta caretta),* which has the largest, most ill-proportioned head of all the turtles and can reach 350 pounds. Sea turtles can live to be 75 to 100 years old and reach sexual maturity at 12 to 30 years old. The loggerhead population is in pretty good shape, with an annual count of nearly 25,000 nests on the southeast coast

Green turtle cruising over manatee grass

of the United States. The loggerhead has large jaws for crushing crustaceans, clams, lobsters, and other morsels. Females lay about a hundred eggs in the summer months, and eight weeks later the 2-inch hatchlings dig out and swim off into the wild sea.

The **green turtle** *(Chelonia mydas)* happens to be the number one choice for making soup because of its tasty green-colored calipee and fat. The Turtle Kraals Restaurant in Key West was adjacent to a slaughterhouse for sea turtles up until 1972, when public awareness caused laws protecting the species to be enacted. The green turtle's tasty flesh is one of many reasons why the population of this creature is so low. It is usually a little smaller (300 pounds) than the loggerhead, and the head seems small in proportion to its carapace. In its young years it is omnivorous, eating jellyfish, crustaceans, and mollusks, but as they age green turtles establish grazing plots in the turtle grass and algae flats and eat little else but vegetation.

The hooked beak and colorful shell of the **hawksbill turtle** *(Chelonia imbricata)* help to identify this species, as do the four plates on top of the head between the nose and eyes. The green turtle has only two plates on

SPECIES IDENTIFICATION

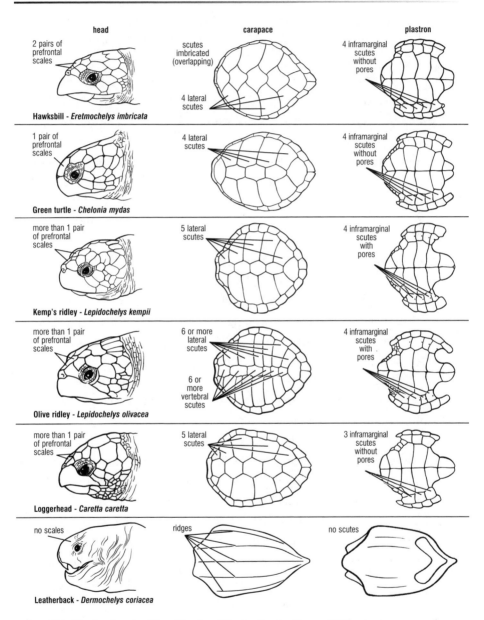

head	carapace	plastron
2 pairs of prefrontal scales	scutes imbricated (overlapping) / 4 lateral scutes	4 inframarginal scutes without pores
Hawksbill - *Eretmochelys imbricata*		
1 pair of prefrontal scales	4 lateral scutes	4 inframarginal scutes without pores
Green turtle - *Chelonia mydas*		
more than 1 pair of prefrontal scales	5 lateral scutes	4 inframarginal scutes with pores
Kemp's ridley - *Lepidochelys kempii*		
more than 1 pair of prefrontal scales	6 or more lateral scutes / 6 or more vertebral scutes	4 inframarginal scutes with pores
Olive ridley - *Lepidochelys olivacea*		
more than 1 pair of prefrontal scales	5 lateral scutes	3 inframarginal scutes without pores
Loggerhead - *Caretta caretta*		
no scales	ridges	no scutes
Leatherback - *Dermochelys coriacea*		

Sea Turtles Species Identification Illustration by Dawn Witherington, as used in The Anatomy of Sea Turtles, *U.S. Dept. of Commerce NOAA* the top of the head. The hawksbill can reach 130 pounds on its diet of primarily sponges. The females will lay three to five nests per season, and return every two to three years. The 100-plus hatchlings make for the water and return when they reach about 10 inches in length. They are said to spend these lost years in the Sargasso Sea, dining on the rich, bite-size flora and fauna available there.

The **Kemps Ridley** *(Lepidochelys kempi)* is the smallest and most threatened of all the sea turtles. Reaching a weight of 100 pounds and a size of less than 30 inches across its rounded shell, this creature has had a population decrease of nearly 75 percent in the last 55 years. It was back in 1947 that 40,000 were counted on the beaches of the western Gulf of Mexico. Now 95 percent of the remaining population comes to a single 17-mile stretch of beach in Mexico between April and June to lay their eggs during the day. The Kemps Ridley's omnivorous habits of eating blue crab, clams, mussels, shrimp, and snails probably brought it into direct conflict with shrimp boats on the Gulf Coast that wound up accidentally drowning many that were entangled in the nets.

Currently federal laws prohibit taking, molesting, or importing these ancient marine creatures. This, along with research and educational outreach about this valuable resource, will hopefully keep these amazing creatures away from the brink of extinction.

As I peeked into the triangular tunnel that led deep into the underwater root system of the red mangrove island, a slow-moving gray shape ambled out into the sunlight. I held my breath and remained perfectly still as it effortlessly paddled by, giving me the eye. It is rare to sight a **mangrove terrapin** *(Malaclemys terrapin)* in the Lower Keys. Not much has been studied in relation to the populations found in the Middle and Lower Keys, but scientist believe that the Upper Keys and the islands west of Key West harbor different subspecies. Mangrove terrapins lay clutches of 8 to 16 eggs in the early spring on sandy berms, and the eggs hatch out some 90 days later. They are not easily spotted in the field, as they do not lie out sunning themselves on logs and usually show only a small, thumb-sized head above the water's surface. The terrapin's diet consists of many different aquatic snails. Since they are not much used as a food source for people, though they were in the past, this subspecies might just be able to hang on and prosper. The home range of the Sand Keys critters is small, about half a square mile, and I suspect that might be true for any of the populations found in the southern Keys.

The **Florida box turtle** (*Terrapene carolina*) is a freshwater species that lives on fruits and insects in the wooded areas of many of the Keys. The rainy season usually stirs up more activity with these creatures, and many are seen trying to cross the streets. The humped dome and bright yellow lines of the carapace make it easy to identify. They lay about five eggs in the spring that hatch out 90 days later with perfectly formed, little domed turtles. These individuals usually have a small, specific home territory and should not be relocated, as they will not fare well.

The **Key mud turtle** (*Kinosternon bauri*) is another freshwater species found in the Lower Keys. The carapace is about 5 inches long, and the slightly wider female will lay several clutches of up to four eggs starting in April. Consuming a diet of insects and scavenged meat, this creature is often found in the freshwater ponds, solution holes, and mosquito-control ditches that have been dug in the Lower Keys. They have a brown oval carapace with black edging on each of the individual plates (scutes) and the underside reveals distinct growth rings in each of the plastron scutes. The relatives that I have handled up north all deserve the nickname of "stinkpot" but all the mud turtles that I have handled in the Keys do not have much of a musk gland odor. As is the case with the Key deer, some scientists argue that this turtle is a distinct subspecies occurring only in the Florida Keys.

Snakes

There are only a few snakes that, if handled gently, can be perfectly docile right from the wild, and the **mangrove water snake** (*Nerodia fasciata*) is one of them. The first time I saw this snake it was in the form of a silver jenny skimming backwards and tail first across a creek in the Content Keys. The snake had the fish in its jaws and was swimming it to a safe eating spot! On another occasion there was one in a slight S curve on the bottom in knee-deep water. We all slowly waded around the creature, and then I slowly put my hand and arm in the water. The snake looked up and leisurely swam into my outstretched arm. Very casually it was lifted from the water for all to view and the words "snake charmer" whispered from their lips.

This is a livebearer that will birth up to 11 young during the summer. This saltwater snake has some physiological adaptations in the skin that help it deal with the salt, but it needs to drink fresh water, and it seems that rain and dew slake its thirst. This snake gets as large as 3 feet long and can have a color pattern like that of a dull copperhead or a banded water moccasin.

The **green snake** *(Opheodrys aestivus)* is a thin and delicate-looking tree climber that is found often in the hardwood hammocks. Approaching 3 to 4 feet in length, this insect eater will occasionally take snails and frogs. It seems to be more active in the summer, when it will lay a clutch of up to a dozen eggs. The emerald green dorsal contrasts sharply with the belly, which can be butter yellow to off white.

During the heat of the summer the **diamondback rattlesnake** *(Crotalus adamanteus)* can be found in the Lower Keys. Most of my sightings have been on the roadside or as the snakes are swimming from island to island. Although poisonous, they are not aggressive and should be given a wide berth. They give birth to live, foot-long babies, which number up to 18 per litter in the summer. I am sure the diet includes a variety of rodents, baby birds, and other creatures. They are able swimmers, and there is a local story about a bridge fisherman who witnessed a duel between a barracuda and a swimming rattler. The rattler, which sacrificed some of its tail in the first round, was able to wrap around and bite the barracuda in the second round. The barracuda seemed to slowly succumb to the poison. The account states that the barracuda floated away belly-up, and the rattler swam away minus some of its tail end.

The **Florida cottonmouth** *(Agkistrodon piscivorus)* would definitely be something to worry about if they weren't so rare in the Keys. In the past 20 years I have heard of only three instances on Marathon Key where this species was a possible culprit in a snakebite that required hospitalization. The cottonmouth has been reported from Key Vaca, Key West, and Grassy Key.

Another rarity, and possibly found only in the Key Largo area, is the **eastern coral snake** *(Micrurus fulvius).* It is definitely more common on the mainland of Florida. A member of the cobra family, this snake can truly cause trouble with its neurotoxin. It is not aggressive and would need to really chew on you to inject its poison. Many are small, 20 inches or less, and the quickest field mark is the bright red, black, and yellow bands that encircle the snake. There is only one other snake that exhibits this pattern, and that is the nonpoisonous scarlet king snake. A quick little ditty to confirm which is which in the field goes "Red on black, venom lack; red on yellow, kill a fellow."

The **red rat snake** *(Elphae guttata)* is found from Key Largo to the Dry Tortugas and probably many of the islands in between. This is a beautiful and easily handled creature that does well in natural areas as well as in developed areas. The yellow-orange blotches on the dorsal side usually culminate in a V- or Y-shaped pattern on its head. They grow to about 4 feet and consume their share of rats, mice, and frogs. They are protected by law.

Indigo snakes *(Drymarchon corais)* are very uncommon in the Keys and in the rest of Florida as well. They were hunted for the pet trade to the point of depletion and have not recovered since. The indigo is a shiny black snake that will hiss in the wild, but rarely will it bite. The species is considered threatened under federal and state guidelines, and the indigo snake is now protected by law. The 8-foot-long adults mate in the winter and lay eggs in the summer. An average of ten eggs per clutch produce 20-inch-long babies in the summer. An 8-foot indigo can eat just about anything it wants, but rats and other snakes are the mainstays of its diet.

The **racer** *(Coluber constrictor)* or black racer will be the most common snake seen trailside, and it is usually moving fast away from any movement. Typical individuals are all black with a white chin patch and reach a size of about 3 feet. As with most all reptiles, they lay up to 22 eggs in the spring, and these hatch about 60 days later.

The **ribbon snake** *(Thamnophis sauritus)* is a unique livebearer that lives only in the freshwater marshes of the Lower Keys. Very few sightings of them have been made over the years, but I imagine that the road out to the Big Torch Key launch site or No Name Key would be a good areas to see these yellow-striped, slender snakes.

When I was first introduced to the **ringneck snake** *(Diadophis punctatus)* it was called the Big Pine ringless ringneck snake. It can usually be found in the same decaying organic leaf litter piles that are also the home of the Florida brown snake. The yellow ring around the neck is less distinct than that of its northern cousin, but the wonderful black-spotted, red-and-yellow underside of the tail is brilliant.

The **Florida brown snake** *(Storeria dekayi)* is a small brown snake that seldom grows to more than 12 inches. When I was young we called this one the decay snake because it usually lives in composting leaf piles and eats earthworms. Later on I realized the name was Dekay's snake and that it was named for one of America's renowned nineteenth-century biologists, Dr. James DeKay.

Probably the rarest of all snakes found in South Florida is the **rimrock crowned snake** *(Tantilla oolitica)*. This small (12-inch) and secretive snake has a black head and coppery brown body. It has a special fondness for hardwood hammocks and the associated vegetation, and is unique in that it has a rear grooved fang. There is no poison gland for the fang and it has not been studied enough to find out its diet or other basic biology. James Lazell writes in his book *Wildlife of the Florida Keys* that "For some reason, this rarest of all Florida snakes, whose habitat is being or has been consumed by human development, is only listed as 'threatened' (Campbell in McDairmid, 1978). I know of no more clear-cut case of endangerment." Key Largo Botanical Hammocks should be a great parcel of forest to give this species a chance of survival.

Alligators and Crocodiles

The **American alligator** *(Alligator mississippiensis)* is a large, mostly black reptile with a rounded snout. The young hatch out at about 6 inches and can grow to 15 feet, but usually average about 6 feet. A good rule of measurement is that every inch between the eye and nose openings equal about a foot in overall length. The alligator's primary water habitat is freshwater areas, although they will travel in the ocean for short durations. They are common in the Everglades, and there is a good population of them in the Lower Keys where the islands have a freshwater lens. In the rainy season young males may be encountered in ocean habitats as they

The crocodile will open its mouth while sunbathing for thermoregulation.

swim to other islands in search of new territories. On Big Pine Key you can usually find a gator at the Blue Hole Observation Pond off Key Deer Boulevard.

There are very few **American crocodiles** *(Crocodylus acutus)* and the majority of the population is found in the Key Largo area. About the same size as a gator, the crocodile can be easily identified because it exhibits a tapered snout and a gray to brown coloration overall. The crocodile is also distinguished by the fact that the fourth tooth of the lower jaw shows itself prominently when the jaws are shut. They also like to bask in the sun with their jaws wide open.

These secretive reptiles usually stay out of sight of humans and prefer the really quiet backwaters of the Upper Keys. This nonaggressive reptile nests in April and May, and the 10-inch young hatch out in the summer.

Birds

During John James Audubon's visit to the Keys back in 1832, his birding dreams were fulfilled on his birthday, April 26, when he saw for the first time a flock of flamingoes near Indian Key. His journals, letters, and five-volume literary masterpiece *Orthinological Biography* are a great resource of information for the Keys as they appeared in the early days. Today it is still possible to see a flamingo in the wild, but they, along with all the other wading birds, have suffered serious population decreases due to habitat alteration and plume hunting throughout the early 1900s.

Only the most common and easily observed birds are listed in this book, as there are over 285 species of birds that occur in the Florida Keys. The Florida Keys National Wildlife Refuge (305-872-2239) distributes an excellent checklist of birds that notes the seasonal appearance of each species and its relative abundance. The Florida Keys Wild Bird Center in Key Largo (305-852-4486) has an excellent local birding guide that indicates good birding locations and directions.

Diurnal Raptors

In the fall and spring there are some great migrations of birds that occur over the Keys as species escape the winter cold fronts. Looking up in the dark blue sky it is possible to see hundreds to thousands of black, pepper-like dots floating along on high thermals. Upon close inspection you can find everything from turkey vultures to peregrine falcons in the skies. The peak fall migration is celebrated with the Florida Keys Birding and Wildlife festival in late September through October, when as many as 30,000 raptors pass through from as far away as Canada and the arctic. The raptors are all heading to various locations including Cuba, the Caribbean, and as far away as Central and South America. Lots of current information about the times and locations of other hawk watches can be obtained at www.hawkwatch.org.

The beautiful soaring and teetering of the **turkey vulture** *(Cathartes aura)* is in sharp contrast to its rugged, red, ugly head. The featherless head is a perfect thing to have if your feeding habits include carrion and other rank appetizers. One of the best field identification marks for the turkey vulture is that the wings in flight show a shallow V or dihedral. Most other birds of its size and shape have a straight-line wing profile, and this will denote some type of raptor. They are an efficient clean-up crew and can pick a Key deer carcass clean to the bone an less than a week. Their keen sense of smell allows them to target rotting flesh from a good distance away. Turkey vultures are summer ground-nesters and use thick brush or tree cavities to protect the two eggs they lay.

An osprey returns to its nest with a meal.

The most common raptor on the drive down U.S. Route 1 will be the **osprey,** *Pandion haliaetus.* The osprey can be seen hovering over the shallows awaiting the precise moment to plunge. It starts its dive headfirst and at the final moment pulls up to bare its talons upon fish that average a foot in length. After a complete submergence you might see them fly away, shaking off the water, with a barracuda, mullet, or needlefish. If it is bringing home the food to its young, it will usually dine on the head first and fly off with the balance of the carcass for the nestlings. The peak of the egg-laying is usually in December, with an average of three eggs laid per nest. About 35 days later the young hatch, and in eight to nine weeks the young will be able to fledge the nest and the parents will teach them how to hunt.

Oftentimes it is an osprey that alerts me that an eagle is nearby. The osprey seems to call consistently and with much agitation, and the eagle responds with its high-pitched series of short squeaks. When I crane my neck to search the skies, the spectacular white head and tail of the **bald eagle** *(Haliaeetus leucocephalus)* are hard to misidentify. Eagles are an uncommon sight in the Keys—there are only a handful of nesting pairs. (The entire state of Florida had 996 active nests in 1999.) Most eagles in the Keys are in the relative seclusion of the backcountry islands. Like the ospreys, eagles also display some spectacular courtship flights in September and October, but unlike ospreys the eagles also interlock talons and free-fall together for hundreds of feet before finally releasing one another to fly off unharmed. Clutches of two eggs are usually laid by December, and the eaglets are usually fledged in four months, after about one month of incubation and three months on the nest. For the next two to three months the immature eagles are taught to master flying and feeding techniques, and soon after that they migrate north. The northward migration shows the height of wanderlust travel—some eagles banded in South Florida were documented a short four weeks later in Canada.

There are another dozen hawklike birds that can be seen in the Keys, but the only other species that nest here are the **red-shouldered hawk** *(Buteo lineatus),* which nests in the winter, and the **swallow-tailed kite** *(Elanoides forficatus),* which is a rare summer nester in the Upper Keys.

The **broad-winged hawk** *(Buteo platypterus)* and the **sharp-shinned hawk** *(Accipiter striatus)* are common winter visitors, but are never seen in the summer months. The small, colorful falcon known as the **American kestrel** *(Falco sparverius)* is a common sight on roadside power lines and poles. These individuals are usually northern migrants that will spend September through March in the Keys and South Florida. The best time of year, if you enjoy seeing the hawks, is in the fall for the migration, when you can challenge yourself with field identification of these fluent fliers. It is during the fall migration that our area can have the highest number of **peregrine falcons** *(Falco peregrinus)* with daily counts of over a hundred individuals. Florida is an important wintering ground for peregrines from as far away as the arctic. One of the largest falcons in Florida, it can usually be seen feeding on the numerous migrant waterfowl present in the winter.

Fish-Eating Water Birds

With a wingspan close to the length of a sheet of standard plywood (90 inches) and weighing in at 3.3 pounds, the **magnificent frigate bird** *(Fregata magnificens)* is one incredible fork-tailed flier. This "man-of-war" bird, or more correctly, "pirate bird" is astounding to watch, with aerial acrobatics honed for harassing others. Terns and gulls with fish in their beaks are tailed so that the fish will fall and the frigate bird can snatch it up. Offshore in the blue waters of the Gulf Stream it is a different story, as the "pirate bird" becomes the "man-of-war" bird. It will then use its aerial adeptness to sight and capture flying fish and other jumping pelagic baitfish as they try to escape tuna and dolphin. The only nesting sites in North

America are found in the mangrove islands of the Marquesas and the Dry Tortugas. One egg is laid in the spring, and the young will fledge 6 months later. The young have an all-white head and chest, females have a white chest, and the males are all black with a distendable blood-red throat pouch.

Looking like a remnant pterodactyl, the **brown pelican** *(Pelecanus occidentalis)* is a common sight everywhere in Florida. The insecticide chemical DDT almost did it in back in the 1960s, but thanks to conservation and repopulation efforts by organizations such as the Suncoast Seabird Sanctuary, the pelican population thrives today. They can be seen feeding in groups or solo diving into the waters and

A pelican can consume 3.5 pounds of fish in a day and live to 35 years.

bouncing back to the surface to strain gallons of seawater from their pouches. I especially like to see laughing gulls perch on the pelican's head hoping a small fry will escape its pouch and become fair game. They breed in every month but October and usually lay three white eggs per nest. Fledging usually occurs at about 12 weeks. The brown pelican can live to be 35 years of age and can fly about 35 miles per hour. The average adult weighs in at 5 to 8 pounds and eats about 3 to 4 pounds of fish a day.

The **white pelican** *(Pelecanus rythrorhynchos)* is a winter visitor to the Keys from its central Canada breeding grounds. It usually stops at Florida

Bay in the Everglades, but can be seen on occasion in the Lower Keys. With a 10-foot wingspan, this big white bird is hard to miss.

In midwinter, rafts of **double-crested cormorants** *(Phalacrocorax auritus)* will be comprised of hundreds of individuals feeding together. One blustery cold-front day I watched a thousand of them chasing down a school of baitfish. The sight reminded me of the Escher print—in which the birds change into waves and then metamorphose into fish—as they flew into and out of the frothy waters chasing fish. It is a common year-round resident that lays four eggs at any time of the year but predominantly in the spring and summer, March through August. Cormorants can be seen drying out their wings after swimming in the water to grab fish with their hooked bills. The **anhinga** *(Anhinga anhinga)* is the freshwater equivalent and obtains its fish prey by spearing them with its pointed bill. They are rarely seen in the Keys, but when they are it is usually flying overhead or at the Blue Hole Nature Trail on Big Pine Key.

The **black skimmer** *(Rynchops niger)* with its small legs and huge bill is a common winter resident. Good areas to see these birds include the waterfront at Key West Harbor and where Sisters Creek and Sombrero Beach meet in Marathon. Skimmers feed in flight by slicing the water's surface with their long lower bills and snapping shut on any fish they encounter. They nest on the mainland of Florida in the summer.

You can see every feather and detail of the **red-breasted merganser** *(Mergus serrator)* as they feed underwater on small fish in the gin-clear shallows. The adult males are rarely seen in their Florida wintering grounds, and the females travel as far as Canada to return to the breeding grounds.

Long-Legged Wading Birds

The big bird you see stalking the flats squawks like some kind of little dinosaur as it flies away. If it was large, white, and had yellowish legs, it was most likely the white morph of the **great blue heron** *(Ardea herodias)*. This 49-inch-tall bird can be found everywhere in the Keys in three distinct morphs: all white, blue-gray, and the white-headed blue-gray, also called Wurdemann's heron. The blue-gray plumage can be seen all over the U.S. and Canada, but the other two are specialties of south Florida.

There is great debate about whether or not these color phases may be subspecies, color morphs, or actually species of their own and with some new DNA studies, we may have some solid answers to this hundred-year-old question. The breeding season lasts from November through July, and four eggs are the average per nest. From recent information gathered, the population of light morphs seems to be holding steady at

Great blue heron

nearly 2,000 individual birds, and the great blue heron (dark morph) numbers about 10,000 individuals statewide.

One of the most remarkable differences between the great blue heron and its shorter relative, the great egret, is in its wingspan. The great blue boasts a 72-inch wingspan, which is 20 inches more than the 50-inch wingspan of the great egret.

The black legs and large size of the **great egret** *(Ardea alba)* are the quickest field identification marks to distinguish it from other waders. Feeding groups of up to one hundred have been observed on the flats in the backcountry in the spring. They lay three or four eggs in a nesting colony beginning in January, and it is at this time that the skin around the eyes turns a brilliant green and the breeding plumes are the showiest. The breeding plumes almost did the population in during the early 1900s, as they were highly sought after for the fashionable millinery trade.

A little bit smaller than the great egret and with bright yellow feet is the **snowy egret** *(Egretta thula)*. Another good field mark is the black bill, which is about half the size of the great egret's. This bird was also almost wiped out at the turn of the twentieth century, but has staged a comeback. They nest from March to August and average two to five eggs per nest. The yellow feet that are so distinctive are used to attract fish by either shuffling them on the bottom or dragging their feet in flight over the surface of the waters and spearing fish that are attracted to the disturbance.

The sight of a wading bird that staggers and flails with outstretched wings on the flats and strikes excessively at baitfish while feeding usually indicates the **reddish egret** *(Egretta rufescens)*. This "drunken sailor" act is humorous and wacky, but is the best field identification along with the reddish head and neck and the pink-red color at the base of the black-tipped bill. Two color morphs are found, dark and white, with the white morph representing about 5 percent of the total population. These are perhaps the least numerous of the egrets. They nest in South Florida in December, laying two to five eggs in nests on mangrove islands.

When a smallish slate blue heron with an all-white belly flies away, squawking vociferously, you can be sure it is a **tricolored heron** *(Egretta tricolor)*. This wader starts to lay its three or four eggs between February and July. This bird is a slow stalker in the shallows and skulks among the mangroves, still-feeding (that is, holding perfectly still until a food item comes within range) on the many small baitfishes around the roots.

The **little blue heron** *(Egretta caerulea)* is an all-dark bird with a black-tipped, blue-based bill. The all-white juvenile is quite approachable while feeding, and I have had them feed right off the bow of my kayak while I was photographing them in the shallows. An interesting plumage change occurs when they molt into the dark adult: A "chevron" of dark feathers on the all-white plumage is evident when the bird is in flight. Many believe that competition for nesting space from the cattle egret between February and August and loss of habitat have contributed to the downturn in the little blue heron population.

Approximately 400 years after Columbus sailed to the new world, the **cattle egret** *(Bubulcus ibis)* thought it was a good idea also. Arriving on its own in South America in the early 1930s, it had migrated north and was documented nesting in Florida by 1953.

Today cattle egrets are found in most of the western hemisphere. They nest from March through August, laying four eggs. This is the smallest of our white herons, just 20 inches tall. The yellow bill of the mature adult is a good field characteristic to look for.

The **green heron** *(Butorides virescens)* is a patient fisherman and has a few tricks up its wings that I have observed closely. As we slowly made our way up the creek using a jungle-gym technique to propel our boats, this green heron flew and landed several feet off our bow. It must have recognized that the kayaks put the baitfish off guard so that they sought refuge in the roots at the waters edge. For nearly a month this same green heron met us in the creek and was quite successful in its fishing endeavors. This bird is often overlooked because it blends in with the surrounding root structure, and its ability to stay perfectly still in any yogalike position makes it hard to detect. They

Punk hairdos of the young green heron

have also learned to use "bait" (shiny litter, plastic, sticks, gum wrappers, foil, and similar objects) to attract small baitfish. They nest prolifically through the spring, laying three or four eggs per nest.

The **least bittern** *(Ixobrychus exilis)* lives up to its name, as there are few sightings of this small, year-round resident. Most birders feel fortunate if they get to hear its cuckoolike, woodwind call. They seem to prefer freshwater areas of the Keys.

The **black-crowned night heron** *(Nycticorax nycticorax)* is a rare sight in the Keys. They seem to prefer freshwater environments, and fish are the main prey items. Mostly feeding at dusk and through the evening, the black-crowned night heron is usually seen resting in the shadows of the mangrove fringes.

If the black-crowned night heron says "quock," then the **yellow-crowned night heron's** *(Nyctanassa violacea)* call would be a "skwok." This common heron is also a night feeder, but usually breaks the rules if a good low tide is occurring, because that is when the crabs and shrimp that they eat are most vulnerable. Nesting from March to June, they lay three or four pale blue eggs, usually on a mangrove island. In the winter, they roost on the lee shores of mangrove islands in flocks numbering up to 20 individuals.

Local Birds with Crazy Bills

The **wood stork** *(Mycteria americana)* will be sighted more commonly in the Upper Keys, as its preferred habitat is the freshwater wetlands of South Florida. An ungainly bird with a huge bill, it feeds by means of a highly refined ability to feel fish near its slightly open bill, and it reacts with a snap in about 1/10,000 of a second! That is faster than the fastest shutter speed on my Nikon, and must make the wood stork an efficient hunter. The estimated population of the species was about 75,000 in the early 1930s, and today it has been reduced to less than 20 percent of that number.

Often confused with the flamingo because of its beautiful pink, red, and carmine colors, the **roseate spoonbill** *(Ajaia ajaia)* stands out like an incredible jewel against the tropical blue sky. Florida Bay and the southwest coast of Florida boast the largest colonies of breeding birds. They nest with other herons and ibises in November or December, and the young fledge in the spring. There are probably 30 to 50 in the Lower Keys, and I see them most commonly as they are finishing with their nesting activities in the spring. There are usually no more that a dozen in a flock, and they feed at the lowest of low tides by sweeping those crazy, spoon-shaped bills from side to side.

The **greater flamingo** *(Phoenicopterus ruber)* will always have a shroud of mystery wrapped around it in the Keys. There is a small enclave of civilization at the terminus of Everglades National Park that bears the creature's name, but many believe the town was misnamed after the numerous spoonbills in the area. Audubon did describe it as being here in his travels, and he also noted what he thought were nesting mounds in the Sugarloaf Key area, but these were never substantiated. Many of the flamingoes sighted in the Everglades in the early 1980s were thought to be escapees from the Hialeah racetrack. Today there are some that seem to return yearly to Florida Bay, and the theory is that they may be migrants from the Bahamas.

From within the tangled roots of the red mangroves, you hear a honking sound, and a white bird with black wingtips erupts from the shadows.... That would be the **white ibis** *(Eudocimus albus)*. It has a red, recurved drinking straw of a bill that it uses to slurp small crustaceans from soft, muddy shorelines. Rarely solitary, this bird is seen in small flocks and is incredibly beautiful against a blue northern sky. This species does nest in the Keys and has the richest blood-red bill and legs during breeding season, from March to May.

Of the seven species of rails, gallinules, and coots found in the Keys, the most likely to be encountered while kayaking near sunset in these mangrove islands is the **clapper rail** *(Rallus longirostris)*. Although I have seen only one—a roadkilled specimen from Big Torch Key—on many occasions I have heard small flocks "clappering" at sunset from various backcountry islands. If you use your imagination, the call of these birds sounds like someone clapping.

Long red legs and a thin black bill confirm that you are viewing a **black-necked stilt** *(Himantopus mexicanus)*. There can be no mistaking this elegant beauty. This uncommon nester is usually seen in shallows where soft mud bottoms are present. The nest is a little hump of vegetation with up to four eggs, and if the tide comes up too high the bird will actually add more nesting material as needed. Most of the small nests I have encountered have been in coves that are laden with seaweed piled high in a rack line.

Shorebirds: Sandpipers, Plovers, Gulls, and Terns

Of the eight plovers found here, **Wilson's plover** *(Charadrius wilsonia)* is an uncommon year-round resident that nests through the summer on isolated beach areas. The **black-bellied plover** *(Pluvialis squatarola)* is another traveler from the arctic tundra and can be seen in its striking black belly, chin, and throat plumage during the spring, as these late migrants prepare to make their way thousands of miles northward.

Bahia Honda State Park Beach is a great area to see many of the 22 types of sandpipers found here in the Keys. The **ruddy turnstone** *(Arenaria interpres)* is a common shoreline dweller. Although most of the mature adults fly off north for nesting in the summer, you can still see some subadults lifting small rocks and beach debris in search of small invertebrates.

Gulls and terns number about 20 species, but the one most likely to catch your ear will be the **laughing gull** *(Larus atricilla).* This abundant year-round resident can be seen at most beaches and fish-cleaning stations looking for a scrap. It has a call like a raucous laugh that seems to be mocking anyone and everything. The head is black-capped, and the bill is reddish during the summer breeding season. Seventy-five percent of the entire Florida population of 18,000 to 20,000 nesting pairs nest in the Tampa Bay area. The state of Florida has about 15 major nesting colonies, and one of these is in the Keys.

The **royal tern** *(Sterna maxima)* is a spectacular plunge feeder with a black cap and orange-red bill. Plunge feeders fold their wings and dive beak first to capture fish. This is the most common large tern and is usually found in the good company of laughing gulls. When you are paddling and you hear a soft *yeek* from the sky, keep scanning the blue heavens for this speedy bird.

One of the smallest of the terns is the **least tern** *(Sterna antillarum).* It is easily identified from March to September as a breeding adult, because it is the only adult tern with a yellow bill. One of the many birds hunted for their brilliant white plumage, it was harvested to the tune of 100,000 a year in the early 1900s. In recent years the Florida population has been estimated at about 8,000 nesting pairs. With habitat destruction and human and canine interference with their natural nesting sites, it is no wonder that 75 percent of the least terns in Tampa nest on rooftops. It used to be a wonderful sight to see them skimming water from the rain puddles in the Winn-Dixie and Eckerd Drugstore parking lots on Big Pine Key. Corporate decision-makers at Eckerd decided to paint the roof black, and that put an end to that. I think it is all about habitat—if we provide a good habitat for the wildlife, it can rebound.

Miscellaneous Mangrove Dwellers

Pigeons and Doves number about a half dozen common species, of which three have been introduced by humans.

The **rock dove** (*Columba livia*) is only some kind of fancy name for the standard New York City street pigeon! When sufficiently well fed, they make great snacks for migrating hawks. Usually they are found in or on the more than 40 bridges in the Keys, as well as other man-made structures.

The **Eurasian collared dove** (*Streptopelia decaocto*) has been found in the United States since the 1980s following an introduction in the Bahamas. During the spring when these birds are breeding they are rather noisy and have a quite an attitude in their flight calls as they approach the nests. Easily identified by the black collar on the back of the neck and the gray-tan body, they can usually be heard calling in the interiors of mangrove forests.

The **mourning dove** (*Zenaida macroura*) is similar in size, color, and pattern to the Eurasian collared dove, but lacks the black collar. It is thought that the two compete for space, and the general feeling now is that the collared dove is taking over the mourning dove's niche in the Keys.

When the **white-crowned pigeon** (*Columba leucocephala*) takes off in flight, it seems to be clapping its wings together, with all of the noise that emanates. The all-white cap on the head is the best field identification mark. Some of these birds winter in the Bahamas, Cuba, and other Caribbean islands where they are sought-after game birds. In fact, about 10,000 were harvested in Jamaica in 2002. They nest in the summer in the Florida Keys, where they—and the food they eat—are protected by law. Nesting begins in the late spring, and two eggs are laid in a minimal stick nest on isolated mangrove islands. The parent birds travel to nearby islands with hardwood hammocks to forage for berries and seeds. This daily migration to and from the islands features a consistent and surprising phenomenon that enables researchers to study the birds' populations: Nearly all the adult breeding males—which have shiny white heads, as opposed to the females' gray-white heads—return to the nesting islands between 8:20 and 10:10 every morning! I once tallied 250 birds in that time frame on one of the backcountry islands.

Another intriguing fact is that these birds feed their young poison-wood berries almost exclusively during the young bird's life. The berries are rich in lipoid proteins, which are very beneficial to the youngsters' growth. How they deal with the toxic characteristics of the poisonwood berry is a mystery.

The **mangrove cuckoo** *(Coccyzus minor)* is one of four species of cuckoos and anis that are sighted in the Keys year-round. They also are be-lieved to migrate between here and the Bahamas and Cuba. In May they begin to set up nesting territories, and can be heard calling as the summer rains start. The nesting starts in late spring, and two eggs are laid on a loose stick nest. I have seen very few mangrove cuckoos, but have heard hundreds of calls every year. The distinctive *gawing* call sounds as if it is part duck and part crow! You may spot the yellow recurved bill and dark mask of this caterpillar eater in the bird's red mangrove habitats.

The **common nighthawk** *(Chordeiles minor)* is one of the four goat-suckers and a herald of the summer mosquito months. This aerial acrobat usually sets up its territory by circling overhead and *peenting* its unique call to all below. This is usually an evening activity, but during the full moon it can be heard all night long. Occasionally it will swoop down to-ward land with grace and speed on a high dive that ends as it pulls out only 10 or so feet above the ground. The swoosh of its feathers as it hits the pull-up zone is astounding. The batlike, floppy flight of this bird is a good field identification characteristic, as are the white bars on the under-sides of the wings. It will nest anywhere.

Another winter visitor to the Keys is the **belted kingfisher** *(Ceryle al-cyon)*, a small, blue-gray bird with a punk-rock hairdo and an attitude to match. The raucous, chattering, ratcheting call can be heard all along mangrove shorelines in the winter. The kingfishers are defining their fishing territories with this distinctive call, and will often have aerial dog-fights. We once saw a chattering pair zoom up the small creek we were on. They came so close to our heads that we all ducked as they swooshed by. These birds are fish eaters and will hover and plunge headfirst toward prey at the water's surface.

The most commonly sighted of the three woodpeckers in the Keys is the **red-bellied woodpecker** *(Melanerpes carolinus)*. Many confuse this bird with the red-headed woodpecker, which has a totally red head. It is easy to distinguish the two: The area around the eye on the red-bellied woodpecker is a whitish-tan. They nest in log cavities and feed frequently in the red mangrove forests.

Moving into the niche of the kingfisher when it departs for northern climes, the **gray kingbird** *(Tyrannus dominicensis)* aggressively defends its mangrove islets. I have seen them chase away eagles, ospreys, and vultures that ventured too close to their nesting territories. There are about 11 additional types of flycatchers and kingbirds, but the gray kingbird is the most common summer mangrove nester. This insect eater lays up to three eggs in a stick nest in May.

Swallows include about ten species that are usually just migrating through the Keys. The **barn swallow** *(Hirundo rustica)* is the most commonly seen swallow, and a few mud nests have been found recently under some Upper Keys highway bridges. The deeply forked tail, pointed wings, and dark blue underparts of this elegant flier can usually be seen in the fall as they travel to their wintering grounds in Central America.

It is 2 AM and the full moon of June is shining down upon you. But that is not what is keeping you awake. What is keeping you awake is the nonstop, "double-CD" set of birdsongs that is emanating from the **northern mockingbird** *(Mimus polyglottos)* outside your window! This is the Florida State Bird, and its signature song will consist of other birdsongs or man-made noises that are heard in its territory. Ringing telephones, backup signals, alarm clocks, and other mechanized noises have been included in their mating songs. There is one in my yard that has a mangrove cuckoo call in its song, as well as the call of the red-bellied woodpecker. When all the singing is over they settle down to a nest or two per summer with an average of three to five eggs.

The **white-eyed vireo** *(Vireo griseus)* is the most common of the seven vireos that can be found here in the Keys. This sparrow-sized, gray-green bird has yellow spectacles, a white eye, and yellowish sides. The bird is a perpetual singer with a call of five to seven notes ending in a staccato *chik.* You have to look hard to spot it in the underbrush.

After wintering in South America, the **black-whiskered vireo** *(Vireo altiloquus)* returns to breed in South Florida in May. This familiar Florida bird is a mangrove dweller and builds its shallow, woven cup of a nest in the spring. Its heavier bill and distinctive black whiskers distinguish it from the migrating red-eyed vireo.

Black streaks on the face and consistent tail wagging distinguish the **prairie warbler** *(Dendroica discolor)* from its common relative the **palm warbler** *(Dendroica palmarum)*. The prairie warbler nests throughout the summer in coastal mangrove swamps. This insect eater has an ascending trill that sounds like a *szee.* The palm warbler is a common winter visitor but returns north during the summer breeding season.

There are no color combinations more enticing than a rich green palm leaf against a deep blue sky. Throw in a blood-red **cardinal** *(Cardinalis cardinalis)* and you have all the primaries in the color palette. Year-round singers, these nonmigratory seed eaters nest in the summer.

Red-winged blackbirds *(Agelaius phoeniceus)* used to only winter in the Keys, but they like it so much that we have a resident population now. This abundant bird is a favorite singer and can be found everywhere in the Keys. During the winter, flocks of hundreds will get together with some of the other ten songbird species roosting in small offshore mangrove islets, and their noise at sunset can be deafening.

Mammals

The **Key deer** *(Odocoileus virginianus clavium)* live on about a dozen islands in the Lower Keys scattered between Big Pine Key and west to Sugarloaf Key. The average height is 25 to 30 inches at the shoulder, and males weigh in at an average of 80 pounds. Females are a bit smaller, with an average of 65 pounds, and fawns are about 3.5 pounds at birth. Compare this with the 200-pound deer that are found in Maine, and you can see how dwarfed Key deer are. After many thousands of years living in these tropical islands they have adapted to this harsh environment by a size reduction and other subtle differences in fur color and bone structure.

When the Key deer was listed as an endangered species in 1967, biologists estimated the population to be about 50 individuals. The current population is estimated at about 800 on Big Pine and No Name Keys. Key deer live to an average age of 8 or 9 years and one was documented to be at least 21 years old.

Key deer

They are on the same seasonal cycle as other northern whitetail deer, with fawning occurring in the spring and mating in the fall. Females breed at two years and males at three years of age. After the spring equinox, when the daily photoperiod is longer, the males will shed their antlers. This co-incides with the birthing of the fawns and prevents the bucks from fighting with the young in their territory. New antlers grow throughout the summer, and the velvet that covers them sheds at summer's end.

Most of the good deer viewing is on Key Deer Boulevard and on No Name Key.

Raccoons *(Procyon lotor)* are ubiquitous and seem to prefer having human structures to scout around on their daily rounds. There are some truly wild ones that live on the outermost islands as well. Miles of open ocean can separate these islands, which have no permanent freshwater re-sources, but the raccoons still survive. The Lower Keys have a much smaller, blonder raccoon that lives by its wits on these ocean islands.

I have watched these bandits eat many crabs over the years but only saw the crab get the upper hand once. A scraggly old coon had a crab in its paws one moment and in a second the crab had his claws on the coon's

The Sea Mammals

Bottlenose dolphin are commonly seen in the waters surrounding the Florida Keys. They grow to 12 feet but usually average 7 to 8 feet long.

Bottlenose dolphin cavort in the Little Pine Key area.

They are year-round residents unlike the manatee, whose seasonal migrations transit many areas of the Florida Keys' waters. Manatee can commonly be seen in the Dusenberry Creek area of Key Largo.

nose! After some tugging the crab was brought under control, and the coon ambled into the mangrove thicket, where sharp popping sounds signaled the crab's demise.

The **Key bunny** *(Sylvilagus palustris hefneri)* is a smaller version of the mainland marsh rabbit. The bushy white tail is absent, the head is wider, and the teeth are quite small when compared to the mainland and Key Largo species. Dr. Skip Lazelle did much research on this creature in the early 1980s, and determined that a subspecies status could be petitioned for. This status was granted, and to thank Playboy Enterprises for funding assistance the surname of the founder has been latinized and used for the animal's scientific name.

The bunny is not often seen. It has a range from Big Pine to Boca Chica Key but usually does not travel far from its small home range of about 10 acres. Late in the day and early in the evening you might spot these on the Jack Watson Nature Trail off Key Deer Boulevard on Big Pine Key.

Other Furbearers

The familiar **European rat** *(Rattus rattus)* is ubiquitous in all man-made shorelines and ports. They are not seen often on these backcountry islands except on those frequented by people.

The **Key cotton rat** *(Sigmodon hispidus)*, the **Key wood rat** *(Neotoma floridana)*, and the **silver rice rat** *(Oryzomys argentatus)* are all unique species that are wild and do not depend on humans or their structures for habitat. The wood rat is a resident of Key Largo and builds its own castle of sticks that can be the size of a small loveseat. The wood rat is the original pack rat, and it will decorate the interiors of its nests with colorful plastics and shiny litter found on their forays. The Key cotton rat and the silver rice rat are found in small numbers because of the shrinking habitat available for wild things.

The **gray squirrel** *(Sciurus carolinensis)* and **opossum** *(Didelphis virginiana)* are found only in the Upper Keys.

As you finish packing up your gear and enjoy the last glow of a salmon-colored sunset, you may notice some wild flying creatures that look like bats. It is most likely these will be nighthawks, which are easily identified by the white bars on the undersides of the wings. If smaller and more erratic in flight, they could be one of the several bat species found in the Keys. All are insect eaters, and the most common is the **velvety free-tailed bat,** *Molossus molossus.* Found in the United States only in the Lower Keys, this bat is common in Cuba and in the rest of the Caribbean. There is a large colony in the Monroe County School Facilities Building on United Street in Key West. If you show up at sunset you will probably run into others looking for some of the estimated 1,300 individuals that live in this roost. These bats can eat up to 3,000 insects per night each, and I am sure that a colony like this is what Richter C. Perky dreamed about when he had his bat tower built on Sugarloaf Key. Unfortunately for Perky and his dreams of a mosquito-free fishing camp on Sugarloaf, the bats he placed in the tower soon escaped and headed for parts unknown.

Walking Insects

There are more than 80 species of spiders that inhabit the Keys. The most common ones that spin the webs encountered on the trails are featured here.

An X marks the spot with the **silver argiope spider** *(Argiope argentata)*. Almost certainly, if you see a web with a white X in the center and a silver-bodied spider on it, you can be confident it will be a silver argiope. It is theorized that this zigzag X makes the spider appear bigger and marks the web so birds will avoid it.

The **spiny orb weaver** *(Gasteracantha cancriformis)* is the most common spider found on the trails. It is a small spider with a black-spotted white carapace. The six red conical spikes that radiate from the body gave rise to its other common name, the **crown of thorns spider.**

There is a **golden silk spider** *(Nephila clavipes)* web on my favorite trail that is about 40 inches across. One day I could see a hole the size of my fist in it. It was assumed that the prairie warbler I had seen stealing insects from the web was responsible for the fly-through. As we sat there motionless for ten minutes, the little yellow warbler flitted 5 inches from my nose as it scouted around the perimeter of the web There is also a small mangrove water snake that lounges nearby on a daily basis. Along with all this is the biggest spider you will find in the Keys. This amazing creature reaches an overall length of 5 to 6 inches and has wonderful burnt orange bands on its legs. The head starts out white and culminates in a red-orange at the tail end. The web of the golden silk spider was even used to make gun sight crosshairs for rifles in World War II, because it exceeds the tensile strength of steel and will not rust!

The **marine water striders** of the *Gerris* species can usually be found in abundance on the calm lee shores of mangrove islands. This is also the preferred area of the mangrove islands for this kayaker and many others. These grayish little striders are often seen in groups of 30 to 100 and reach about 0.25 inch in length. They zip around the surface in crazy zigzag circles in tight clusters the size of pie plates. I have never seen them eat nor have I seen them being eaten.

Flying Insects

Dragonflies belong to an order that is 300 million years old. The large state of Florida boasts over 150 species, with those in the Keys representing a small portion of those. Dragonflies eat mosquitoes in all stages of their life cycles. All dragonflies have four wings that enable them to fly forward and backward. Many mating pairs can be seen in flight in the spring. One of the most unique dragonflies found in the Keys is the **marine dragonfly** *(Erythrodiplax berenice).* This dragonfly has a nymphal stage that lives in salt water and can tolerate salinity levels twice those of seawater (64 parts per trillion). All other dragonflies utilize fresh water to lay their eggs, and only a few can tolerate brackish waters.

A Florida summer vacation just wouldn't be the same without being able to tell an outrageous **mosquito** (*Aedes* species) story. With over 36 Florida Keys species that feed on human blood, it is no wonder that in 1997 $5.9 million was spent by the local Mosquito Control Board to combat the pest. Currently that budget is closer to $9 million, and most of the eradication efforts are focused on the **black saltmarsh mosquito** *(Ochlerotatus pantaeniorhynchus).* The locals build up a resistance to the bites, but it seems as if the new visitors really swell up until they get used to the toxin they produce.

DEET-based products are a good deterrent, but I would avoid skin contact with this chemical over the long term, and if you use it on your skin you should wash thoroughly after returning from the field. I prefer citronella-based insect repellents, or—if they are really gonna be bad—the Buzz-Off bug suit. This is basically a hooded sweatshirt made of no-see-um netting, and although it can limit visibility it really keeps them off you so you can concentrate on other things. If I am going be photographing in the swamps, I will also bring some ear plugs, as the buzzing and whining can really destroy your concentration.

No-see-ums are little specks of pepper that have a wallop of a bite. The mosquito injects a mild local painkiller as it searches for a vein, but the no-see-ums, with their sharp-edged chompers, cause quite a bit of pain. Usually found in good numbers at sunset and sunrise when the winds die down, they can create havoc with their annoying little jaws. Skin-So-Soft is an Avon bath oil product that seems to keep them in retreat. Anything oily on the skin seems to make them slide off and not be able to chew. There are about six species of no-see-ums, and the most common one is the gray saltmarsh punkie.

There are four little green-headed flying jaws that are at home anywhere in the backcountry. The deerflies and horseflies aren't partial to deer either, they like humans also, and will usually patiently circle you until you have your hands full with a kayak and then go for any exposed flesh. They do have a nasty bite, but most people recover quickly from the sting. For some reason that is not clear to me they seem to like the underside of the dark blue Bimini top on my charter boat, and a dozen will be waiting for me after some of my summer backcountry trips.

Butterflies

Butterfly season occurs in June and July, when a majority of the winged creatures can be seen in the adult stage. This is the time of the great butterfly count that occurs nationwide, during which as many as 350 counts occur across North America. According to a quick review of the *Butterflies Through Binoculars* book, there are about 90 species in Florida and 30 that are found at the southern tip of the state. I have included here just a few of the more common ones, as well as some of the least common found in the Keys. The book on butterflies and the contact information for the North American Butterfly Association can be found in the Bibliography and the Internet reference sections.

The **zebra long-wing** *(Heliconius charitonus)* is an easy one to identify with its bold yellow stripes on a black field. The wings are so long on this creature that when it flies it seems to be jumping up and down on a trampoline rather than effortlessly searching for its preferred food, the passion flower.

The pale yellow wings of the **cloudless sulphur butterfly** *(Phoebis sennae)* are a beautiful contrast against the blue sky and waters. It is always a surprise to spot them floating up and down as you paddle across the open water toward your next mangrove island. All three species in this genus have a rich yellow wing color, and can be seen feeding on royal poincianna trees, black bead, and clovers.

The **great southern white** *(Ascia monuste)* can be seen in the mangrove fringes, where it feeds on saltwort and other salt marsh plants. I have seen these 1.5-inch-long, off-white butterflies in great numbers on some of the backcountry islands in June. It is usually found from Georgia south, but during times of population explosions specimens have been noted as far away as North Dakota.

Considered to be the rarest butterfly in the state of Florida, the **Miami blue** *(Hemiargus thomasii bethunebakerii)* is found only at Bahia Honda State Park in the Keys. It was previously known from several other parts of the state, but has suffered such a decline that Bahia Honda State Park seems to be its last refuge. This butterfly is about the size of your index fingernail. A wide white band distinguishes it from the three others like it with four adjacent black spots on the undersides of the wings. This coloration is easily seen as the creature is resting with its wings folded upright. It is estimated that only 2 percent of the young reach adulthood, and the young are quite dependent on the seaside shrub known as knickerbean. Please stay on the marked trails and contact the rangers for the best location to see this highly watchable, rare butterfly.

There are ten swallowtails found in the Florida area. The rarest one, which is restricted to Key Largo and Elliot Key, is the **Schaus' swallowtail** *(Papilio aristodemus)*. There are two other swallowtails in the Keys that it can be confused with, and field identification is difficult. The main limiting factors for this species are habitat and food. It prefers shady hardwood hammocks and the preferred food plant is torchwood, which was harvested extensively in the early years for its fire-starting abilities.

Sponges

Aristotle, the great philosopher, first documented that these plantlike creatures were actually creating currents with internal hairlike appendages called flagella. Sponges do this in order to create a water flow that provides food and oxygen through the convoluted channels inside the structure. Humans soon realized that this amorphous blob was actually a colony of specialized cells that filter-feed plankton and bacteria from the ocean. Some of the sponges can actually filter 10,000 times their body size, and if you see a gallon-sized sponge on the bottom you can guess that it can daily filter enough water to fill a small swimming pool!

Filtering the oceans is just one of many important contributions that sponges make to life on our planet. Because of their incredibly convoluted surface area and inner chambers, a large number of other organisms actually live inside sponges, which provide an invaluable condominium for these sea creatures. Around the exterior and the base of many sponges you can find crabs, lobsters, fish, seahorses, and many other lifeforms. On the inside, within the convoluted channels, live brittle stars, shrimp, and other small invertebrates. The Mote Marine Lab website states that 16,000 species of creatures were found in one loggerhead sponge. I suspect that this was one of the specimens that grow to 6 feet in diameter. There is a unique oriental wedding gift that consists of a pair of dried shrimp that are enclosed within the skeleton of a sponge. These shrimp get inside the sponge through a small opening and as they grow they become too big to crawl out through the tiny holes. They are usually joined by a mate and live their entire lives within the sponge together. This is supposed to signify many things for the newlywed couple and is a gift for peace, prosperity, and happiness together.

In the fields of medical science and research, sponges have been found to have antibacterial, antifungal, antimalarial, and anticancer constituents. In fact, one of the first drugs for treating cancer was from a Cytocine sponge. Recent developments have also given hope for a diabetes cure through sponge lipids discovered in a study at the University of Florida. The sponge lipids were used as a catalyst to redirect cell activity to regulate and reduce cell inflammation that causes diabetes, multiple sclerosis, and rheumatoid arthritis.

There are about 15,000 species of sponges documented throughout the world today. Just imagine how important they all could be if just one held the miracle cure to your health in the future. There is a group in Australia that has 2,500 species in a collection, and from this assemblage has discovered 400 novel compounds and reported upon them in 100 scientific papers.

Sponges have also been collected for commercial use in the Keys since the early 1850s. In the early 1900s there were over 300 boats and 2,000 men working in the sponge trade. Can you imagine what the Key West docks were like back in those days? There is an old black-and-white film that depicts the conflict between the Greek spongers and the Key West spongers. The film stars Robert Wagner and it is called *Beneath the Twelve Mile Reef.* It is a Hollywood classic but really does not shed much light on commercial sponging history, except for its reference to the Monroe County law that prohibits divers from taking sponges. This law was passed to exclude the Greek spongers, who utilized hardhats and compressed air to work the sponge beds. Monroe County spongers used in the old days, and still operate today, with curved, 5-inch-wide metal forks attached to long poles. These are used to make sure the sponge is the 5-inch legal size before they rip it off the bottom. Usually there is some portion of the sponge left to regenerate another colony, but the sponge industry in Tarpon Springs on Florida's west coast—which is where the Greek spongers relocated—has a higher regeneration rate than the 33 percent regeneration rate of sponges in the Keys.

Sponges' skeletons are composed of siliceous-, calcareous-, or spongin-based structures. The sponging-based skeleton is found in about six of the local Keys species, and these are the ones that are harvested by today's spongers. Known as sheep's wool, lamb's wool, yellow, and grass sponges, they account for a million-dollar-per-year business for the tourism and cosmetics markets.

The descriptions and the categories of sponges below are given to provide an idea of the diversity of species that can be found in the Florida Keys. Many of the common names are used to describe differing genuses and species, and the only sure way to identify some of these is to examine the skeletal spicules with a microscope. Some sponges will have up to four different color variations, proving that color alone is not a good field identification characteristic. There are over 500 species found in these tropical waters, and a few that are relatively easy to identify are discussed below.

Barrel and Vaselike Sponges

The **loggerhead sponge** *(Spheciospongia vesparia)* is a big, tirelike structure on the bottom. Usually the excurrent pores are in the center of the circle, scoured black by current, appearing like a dark hubcap on an old gray tire. The tiny in-current pores that surround the exterior have a fine layer of dustlike sediment surrounding them. In the shallows during the new-moon low tides, you can sometimes see the boiling current of water being forced through the "chimney" in the sponge colony.

Loggerhead sponge

What is that thing that looks like a bowl or vase attached to the bottom? It is a **vase sponge** *(Ircinia compana)*, which has a calcareous skeleton that remains intact upon the sponge's death. This can be seen washed up on the beaches, and some believe—as did Robinson Crusoe—that it makes the perfect sun hat.

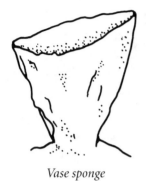

Vase sponge

Tube and Ropelike Sponges
The **candle sponges** *(Verongia longissima)* are branching candelabras on the shallow ocean floor. Usually dark brown with a 2–3 inch opening at the top of each branch.

Black organ pipe *(Pellina carbonaria)* is always a good sign for rocky habitat with good current. These small erect 1-inch-wide black tubes are usually no more than 10 inches in height. Whenever I see these while snorkeling there is sure to be rocky habitat with structure that would hold numerous fish and lobster.

The **branching vase sponge** *(Callyspongia vaginalis)* ranges in color from soft purple to gray-green and is usually found in waters 6 feet deep or more. These sponges usually have little anemone-like creatures called zoanthids living in the small pores and at dusk and through the evening you can see the spiny arms of brittle stars reaching out to capture plankton. The erect individual tubes usually branch forth from a central base.

Purple bleeding sponge *(Iotrochota birotula)* is also referred to as Green Finger Sponge in some guide books and when this multi-branching colony is squeezed it will exude a purplish-black secretion.

Oval and Erect Shaped Sponges
The sponges that have spongin as their skeleton and are commercially harvested include the **lamb's wool** *(Hippospongia lachne)*, **yellow sponge** *(Spongia barbra)* and the **black ball** or **cake sponge** *(Ircinia strobilina)*. All of these appear to be a dark black blob on the bottom. Anything that looks like a little black cannonball on the bottom can probably be grouped in the commercial category.

All sponges stink as they decay in the tropical sunshine but the **stinker**

sponge *(Ircinia fasciculata)* can reek while it is still a living creature. This sponge grows in a clumpy formation with nodules or lumps of smaller tubes of varying sizes haphazardly attached to the perimeter.

A "squeezable intolerant" species is known as the **bleeding sponge** *(Oligoceras hemmorages)*. This sponge actually exudes a dark blood red liquid substance if compressed or damaged. This 4–5 inch sponge can be found growing in shallow water on hard bottom. It has a lumpy shape with bulbous projections.

White sponge *(Geodia gibberosa)* can be found in the shallows but not in great numbers or by itself. It is usually associated with other encrusting organisms.

The blue color of the **heavenly sponge** *(Dysidea ethereal)* matches the sky and is not easily confused with other sponges. It is common around grass beds and seldom grows larger than a few inches. It looks like a cluster of little blue mutant mittens.

Encrusting and Bloblike Sponges

The **chicken liver sponge** (Chondrilla nucula) seems to be a whitish, small, globular colony about 2 to 4 inches in size that attaches to the undercut areas of mangrove islands. It can also be found quite commonly in the grass mats floating on the surface, where it will be attached to turtle grass. It truly looks just like a raw chicken liver when found on this grass.

The **viscous sponge** *(Plakortis angulospiculatus)* seems to have just been poured, and we caught it slowly rolling away as a blob. This brownish sponge seems as if the current shapes the creature into its form.

The **fire sponge** *(Tedania ignis)* lives up to its name as an irritant. This reddish sponge is usually no bigger than a football and has small, 0.5-inch openings for the excurrent pores. The spicules are able to pierce skin and break off in your epidermis like fiberglass shards. These cause itching and swelling and in some extreme cases one can lose a layer or two of epidermis after it blackens and peels off.

The **orange lumpy encrusting sponge** *(Ulosa ruetzleri)* is just one more of a dozen red-orange sponges that live in the red mangrove root system. A good rule of thumb for many things found in the ocean is: "If it is red like a STOP sign, there is a good reason for it!" Red and orange colors are a warning that says: "stay away," or "don't attempt to eat me," or "I am armed."

The **variable sponge** *(Anthosigmella varians)* is a suitable name for many of the sponges because they have an outside form that is, well, quite variable. Different colors, forms, and patterns can be exhibited by the same species due to age, current, available sunlight, water chemistry, and the presence of differently colored symbiotic algae living in their tissues.

The **green sponge** *(Haliclona viridis)* is a dark forest green and is usually solitary and growing in a bloblike form on the bottom. It is kind of a solid structure and usually has many boring and digging creatures that associate with it.

Pink mangrove sponges *(Acervochalina molitba)* are stubby, slightly curved, and small branching colonies that are usually found on red mangrove roots. The dusky pink colonies can reach several feet in diameter.

Jellyfish

The **Portuguese man-o'-war** *(Physalia physalia)* is an oceanic species that may sometimes be found washed up on the shores by the strong southern winds. These jellyfish look like a bluish-edged, clear plastic bag with tentacles that may stretch up to 70 feet in length. The tentacles secrete a powerful venom that can cause painful swelling and other allergic reactions.

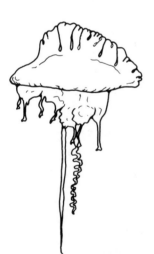

The floating portion of the animal can be 3 to 9 feet in size and it can have symbiotic fish, expecially *Nomeus* species that live among its tentacles.

The **by-the-wind sailor** *(Velella porpita)* is the smaller cousin of the man-o'-war jellyfish. It is a small, 2- to 3-inch floating, oval disk with an S-shaped curved sail on top. It is mostly clear with small tentacles that fringe the perimeter. Sometimes we can find these in great numbers in the weed rack lines that get pushed against the mangrove shorelines.

Where there is one there are usually more **moon jellies** *(Aurelia aurita)*, as they are swept through on the eddies and currents of offshore wa-

Portuguese man-o'-war

ters. These 12- to 18-inch-long, bowl-like creatures have thin, wispy tentacles that can give a
mild sting. Peer closely around the perimeter of
the animal and you might find several small fish
hitching a ride. Another good field identification
characteristic is the four oval gonads radiating
from the center of the disc.

Moon jelly

The most common jellyfish on the flats is the
upside-down jellyfish of the *Cassiopeia* genus.
This "queen" of the ocean floor can be found in
great numbers lying upside down on the bottom
where there is little current. Shallow, calm water
where sunlight penetration is at the maximum is
also a necessary ingredient for these creatures to
survive. They look like an eight-armed anemone
with frilly tentacles that vary in coloration from
green to gold, black, and yellow. All these colors

Upside-down jellyfish

represent the 80 or so species of algae that live as symbionts within the animal's tissue. Look closely at the upside-down bell and you can see it
pulsing.

The **cannonball jellyfish** *(Stomolophus meleagris)* can be found in the
water in nearshore habitats during the summer. This 8- to 9-inch, ball-like
jelly has short, stingless tentacles and a yellow-brown exterior edged with
a brown band. Small silvery jacks swim along with it and scurry to the inside of the bell when threatened.

Corals

To simplify things as far as the reef
corals go, I will refer you to more
comprehensive volumes (in the
"Suggested Reading" appendix)
written about the more than 75 different species found here in the

Parrotfish feed on algae growing on coral.

Keys. To keep it simple I will describe the two main types of corals found
on the ocean side of the Keys. Hard corals (75 species) are boulder and

branching types that are actually reef builders. Soft corals (50 species) are sea fans and sea plumes, which have small, treelike forms and are attached to the bottom by a stalk.

In the shallow seas and bay areas you can find a handful of each of the two groups of corals. The **lesser starlet coral** *(Siderastrea radians)* can be found from the intertidal line to about 20 feet deep, growing in irregular and encrusting shapes. The most common hard coral on the shallow flats is the **golf ball coral** *(Favia fragum)*. It does indeed look just like a small gold golf ball when young, but the colony can reach 1 to 2 feet in width. In the summer months it may expel its symbiotic algae to reveal a reddish-purple skin tone. About the size and shape of a small baby's fingers, the **common finger coral** *(Porites furcata)* can be found in living shoals or in small colonies in shallow water.

Sea plume

Anchored to the substrate with the equivalent of a miniature tent stake, the **rose coral** *(Manicina areolata)* can actually flip itself right side up, if overturned by a storm, by using its polyps. The overall oval shape with wavy sides makes this colony unique on the flats.

The **ivory bush coral** *(Occulina diffusa)* is a delicate beauty that grows in small colonies of slender, 0.25-inch-thick, branching limbs. Often covered with other encrusting invertebrates, it can be found on sponge flats and other hard-bottom areas. The colonies grow to about volleyball size and have multiple branching stalks about the diameter of a pencil.

The soft corals found in shallow nearshore waters include 7 of the 50 species that can be found in the Keys. As with the hard corals, the most diversity can be found near the waters that are bathed by the Gulf Stream, not the waters that are washed by Florida Bay.

The three basic groups are: **sea plumes** and **sea feathers** of the *Pseudopterogorgia* species; the

Sea fan

sea fans of the *Gorgonia* species; and the **sea whips**
of the *Pterogorgia* species. The things that appear
to be trees or shrubbery on the bottom fall into the
plumes, feathers, and whips categories. Of course,
the plumes have a central stalk with many single
branchlets jutting off the central core. The feathers
are nearly the same, except the branchlets are all
on one plane, as on a bird's feather. The sea whips
are usually triangular in cross section and have
small polyps interspersed along the edges. The sea
fans are self-descriptive as they are flattened and

Sea whip

attached to a central holdfast and are usually waving back and forth in the
ocean's surging currents.

Anemones

Waving its slender tentacles on the shallow ocean floor, the **pink-tipped
anemone** *(Condylactis gigantea)* stands out as something different on the
bottom. The color varies from pink to scarlet, off yellow, gold, or whitish,
but they nearly always have bulbous tips that are pink, purple, or green.
Found from mangrove roots to 100-foot-deep coral reefs, these gentle
creatures capture prey with their stinging tentacles
and then slowly retract the food into their
mouths—which is the only way in and out of the
creature's stomach. Small larval fish and invertebrates make up a majority of the diet. If you ob-
serve closely you can often find one of the five
symbiotic associates that lives in harmony among
the anemone's tentacles.

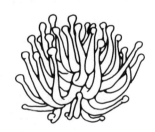

Anemone

The **Peterson cleaner shrimp** *(Periclemenes
yucatansis)* is one of the three shrimp species that are symbiotic with the
anemone. It is about 1 inch in length and has a translucent body with a series of pinkish saddles on the back and tail. The other two symbionts associated with this anemone are a blenny and a species of crab.

The **collared sand anemone** *(Actinostella flosculifera)* has sometimes
fooled me into thinking that it was just another Cassiopeia until I had a

closer look. Its fringed disk is about the same size and color as that of the many Cassiopeia that sometimes surround it in the shallow sunlit seas. It will retract into the substrate if molested.

Most commonly found colonizing red mangrove roots, the **pale anemone** *(Aiptassia pallida)* has a slender stalk and splayed-out tentacles that are about half as long as its stalk. These tend to grow together in dense colonies.

Where you find one **sun anemone** *(Stoichactis helianthus)* there are usually more nearby, sometimes to the point that they will form a living "shag carpet" 2 to 3 feet in size. One overcast day in June when the surface waters were flat calm, I could see literally dozens of individuals standing out from the bottom as they appeared to fluoresce in the overcast light. This species also has various species of crabs and shrimp that are symbiotic.

The **ringed anemone** *(Bartholomea annulata)* is a clear-tentacled creature with white corkscrew markings on the tentacles. The sting from this creature can be mildly toxic if it comes in contact with sensitive skin, and there are several symbiotic shrimp that may be seen in the tentacles.

Worms

Crozier's flatworm *(pseudoceros crozieri)* has some crazy black, zebralike stripes on a yellow-gray field. The worm itself is a 1.5-inch flat oval that conforms to whatever it may be grazing upon. Frequently it grazes on the grapelike sea squirts and seems to conform perfectly to the bubbly exterior.

The **green bristle worm** *(Hermodice carunculate)* lives under small rocks and ledges. Usually a nocturnal predator, it can feed in the daytime and has some venomous stingers on its flanks. It is about 4 to 6 inches long, and its segmented body is greenish in coloration. It is seldom seen unless rocks are turned over.

It is rare to see the **shaggy parchment tube worm** *(Onuphis magna),* but its tube can be found on sandy bottoms throughout the Keys. The white tube is 1/8 to 3/8 inch wide and is composed of calcium carbonate pebbles and other organic debris that it cements together. It can project an inch or two above the substrate and looks like a sugar-encrusted drinking straw.

Atlantic palolo *(Eunice schemacephala)* worms are nature's original miners. These burrowing worms reach about 6 inches in length and use complex jaws to burrow in calcium carbonate substrate and coral structures. Within 3 days of the last quarter moon in June and July they shed their reproductive parts in a process known as *epitoky*. The hind end of the worm (the *epitoke*) is a modified, self-propelled, egg-carrying structure. It breaks away and zooms to the surface, where it leaves a V-shaped wake as it travels along. Tarpon have been known to eat nothing but palolo worms when the worms swarm with the outgoing tides. After years of observation, Simon Becker, a flats guide and friend of mine, has been successful in producing an imitation for fly casting that is fairly successful when fished correctly. The Samoans and other Pacific islanders traditionally skim palolo worms from the ocean to feast on during the summer full moons.

The **luminescent threadworm** *(Odontosyllis enolpa)* makes a light show during its spawning migration from rocky sponge flats to the surface of shallow bays. Although I have seen this phenomenon throughout the year, it peaks in the spring and summer. The female glows with a blinking greenish light as she swims in a cookie-sized circle. Smoky, glowing trails are left in her wake. The glowing, sperm-laden males blast toward the eggs and unite in a bioluminescent explosion. The peak activity seems to be evenings following a full moon, about 30 minutes after sunset. Some nights we have seen 40 or 50 of the glowing unions at one time

I have only seen the **lug worm** *(Arenicola cristata)* exposed once. It was after a severe cold front in February, and the 12-inch-long pencil-sized, segmented creatures were lying torpid on the bottom in the bright sunshine. They lay translucent, gelatinous egg cases that slowly undulate on the muddy bottom. These sediment-covered egg cases are the size of small balloons and can sometimes be attached to the worm's burrow entrance.

Radiating out from a central point the 8-inch long skinny arms of the **medusa head worm** *(Loimia medusa)* search for small benthic food items. There may be as many as a dozen tentacles that stretch out over the sandy bottom looking for prey to capture. If you gently touch them they will retract into the buried tube.

The **feather duster worm** *(Brachiomma nigromaculata)* can be seen growing on submerged mangrove roots in the company of other invertebrates and algae. The radiating featherlike appendages quickly collapse, like an umbrella, into a parchmentlike tube at the slightest disturbance. The color varies from white to pink, and since they live together in colonies they will appear in great numbers where found.

Mollusks

Worldwide the mollusks comprise a uniquely diverse group of creatures that includes more than 85,000 different species. Over 350 species commonly occur in South Florida and include octopi, snails, clams, sea slugs, squid, and chitons. The following are some of the more common species encountered.

Queen conch

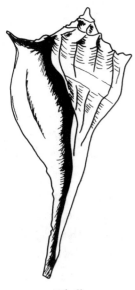

Whelk

The state-protected **queen conch** *(Strombus gigus)* is also the symbol for Monroe County. This large snail has a luscious pink, flaring lip and reaches pie-plate size. Found from Bermuda to South Florida and throughout the Caribbean to Brazil, this giant snail is an important link in the food chain, feeding humans, sea turtles, rays, and octopi. Harvested to excess in the late 1970s, it was put on the protected species list in 1985. After a 20-year ban and several mariculture attempts, the population still has not rebounded enough to harvest locally again. Queen conchs lay egg masses of about 350,000 and hatch out to a planktonic phase in 3-5 days. After about a month of planktonic drifting, they settle out to the bottom and change into a snail-like form as big as a grain of sand.

The thicker lip and body of the **milk conch** *(Strombus costatus)* distinguish it from the queen conch. This conch rarely gets bigger than softball size, and has blunt spines on its exterior. The underside of this mollusk has a milky white appearance.

Fighting conchs *(Strombus alatus)* are about 4 inches in size and have a distinct orange coloration to the shell and lip. Unafraid to the point of aggression, this snail will attempt to dislodge itself from your hand with violent swings of its toenail until released.

The **hawkwing conch** *(Strombus raninus)* is beautifully etched with horizontal lines and the flared lip has a unique wing-tip point at the tip.

There are about four species of whelk found in the Keys, and the most common is the **lightning whelk** *(Busycon contrarium)*. In the wintertime it is common to see the egg cases of these snails attached to the substrate in the shallows. The egg case looks like a spiraling snake comprised of human-sized vertebra-like disks.

The **true tulip** *(Fasciolaria tulipa)* is certainly the snail most often seen while kayaking, and this may have to do with its predatory nature. These cannibals will eat any other snail they encounter, and if you put one in a holding bucket with other conchs you will see that snails can "hop to it" when it is a matter of life and death. The tulip has a rounded, smooth shell that tapers to a fine point.

As the name implies, the **horse conch** *(Plueroploca gigantica)* gets as big as a horse in the world of snails. This conch reaches 20 inches and has a narrow spindle and a tapered conical spire. I have observed its orange foot and mouthparts eating queen conchs in the Dry Tortugas.

The **king crown conch** *(Melongena corona)* is a small, shallow-water snail that has unique crownlike spires around the whorled top. The clean discarded shells are used by hermit crabs, and the live animal has black and white mottled skin with abundant algal growth on the shell. They lay thin, round egg cases the diameter of a pencil, which look like little white plates in a drying rack. Look for them on mangrove roots in the spring at the tide line.

The predatory **moon snail** *(Natica canrena)* can drill holes in other snails and scrape out the unprotected flesh. This snail has a large foot and can engulf prey to dissuade escape as it drills away. The sand collar egg case is commonly found on the flats and if it is held to the sunlight the individual eggs can be seen. The collar is wavy around the perimeter, and smooth and fluted on the inside circle.

Peering closely around the red mangrove roots you can usually find the **mangrove periwinkle** *(Littorina angulifera)*. This small, dark, conical, inch-long shell blends in well with its surroundings as it slowly grazes on the algal growth on the mangrove root system.

Glowing marginella

Glowing marginella *(Marginella pruniosum)* are beautiful pinky nail-sized, pill-shaped snails that are always grazing in the detritus layer. The area where the snail comes out and contacts its exterior shell is polished completely smooth to the point of glowing, hence its name. If disturbed, the animal will withdraw into a vertical slit on the underside of its shell.

The **coffee bean snail** *(Melampus coffeus)* is peanut-sized and coffee brown in color with cream bands. It can be found in the shade of tide-exposed red mangrove roots grazing in the mud.

Sometimes the rocky nearshore habitats are covered with **black horn snails** *(Batillaria minima)*. These 0.5-inch-long, skinny black snails seem to be able to handle the baking, sun-dried, rocky shorelines well. Literally thousands can be found along 50 linear feet of shoreline in some ocean-side areas.

The rocky shorelines with tide pools are the best habitat to encounter one of the four species of **nerite** *(Nerita* species). This marble-sized univalve is usually firmly attached to the substrate when the tide is out. In the shady areas closest to the shoreline you can find clusters of the **bleeding tooth nerite** *(Nerita peloronta)*, which has a red and black zigzag pattern on its exterior. On the inside of this shell you will find two small white teeth on a splotch of red, which give the snail its common name.

The tide pools and riprap shorelines near the bridges are excellent habitat for the **fuzzy chiton,** *Acanthopleura granulata.* These wave-washed shorelines are no threat to the armor coating and huge foot that carry this grazing mollusk along inch by ponderous inch. This oval-shaped snail has a rough-skinned foot extending around the perimeter of eight jointed armor plates.

Common Bivalves

Seemingly paper thin and growing in clusters by the dozens, the **mangrove oyster** *(Crassostera rhizophorae)* is commonly spotted on red mangrove roots and dock pilings. Huge clusters can be exposed at the lunar low tides, and I have seen raccoons attempting to eat them on the half shell with no success. The **coon oyster** *(Lopha frons)* is also found on mangrove roots. Its shell is ridged and fluted and this makes it easier for the raccoons to pry it open. It is common to find the empty shells of the **southern quahog** *(Mercinaria campe-chiensis)*, but in all my years here I have never encountered a live specimen. The classic clam shape is easily identified, and the radiating ridges tell you it is from the tropics as

Coon oyster

does the "missing" purple interior splotch common in northern quahogs.

The literature states that the **amber penshell** *(Pinna carnea)* can have the most beautiful black pearls within the mantle of this bottom-dwelling mollusk. The shell is triangular and up to 11 inches tall. They are common in the backcountry waters in water depths of 15 feet or more. While snorkeling in these areas, you may notice the wide portion of the fan-shaped shell projecting from the substrate. Its color is a wonderful mix of oranges and yellows.

Zebralike stripes and a winglike appearance identify the **turkey wing** *(Arca zebra)* shell. They are usually attached to rocky surfaces in the intertidal zones. The delicate beauty of the tellin family of shells could fill a book, and in the Keys you could find more than five distinct species. One of the more common is the **sunrise tellin** *(Tellina radiata)*, which can be found burrowed in the grass flats with only the siphon protruding. The shell has a sun ray pattern on the exterior and is about an inch long.

Crabs

There are about 35 species of crabs that can be found throughout the South Florida area. A handful of these are edible, with the **blue crab** *(Callinectes sapidus)* and the **stone crab** *(Menippe mercenaria)* being the most popular.

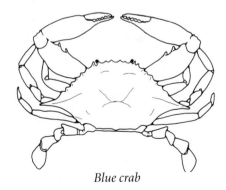

Blue crab

Both are rather pugnacious in the water, and the blue crab will attack anything, even if it's one thousand times its size. The stone crab is Florida's only renewable marine resource. This is because only the claws are taken, and the rest of the crab is put back in the ocean to grow new claws. It takes about two years for the crab to molt claws that are of legal size. In Monroe County there are about 750,000 traps, and between 1993 and 1996 the average annual catch was about 2.5 million pounds.

The most common hermit crab that you will find in abandoned shells will be the **green-striped hermit crab** *(Clibanarius vittatus).* This crab can be found from the roots slightly above the water level to the bottoms of 30-foot-deep channels. It will usually take over the empty shell of a king crown conch or a tulip snail. As its name suggests, it has green and white stripes, which are noticeable on the legs as it retreats into the shell.

The **land hermit crab** *(Coenobita clypeatus)* is always a surprise. When you think you might be on a deserted island, suddenly you realize you are not. They scrabble around in the underbrush making lots of noise and,

Hermit crab

when you finally realize what they are, you start to look around and realize you're surrounded by 'em. There can be up to a hundred in the smaller colonies, and they seem to like to hang out together in the cool shade. Most active in the midmornings and late evenings they leave their telltale trails in the sand. Snail shells like queen conch, tulip snail, and whelk shells are commonly used by the

land hermit crab, but they will have other unique coverings, including one that used an old glass inkwell.

In the springtime great migrations of the **great land crab** *(Cardisoma guanhumi)* travel from their earthen burrows to shallow, seagrass-studded waters. This is where the females will deposit their eggs and the young will metamorphose into land-dwelling creatures. Hundreds of these can be seen crossing the roads as they make their way back to the ocean. Some of the areas where you can see these in the Keys are at Geiger Key (MM 10.8) and at the entrance road to Biscayne National Park.

The **giant hermit crab** *(Petrochirus diogenes)* can usually be found in a huge queen conch or horse conch shell. These monsters graze on the bottom looking for shrimp, smaller crabs, and just about anything that gets in the way. Their claws can be the size of tennis balls and have a rough, pebbly, pinkish coloration. You may notice the colorful and encrusted **southern spider crab** *(Libinia dubia)* clinging to the undersides of rocks, coral heads, and ledges. The unique claws on these crabs are like huge pincers with a

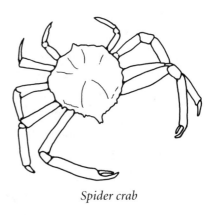

Spider crab

knobby projection jutting down from the upper claw. Their spindly legs have extremely sharp points, which they use to cling and crawl along the rocky structures on the bottom.

The smaller ledges and sheltered rocky bottom areas will have the **arrow crab** *(Stenorhynchus seticornus)* in residence. The toothpick-thin legs and long pointed nose of this crab make it easy to identify. It doesn't move much, but just kind of hangs out in the shelter of rocky formations. It has short little spiny projections on its nose (rostrum) where it sometimes stores extra food particles. So, when it's hungry later, it can pick its nose.

During the low tides up in the mangrove roots, it's a good observational challenge to sit and just watch for five or ten minutes. Soon your eyes will key on many little things moving. A white claw about an inch long waves in the sulfurous air every two or three seconds. This is the claw of the **fiddler crab** (*Uca* species) as it defines its territory and tries to capture the attention of a mate. In some areas you'll see up to 50 or 60 of these within view of your vantage point.

Are they tarantulas? Is that a tree frog? What are those things crawling around in the red mangrove tree roots and branches? Blending in with the dark bark of the mangroves and about quarter-sized, the **mangrove tree crab** *(Aratus pisonii)* hides on the backsides of the roots and branches as you paddle through the creek areas. If you sit still for just a few minutes, they will slowly creep up and down the branches, looking like

Mangrove tree crab

small spiders or frogs. There are about five to seven different species of these mangrove dwellers, the most common being the **marbled marsh crab,** *Sesarma ricordia.* We have counted up to 80 of these omnivorous creatures on a single tree branch in some of these mangrove creeks. They can swim, but with a kind of sideways sweeping motion. They are rather shy but can be caught if you place your hand on a branch near them. Next, use your other hand to slowly coax them into retreating toward your hand on the branch. They will gingerly walk onto your hand and try to scurry up to your shoulder. From this proximity you can really see the distinct spines at the corners of the eyes that distinguish this species from the rest.

The life of the party usually will stick something on his head to make others laugh, and the **decorator crab's** *(Microphrys bicornutus)* habit of camouflage has the same effect. There are about three or more crabs in this group that will attempt to camouflage themselves with algae and bits of grass. This material is attached to the back of the carapace with springy hooks of hair similar to Velcro. This species is similar to a spider crab with its long spindly legs, but has a triangular shell and a bifurcated rostrum (two-forked nose).

The **Swiss army knife crab** or **flame box crab** *(Calappa flammea)* gets an acknowledgment for the most unique claws. There is a serrated knife, a can opener, pincers, and a clam opener that are easily seen, and many other prying and pinching combinations. This bulldozer-like crab is usually buried in sand and searching for clams. If you have the opportunity to view one in shallow water, you will notice that its excurrent breathing water shoots a jet like a water fountain. The highly ornate claws identify this creature.

The **pea crab** *(Dissodactlyus* species) is so small that about seven of them could fit on a pea. Easily mistaken for small chunks of bottom sediment, these crabs are found on the exterior of sea biscuits and heart urchins. Gently pick one up and shake off most of the sediment, and you may find several in amongst the stubby spines of these bottom dwellers.

Shrimp and Lobsters
Pink shrimp *(Penaeus* species) were touted as "pink gold" in the 30 years of commercial harvest that started in the 1950s off Key West. The average

annual harvest was close to 10 million pounds until the early 1980s, when the industry slowed because of a declining catch and the rising cost of operations. Shrimp landings have been sporadic recently, but there was a decent harvest of 6 million pounds in 1996. If you are paddling at night and shine a flashlight into the shallow waters, you will see the golden-amber glow of shrimp eyes as they graze on the algae flats. The cold fronts of February that coincide with the full moon tides are peak shrimp movement times. They usually move from the shallow flats to the deeper waters of Hawks Channel.

The **cleaner shrimp** (*Periclimenes* species) are unique shrimp that actually assist in the cleaning and maintenance of anemones, fish, and even moray eels. There are about twelve species of these, and eight set up shop on specific types of anemones. Once on an individual anemone, that particular shrimp will be recognized as part of the anemone. It can do this because it can cover itself with the slime of the anemone, and this protects it from predators and anemone stings. It is individually specific so that, if you were to put that shrimp on another anemone of the same species, it would take a while and a few stings before it got acclimated to its new host. The other four types of cleaner shrimp are rather unique and usually set up their cleaning stations at the edges of coral heads.

The **banded coral shrimp** (*Stenopus hispidus*) is the most easily identified with its red-and-white-striped body. Its long white antennae beckon fish to come close and lay still so that it may swim over and clean the epidermis of parasites and loose skin or scales. Its body is covered with spines, and the claws have purple bands with red borders.

The translucent and iridescent **mantis shrimp** (*Squilla empusa*) is a creature of the evening. There are about 60 species of this shrimp in the Keys area, and they all have a perfectly circular tube for a burrow. Lightning-fast and with a razor-sharp edge on the claw, they search for unsuspecting fish and other soft-bodied invertebrates as night approaches.

The **ghost shrimp** (*Callianassa* species) are crepuscular creatures that feed at dusk and dawn. You can see their homes as you paddle along the grassy flats. These look like slow-motion, miniature sand volcanoes as the shrimp burrow into the soft sediment, and the tops of their burrows will be littered with sand-colored fecal casts. These burrows will have several exits so that, when they are feeding on the flats and are chased down by bonefish and permit, they will usually have a quick retreat nearby. They attain a length of 3.5 inches.

The **spiny lobster** *(Panulirus argus)* is a $30 million-a-year resource in South Florida. Half a million traps are placed on the ocean floor to at-

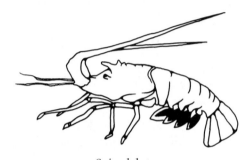

Spiny lobster

tempt the capture of millions of pounds annually. The yearly catch averages about 5.5 million pounds, and it swings from a low of 4 million to a high of 7 million. This edible crustacean has no claws, but hundreds of tiny, recurved spines on its body give it ample protection from predators. It takes about two years for a lobster to grow to legal size (3-inch carapace), and during that time it will molt about 25 times.

The **slipper lobster** *(Scyllarides* species) looks like a little bulldozer with a lobster tail. This species reaches a weight of about 2 pounds and primarily lives in

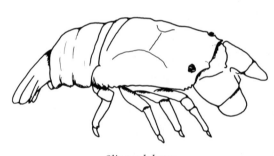

Slipper lobster

the coral reef. It is nocturnal and is most often found in lobster traps that are set on the ocean side of the Keys.

Spiny-Skinned Creatures

There are about eight species of sea stars that are found in every niche in the underwater environment. One of the largest, growing to about 12 inches in diameter, is the **Bahama sea star** *(Oreaster reticulates)*. This is found on the grass flats in shallow water, where it grazes on the plant and animal life living amongst the grass blades. It can actually distend its stomach out and scour clean large areas of turtle grass. This species is legally protected from molestation and harvest. It is very beautiful with its netlike yellow pattern over an orange or burnt red base. The **brown spiny sea star** *(Echinaster spinulosis)* is the most commonly found in all of the backcountry areas. You can see it grazing on the red mangrove roots, on the grass or muddy bottoms, or in the bottoms of tidal creeks. Sea stars have a water vascular system that supplies the pressure necessary for their tubular feet to expand and contract. They crawl along on these tube feet in a slow-motion search for clams and other attached animals and plants.

You will rarely see the **chocolate brittle star** *(Ophioderma cinereum)* or any of the eight other brittle stars found in the shadows and amongst the rocks. Their five long, snakelike arms will extend out from underneath the rocks and crevices at night and capture plankton with their small tube feet. These arms, if broken off, will be regenerated. Some sand-dwelling brittle stars will be completely covered with sand except for the small tips of their arms that reach out and capture prey such as small fish, plankton, and just about anything else that floats their way.

The sea urchins are commonly found in all nearshore environments. There are about 15 species of these grazers, and the most easily identified are included here. The **long-spined sea urchin** *(Diadema antillarum)* was very common until a waterborne pathogen struck the Caribbean and caused a huge population decline in the early 1980s. This species is just starting a comeback and can be seen in the surrounding waters in small numbers. It has long black spines that can reach 8 inches in length. The spines are venomous and can easily puncture skin and cause a painful irritation like a bee sting, which usually subsides within an hour.

The **sea egg** *(Tripneustes ventricocus)* is commonly found in grass beds, sometimes with bits of grass or shells stuck to its exterior. The whitish spines are numerous, short, and harmless on this algae grazer. The eggs, which can number in the thousands, are eaten by the locals of the West Indies. In the rocky shore areas you can encounter the **rock-boring urchin** *(Echinometra lucunter)*. It is usually found in a perfectly matched hole it has scraped clean on the interior. The spines are stout and generally reddish brown. The relatively thick, clublike spines of the **slate pencil urchin** *(Eucidaris tribuloides)* are a unique field characteristic for this grazer. It eats a variety of stuff including algae, grass, and sponges.

The **inflated sea biscuit** *(Clypeaster rosaceus)* is a palm-sized, rounded, brown creature that grazes in the sand or turtle grass areas. Oftentimes it is covered with bits of shell fragments or vegetative debris. The seabiscuit has small, nonpoisonous spines covering its body, and the pea crab is a symbiont that can be found on its underside crawling amongst its spines.

What could be more fun than a creature that looks like donkey dung and jets a stream of water from one end when lifted from the water? This

Sea cucumber

pretty much sums up a description of our sea cucumbers, of which there are about ten species. The most common is the **Florida sea cucumber** *(Holothuria floridana),* which inhabits grass beds where it moves at a ponderously slow 6 or 7 feet per day. Sea cucumbers use branching tentacles to gather sand into their mouths and digest the organic material from this mud. The branching tentacles are all you can see of the **striped sea cucumber** *(Thyonella gemmata),* which reaches about 6 inches in length. This sea cucumber is always buried in the soft sand and mud bottoms, and currents will carry nutrient-laden detritus into its tentacles. On the miles of grass flats you may notice little hills of sand that resemble miniature volcanoes mixed in among the grass blades. These pie-sized sand mounds are the aftereffects of the **burrowing sea cucumber,** *Holothuria arenicola.*

The **five-toothed sea cucumber** *(Actinopygia agassizzi)* is another common sea cucumber found in the grass, but it can be distinguished by the ring of five calcareous teeth around the anus. These teeth are quite conspicuous as the animal breathes, since it also respires through its posterior. Since we are on the subject, there is one more unique thing about this cucumber's posterior: It can sometimes have a pearl fish living in its anus. The pearl fish is a tapered, slender fish that escapes the cucumber at night to feed and wriggles back in toward daylight to hide.

Tunicates

The tunicates or sea squirts are common encrusting creatures that inhabit all kinds of marine habitats. They can completely overgrow the bottoms of boats, mangrove prop roots, and other submerged structures. This colonizing animal varies in size and shape, but will always have an excurrent and incurrent opening to facilitate feeding and breathing.

There are about 20 varieties, but the most common are the oval, grapelike clusters found on submerged mangrove roots. The **painted tunicate** *(Clavelina picta)* is about 0.75 inch in size and is found in colonies of up to a thousand individuals covering 10 or more inches of prop root. They are translucent with a purplish or reddish ring at the circular openings. The **mangrove tunicate** *(Ecteinascidia turbinate)* is most common and about 1 inch in size. Colonies can cover 5 to 9 inches of the red mangrove prop

Sea squirts

root, and its distinguishing characteristic is a soft orange color with an orange-rimmed opening. There are certain compounds found in this animal, known as ecteinascidins, that are utilized in powerful anticancer drugs.

Marine Algae

Green algae comprise some 75 different tropical species that can be found over almost all ocean depths, from sandbars that are exposed at low tide to over 500 feet deep in the clear waters of the Bahamas.

The three species of **sea lettuce** *(Ulva* species) can be found in the shallows where there is usually a high nutrient content. Mangrove islands that have roosting bird colonies usually have an abundance of nutrients from the bird guano. This contributes immensely to the proliferation of the filamentous and green leaf algae. Many people in ocean-oriented communities eat the sea lettuce raw, for soup stock, or in mixed green salads.

The little green umbrella on a slender light green stalk is one of the two species of the **mermaid's wine cup** *(Acetabularia* species). These delicate-looking, single-celled algae remind me of some fantasy-land forest. Many people have noted that the "wine cup" looks more like a martini glass.

Mermaid's wine cup

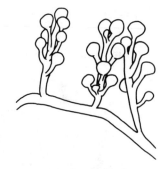

Caulerpa algae

Feather algae

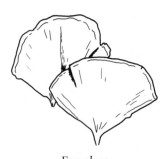

Fan algae

Grape, feather, fern, mushroom, and little cactus are all common names for the 13 different growth varieties that the **caulerpa algae** (*Caulerpa* species) may exhibit. This genus can literally carpet the bottom with its extensive and unique growth forms. It is fairly fast growing, and I have noted it overgrowing a grass flat and then dying off, all in a span of 2 months in the spring. In the Philippines, some of these species are eaten in fresh salads. Someone once told me that every marine algae is edible, but I have never personally verified that assertion.

The short tufts of **green horsetails** (*Batophora oerstedi*) and the **squirreltails** (*Dasycladus vermicularis*) look so much like shag carpet that many use that as its common name now. At dead low tides, when little water movement occurs, or when the algae is squeezed, you can actually see the distinctive yellow-green, dyelike substance in the water surrounding the plants. This algae will carpet entire areas of the substrate.

Beautiful little green, grape-sized bubbles identify one of the three species of **bubble algae,** members of various *Valonia* genera. Each bubble is a single cell that may be found attached to the bottom in clusters, or free-floating individually in the water column. A free-floating specimen held in your hand seems to be an egg of some sort, rather than the living tissue of a plant.

Resembling tiny green fans attached to the bottom, **fan algae** (*Avrainvillea* and *Udotea* species) include about eight different species that can be seen undulating in the wave action of nearshore waters.

Those little tufted, treelike structures growing in forestlike stands are

Neptune's shaving brush (*Pennicilus* species). They are relatively abundant in most shallow areas.

Look closely at the substrate in these areas, and you will realize that the sandy bottom is actually composed of tiny fragments of the calcium carbonate skeletons of various algae. The one that looks like oatmeal flakes is probably the most common and is known as **disk algae** or **oatmeal algae** of various *Halimeda* species. There are about nine species of this algae, and its tangled brushlike growth harbors tons of little creatures, including baby octopus, brittle stars, amphipods, and many other larval-stage marine creatures.

Neptune's shaving brush

More than 34 species of brown algae can be found in these tropical seas, and the most commonly seen will be one of the seven species of **sargassum weed** (*Sargassum* species). These algae can be attached to the bottom or free-floating, as in the Sargasso Sea, with rafts that periodically wash ashore during the southerly winds of summer.

Oatmeal algae

The sargassum that is attached to the bottom can form dense, kelplike forests on the shallow ocean floor. It will float to the surface because of the air-filled bladders in its branches, and it provides a wonderful habitat for many marine creatures, including seahorses.

The Sargasso Sea, which is in the middle of the Atlantic Ocean, supports an entire ecosystem of uniquely adapted creatures that live in the branching weeds. Many can be shaken out onto your paddle and you can view perfectly camouflaged

Sargassum weed

shrimp, frogfish, crabs, nudibranchs, and other creatures. A word of caution is in order, because also associated with these weedlines are stinging blue jellyfish, such as as man-o'-war and by-the-wind sailors.

Does your mask fog up when you are diving or snorkeling? There are some over-the-counter remedies for this problem, but if you are "out there" and in need, then many of the *Dictyota* species of **brown algae** can help. These branching, brown, and flat algae can be used to provide a slippery layer on the glass surfaces of your mask so water vapor cannot condense and cause fogging. This algae exhibits a slightly slimy feel when handled.

The stuff that looks kind of like tannish-yellow ribbon candy in little semicircular tufts is a brown algae called **petticoat algae** (*Padina* species). Distinct banding on the leaves denotes different rows of microscopic hairs and reproductive structures. The two *Padina* represent the only varieties of brown algae that have calcified skeletons.

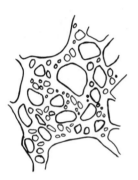

One of the most distinctive growth forms and my personal favorite is the **waternet algae,** *Hydroclathrus calthratus.* Its spongy texture and Swiss cheese, netlike structure are hard to miss. It forms large, free-floating structures that are usually found covering shallow bottoms. At first glance it appears to be a disheveled fishnet.

Waternet algae

The **red algae,** which number about 90 species local to the Keys but more than 4,000 species strong in tropical reef communities worldwide are the least studied of all the algae. They can be found at depths ranging to 800 feet, but we shall concentrate on four that live in the shallows.

As you paddle and coast with the tide you notice that a big red clump of something is also moving right alongside. You peer closer and realize it is a big tumbleweed-shaped mass known as **redbeard algae** (*Gracilaria tikvahiae).* As you watch, it seems to be rolling around as if in a dryer and there are many mollusks and shrimp hitching a dizzying ride. During certain times of the year, with the different currents and wind directions, you can find many species of algae "tumbleweeding" around the flats transporting small creatures to and fro.

Some of our extensive seagrass meadows have what we used to refer to as "Yankee snail trails." These are the evidence that someone from up north was trying to navigate the shallow backcountry waters and ran aground. These carved-out gutters usually don't grow back quickly, and it seems that they usually fill with a red algae called **laurencia** (*Laurencia* sp.) and **eucheuma** (*Eucheuma isiforme).* Eucheuma is a yellow-red, rubbery, branching alga that in some countries is used to make a porridge that re-putedly is an aphrodisiac. Carrageenan is an emulsifier that is derived from Eucheuma and is used in many everyday food products, such as ice cream and other dairy products.

In some areas the red mangrove roots have a fuzzy coating of algae en-crusting the roots. This is usually a diverse assortment of red algae that in-clude two species of **bostrychia.** Recognize the last part of the scientific name? Just like the Chia Pet that grows a fuzzy exterior when watered, this algae encrusts the roots so you can still see their structure underneath.

The final grouping of red algae consists of 20 or more species that are in the Corallinaceae family. These are known as the **red coralline algae** be-cause of the calcium carbonate-hardened skeleton and the rosy colors. They can form dense layers in the shallow waters, and lots of invertebrates use its structure for safe habitat and for feeding grounds. The most common species of this group is *Goniolithon stricta.* The thin-branched skeletons are commonly found in the intertidal tide pools on the ocean side of the Keys.

Flotsam and Jetsam

Over the years many interesting things have been found in and around these mangrove islands. Some are manufactured items and withstand the rigors of this ocean environment, such as bottles and cans. There is a fa-vorite little creek of mine where we can usually find a Busch Bavarian Beer can that has the old style pull-tab. In bold blue lettering on the can it proudly proclaims: "New, All-Aluminum can." They are usually at the bottom of the creek and well preserved, even though they may have been on the bottom for over three decades.

Occasionally you will run across some very old bottles that may date as far back as the Colonial era, when demijohns transported cooking oil, water, and other necessities. I found one of these way up inside a tiny little mangrove creek in the backcountry while snorkeling. There are lots of those little green Coca-Cola bottles that will tell you where they were bot-tled if you look on the bottom; Key West had a bottling plant from 1900 to 1924.

Other items salvaged have included dinghies, push poles, lifejackets, glass fishing net floats, coolers, scuba tanks, entire docks (after hurricanes), and a full set of scuba gear!

Drift seeds and sea beans can be found in the rack lines at the beaches and among the sparse root systems of the red mangrove. These floating seeds are usually from giant vines and trees that line the mighty Amazon and other waterways that lead to the oceans. A great website devoted to identifying the seeds can be found at www.seabeans.com. Bamboo from Central and South America gets caught up in the Caribbean Sea currents and will sometimes be strained out of the ocean by our islands.

The National Oceanic and Atmospheric Administration (NOAA) occasionally conducts research in which they will toss a Styrofoam drift meter called a radiosponder into the ocean at various locations. Key West seems to be the starting point of many of these small, rectangular white blocks that are about the same size as a 12-pack of canned beverages. The one I found on Molasses Key had been dropped 12 days previously in Key West. The meter has a plastic postage-paid envelope stuck inside with instructions to send it to the National Weather Service in Missouri for reconditioning and data downloading.

There are not many pieces of flotsam that have their own postage-paid envelopes, but I did find one that had a phone number. It was a great message in a bottle from a young girl in New York who was visiting Bahia Honda State Park. It was bobbing off No Name Key, and a client found it and read it aloud to all of us on the trip. She included her phone number and since we had a cell phone among us, we called and left an inspired group message on her home machine telling her where and when we found her novel experiment.

The most incredible thing I ever found was something that I had lost 2 years prior. One dark night while in my sailboat motoring north against a 22-knot headwind in 3- to 5-foot seas, I had the rug pulled out from under me. This catamaran has a drop-in center cockpit that is 4 by 8 feet that sits on the crossbeams. The cockpit has an engine mount with a new 9.9-horsepower outboard. Somewhere in the middle of my transit through Florida Bay, on my way to Cape Sable, a rogue wave ripped my cockpit and engine from the beams. Many things washed off the deck and into the blackened sea. The rest of the boat held together for me to sail home the next day, but I was never able to recover the engine or cockpit, among other things. I plotted my position to be somewhere near the halfway point of my trip—nearly 20 miles from home. Somehow, 2 years later, the engine must have shaken free from the cockpit and she floated to the surface. Miraculously it floated and was carried through a backcountry of island obstacles, grass flats, and deep channels for 12 miles. It showed up on a stretch of Little Pine Key's shoreline where we usually run our custom backcountry charters. This had me scratching my head for a week trying to figure out the significance of the event. My waterfront house was only about 3 miles downwind from the cockpit's location, and I can't help believing that if I had waited just a week or two longer she would have floated right back to her dock!

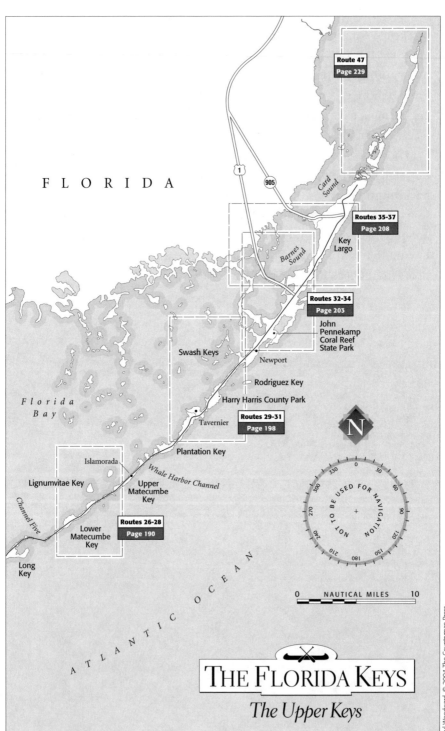

FLORIDA

Route 47
Page 229

Card
Sound

Routes 35-37
Page 208

Key
Largo

Barnes
Sound

Routes 32-34
Page 203

John
Pennekamp
Coral Reef
State Park

Swash Keys

Newport

Rodriguez Key

Harry Harris County Park

Florida
Bay

Tavernier

Routes 29-31
Page 198

Plantation Key

Islamorada

Whale Harbor Channel

Lignumvitae Key

Upper
Matecumbe
Key

Channel Five

Lower
Matecumbe
Key

Routes 26-28
Page 190

Long
Key

ATLANTIC OCEAN

N

NOT TO BE USED FOR NAVIGATION

0   350   30   60   90   120   150   180   210   240   270   300   330

0   NAUTICAL MILES   10

THE FLORIDA KEYS
The Upper Keys

Paul Woodward, © 2004 The Countryman Press

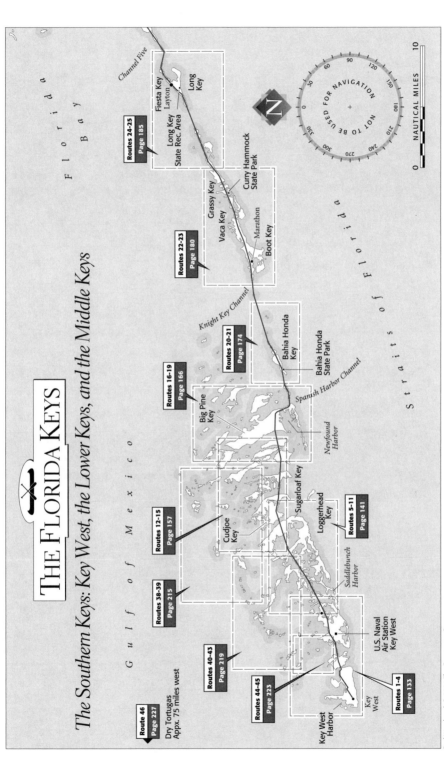

THE FLORIDA KEYS

The Southern Keys: Key West, the Lower Keys, and the Middle Keys

Route 46
Page 227

Dry Tortugas
Appx. 75 miles west

Routes 44-45
Page 223

Routes 40-43
Page 219

Routes 38-39
Page 215

Routes 12-15
Page 157

Routes 16-19
Page 166

Routes 24-25
Page 185

Routes 22-23
Page 180

Routes 20-21
Page 174

Routes 5-11
Page 141

Routes 1-4
Page 133

Gulf of Mexico

Florida Bay

Straits of Florida

Channel Five

Fiesta Key
Layton
Long Key

Long Key State Rec. Area

Curry Hammock State Park

Grassy Key

Vaca Key

Marathon

Boot Key

Knight Key Channel

Bahia Honda Key

Bahia Honda State Park

Spanish Harbor Channel

Big Pine Key

Newfound Harbor

Sugarloaf Key

Cudjoe Key

Loggerhead Key

Saddlebunch Harbor

U.S. Naval Air Station Key West

Key West Harbor

Key West

N

NOT TO BE USED FOR NAVIGATION

0   NAUTICAL MILES   10

PART III
The Launches

W<small>HEN IT COMES</small> to the ocean, it is all about access. Our thin ribbon of highway allows for some unique access points for some great shallow-water paddling. There are many stretches where you can just pull your car over and walk several yards and be able to check the temperature of the ocean. This, combined with the quality and diversity of our tropical ocean environment, makes it a paradise for paddling.

The launches that follow are organized from Key West to Key Largo and have been compiled to give you an idea of where the best access points are. You will see that there are more launches than tour descriptions, and that is because with these access points you can explore on your own. Everywhere one looks along the Overseas Highway is a potential trip, and every stretch of water holds a unique experience.

1. Simonton Street Launch

This launch site is nestled between the Hyatt Hotel and the Pier House Resort at the north end of Simonton Street. It is a small city beach that has paid parking and great access to the waters west off Key West. Simonton Street runs east to west, parallel to Duval Street. This sandy ramp offers easy access to a great sunset view and a quick trip out to the anchored boats near Sunset and Christmas Tree Island. Entering Key West on U.S. 1, bear right onto North Roosevelt Boulevard (U.S. 1) and continue for about 4 miles. It changes into Truman Avenue after the intersection with Eaton Street. Following this, you will start to see signs for Duval Street. At the intersection with a traffic light that has a Duffy's Restaurant on the left and a moped store on the right, you will find yourself at Simonton Street. Take a right at the light and follow it to the end of the road and the public beach. GPS coordinates for this launch are N 24°33.717, W 81°48.333.

2. Smather's Beach

This is the city beach and can be crowded in season. As you enter Key West from U.S. 1, bear left on Route A1A toward the beaches. Follow Route A1A for approximately 2.3 miles, and you will pass Mile Marker 1. On your left you will see a palm-studded shoreline with a rocky spit. This is a good launching spot on all but the lowest of tides. Parking is easy and close to the launch site. The Global Positioning System (GPS) coordinates for this site are N 24°33.156, W 81°45.933. From here you will see the first of ten poles that denote the swimming area that stretches across blue water for a mile. The least congested area is the easternmost portion of this long stretch of beach. The westernmost portion of the beach has restroom facilities and is adjacent to the water sports rental area and the food and beverage concessions. The coordinates of the westernmost area of the beach are N 24°33.017, W 81°46.577.

3. The Riviera Canal

This launch is an alternative to Little Hamaca City Park and is easily accessed from Flagler Drive. As you enter Key West from U.S. 1, bear left on Route A1A toward the beaches. The first light you reach will be Flagler Drive; take a right at the light. Follow Flagler Drive through the first traffic light at Kennedy Boulevard. A short distance on your left will be a center turn lane for 11th street. Take a left on 11th and follow a short distance to the boat ramp at the terminus. The Riviera Canal GPS numbers at the boat ramp are N 24.33.590, W 81°46.112.

4. Little Hamaca City Park

This is a quaint wooded park in the middle of the city with some great birding. Follow the directions for the Riviera Canal launch, but instead of turning onto 11th street, follow Flagler for another 0.2 mile to Government Street. Take a left on Government Street and proceed to the STOP sign. Straight ahead there will be a gate to the park entrance. Follow this road as it winds by the airport landing field. This area is good for bird viewing, as the larger raptors favor soaring in this area. The salt ponds on the right are great for waders. About 0.5 mile down the road is a small parking lot, where you will have a moderate portage through small, winding wooded trails and raised boardwalks. To the left of the dock is a small creek that makes for an easy launch. The GPS numbers for the dock are N 24°34.497, W 81°43.951.

5. Florida Keys Community College

GPS coordinates: N 24°35.082, W 81°44.780. This launching site on Stock Island offers a great location for easy access to some of the distant back-country islands. Leaving Key West on U.S. 1, take a left at the first traffic light onto Stock Island. This is College Road, and you will pass the Monroe County Correction Center, the dump, and the grade school on your left as you travel 1 mile to the college entrance. As you enter the school's main entrance from College Road, bear left at the traffic circle and wind through the parking lot toward the pool and aquatics area. You will find the shoreline accessible behind the Public Safety Building just beyond the pool. This parking lot looks out over a clean horizon of ocean, with the islands to the north. The parking lot has a bit of a drop (3 to 4 feet) to the water's edge, so it is nice to have assistance with your boat here.

6. Public Ramp MM 5.3

On the ocean side of U.S. 1 as you are leaving Key West, you will encounter a boat ramp that allows access to the bay between Boca Chica and Stock Island. The boat ramp is at MM 5.3 across from the Texaco gas station. This ramp sees heavy use, so park well out of the way of the other cars and trailers. The GPS numbers for this launch are N 24°34.571, W 81°43.673.

7. Boca Chica Channel (West)

The bay side of the highway on the western side of Boca Chica Channel has plenty of off-road parking and can be crowded with picnickers, wind-surfers, and sun worshipers. This site is a good alternative to the eastern side of the bridge if you are not going to cross the Boca Chica Channel. To beat the crowds and facilitate your launch, you can use the little gated road adjacent to the Key Haven Borrow Pit. This is at Mile Marker 5.5, and the GPS coordinates are N 24°34.571, W 81°43.673.

8. Boca Chica Channel (East)

The launch at the east side of Boca Chica Channel (N 24°34.710, W 81°42.736) has an excellent lee shore when there is a strong east wind. There is plenty of parking and easy access to the water. There are usually people fishing at the embankment and a car or two on the roadside. Leaving Key West, you pass over the Boca Chica Bridge at MM 5. Just over the bridge, after about 100 yards, you will see a center U-turn spot where you can turn back to the bay side of the bridge. Pull over just before the bridge and get ready to head out. The west side of the Boca Chica Bridge is also a good launch site, but there is usually a lot of traffic at this location.

9. Big Coppitt Public Ramp

The Big Coppit Launch is truly at the end of the road, and it seems it would be pretty easy to drive right into the water if you weren't careful. Coming from Key West, take a left at MM 10, where Bobalu's Restaurant is located. This is Fourth Street, and you will follow it for a few blocks until you turn left onto Avenue F. Follow Avenue F 0.3 mile until it intersects Barcelona Drive. From here you will take a right and follow Barcelona Drive for a little less than 0.5 mile to the ramp. Just before the ramp on the right is a small local convenience store. The GPS coordinates for this launch are N 24°36.105, W 81°40.025. On your return to this launch, keep your eyes on the large Norfolk Island pine that grows above the regular tree line.

10. Geiger Key Launch

GPS coordinates: N 24°34.925, W81°38.802. This launch site is just up the road from the Geiger Key Marina and Bar. Coming from Key West on U.S. 1, take a right just past the Circle K gas station at MM 10.8. Follow Boca Chica Road for about 1.7 miles until you see a left turn marked with a sign for Geiger Key Marina. Take that left onto Geiger Road and follow the road until you just pass the marina. A large chain link fence surrounds this boat launch, which has plenty of parking.

11. Geiger Key Creek

This launch is about 2.5 miles down Boca Chica Road, where you will encounter beach parking on your left. The GPS numbers N 24°34.208, W 81°40.161 are for the bridge as it goes over the creek. You can pull over anywhere on the beach side and launch off the rocky shore. At this point you can head left up the shoreline to the Geiger Creek entrance or head right and parallel the beach and shore for about 3 more miles. The last point where you can park on Boca Chica Road has the GPS coordinates N 24°33.789, W 81°40.643.

12. Shark Key Boat Ramp

This site offers easy access to the Similar Sound area. Leaving Key West on U.S.1, travel to MM 11. On the ocean side of the highway will be a pull-off and boat ramp. The GPS numbers for this site are N 24°36.081, W 81°38.830.

13. Saddlebunch #3

GPS coordinates for this launch are N 24°37.374, W 81°36.208. This is a pull-over on the ocean side of U.S. 1 at Mile Marker 14.2 that allows access to the underside between the new and old bridges on the Key West side. It is a little rough and rocky, but the incline is easy, and the haul from the rooftop to the water's edge is short.

14. Saddlebunch #5

This launch, at GPS coordinates N 24°36.764, W 81°37.379 is on U.S. 1 at MM 14.3. On the Key Largo side of these bridges is a slight incline that allows for easy access to the water between the old (1943) bridge and the new bridge. A short walk brings you to lots of roadside parking.

15. Mile Marker 16

GPS coordinates: N 24°36.081, W 81°38.830. This launch site seems to be the center of the universe when it comes to great access off the highway. Right at the milepost on both sides of the road is excellent access to several routes. Both shores have fossilized Key Largo limestone boulders that can tear up boats, but if you take your time you can gently launch into

---

Fort Zachary Taylor State Park, Key West. Launch site for paddlecraft is now available; call 305-292-6713. This spot also offers easy access to wonderful snorkeling and patch reefs off Key West.

---

some enchanting shallow bay habitats. Any vertical structure in the ocean seems to become colonized rapidly, and these rocky shores hold anemones, mangrove snapper, and many colorful invertebrates. It is inspiring to pull off the main highway and see pink-tipped anemones in 12 inches of gin-clear water. There is one other reason that I call this launch the center of the universe: It happens to be within aroma distance of Baby's Coffee (MM 15), where they roast coffee beans daily and have the best variety of fresh-brewed coffee.

16. Sugarloaf Marina

This site is located on the bay side of the highway at MM 17. Several outfitters use this area to launch guided tours throughout the Sugarloaf areas, and the marina store rents and sells kayaks and accessories. Call the marina at 305-743-3135. A blinking yellow caution light is at the intersection, and the small-boat launch is located behind the tackle shop and marina. At this time there is a fee of only $1 to launch kayaks and park. The small store next door has excellent fresh-made sandwiches and beverages for your excursion.

17. Sugarloaf Creek Bridge

This launch site is a bit off the beaten path. At Mile Marker 17, at the blinking yellow light, pull onto Sugarloaf Boulevard (oceanside), directly opposite Sugarloaf Lodge. Follow this road about 2 miles, and you will find a STOP sign. Take a right at the STOP sign and go another 2 miles, where you will reach a small bridge. Sugarloaf Creek is also known locally as Sammy's Creek, because this is where the Sammy family had lived since the 1950s. As of 2003 there was no one residing there, and an antenna farm was strung out on the oceanfront property with security personnel nearby. The bridge that traverses the creek is a favorite among fishermen, and there is ample parking on the west side. Getting your craft down to the water's edge is a challenge, as the steep, narrow embankment looks menacing, but if you take it slow and have assistance it is well worth the effort. This access point puts you into watery wilderness in minutes.

18. Upper Sugarloaf Sound (Northeast)
This launch is located right on U.S. 1 at MM 18.7. The access is a small opening in the mangrove shoreline on the bay side of the highway. This sound is constantly awash in mullet mud, and offers a great lee shore in an east wind. The GPS numbers for this site are N 24°39.317, W 81°32.352. There is also an old, abandoned dock on Park Key at Mile Marker 18.3. This may be slated as a paddlecraft launch in the future, but for now it is barricaded with two big yellow concrete structures. It is also posted with NO TRESPASSING signs from Monroe County.

19. Mile Marker 19 (Ocean Side)
At this site, there is a yellow striped traffic barrier a short distance from the highway. Coming from Key West this site is on the right side of U.S. 1. Immediately to the left of this barrier is a short, poisonwood-laced trail that has an easy launch site for access to Sugarloaf Sound. The GPS numbers are N 24°39.345, W 81°32.202.

20. Tarpon Creek
This launch is accessed at MM 20 on the bay side of U.S. 1. Coming from Key West, go right at Pirates Cove Road and continue until the pavement ends. This road is quite rough in several places and does require the use of a truck with big tires and good clearance, but it brings you right to the old, burned-out bridge over Tarpon Creek. The GPS numbers for this site are N 24°37.853, W 81°30.930. This was the old highway that previously led to Key West and has not had any maintenance in several decades. There is great birding on this road, and it is also a good fat-tire bike ride.

21. Cudjoe Key West Shore
This launch site is easily accessed from U.S. 1 at MM 20.5, where the Sugarloaf–Cudjoe Bridge meets Cudjoe Key. This appears to be an old boat launch that has been taken out of service. There is some great old, fossilized

Key Largo limestone here that was used for the retaining wall. The bay side of the highway has parking for several cars and is off the highway enough that you do not feel the wind shear from the oncoming traffic. This site also provides a great lee shoreline when the strong easterlies are blowing. The GPS coordinates are N 24° 39.769, W 81°30.774.

22. Cudjoe Key–Blimp Road
This launch is accessed from U.S. 1 at MM 21.3. There is a center turning lane at the junction where you turn north onto Blimp Road. Blimp Road runs due north and dead-ends at the boat ramp after 1.8 miles. There is ample parking and easy access to the backcountry islands from here, and for that reason there may be many cars with boat trailers at this spot. Make sure to leave the circular area near the end of the road clear to allow trucks with boat trailers ample room to turn around. The GPS numbers for this launch are N 24°41.686, W 81°29.982.

23. Spoonbill Sound Hammocks
At MM 22.2 on the bay side of Cudjoe Key is a little parking lot with a great boat ramp and kayak launch. The ponds located on the right before the launch are great for birding, and Alan Maltz, a famous Keys photographer, has produced many fine works of art here. There are some overgrown hiking trails that offer a closer look at these salt ponds. The GPS coordinates for this launch are N 24°39.731, W 81°29.214.

24. Summerland Key
This launch is accessed from U.S.1 at MM 24.9. Directly across from the Mobil gas station is Horace Street. The old Monte's Restaurant sits on the corner to your right as you turn onto Horace Street. Your second right is North Side Drive and you follow this for a short distance until you see Niles Road on your left. Follow Niles Road to the end after about a 1.5-mile transit. At the end of the road, a wonderful vista will greet you with a small, rocky launch site on your left, perfectly suited for launching kayaks. The yellow fence on the right side of the terminus marks the entrance to a U.S. Fish and Wildlife Service property that has an old wooden bridge connecting it to Wahoo Key. The GPS numbers for this site are N 24°41.058, W81°26.662.

25. Ramrod Key Swimming Hole

This launch, at GPS coordinates N 24°40.172, W 81°24.952 is one of those hidden local secrets. It is on the west shore of Ramrod Key, so it provides good protection when the east winds blow. Traveling from Key West after crossing the Niles Channel Bridge, you will be on Ramrod Key. Your first left (MM 26.7) will be Mako Road, which you will follow to Johnson Road. Bear left and follow Johnson Road, which jogs to the right and ends at a dirt road. To the left will be the old canal, which offers easy access to Niles Channel and doubles as a great swimming hole.

26. Middle Torch Key Causeway

This launch site is a great location for access to the Torch Keys. Coming from Key West on U.S.1, take a left at MM 27.8 onto Middle Torch Key. This road jogs along for several miles, and then you will see a sign for Big Torch Key, where you turn left. The beginning of this transit will be a causeway with several large culverts running under the road. The second and third culverts are easy launch sites that also double as spa-sized swimming holes at high tide. When the tides run well here, you may see some of the locals swimming and riding the currents through the culverts. Every year when the cold fronts blow the shrimp off the flats and into deeper water, I bundle up with a flashlight and shrimp net to see if a mass migration has occurred. I have never seen more than a handful sweep by with the currents, so I swear I will try again next year. The GPS coordinates are N 24°41.425, W 81°25.083.

27. Big Torch Key

This launch (GPS coordinates N 24°43.279, W 81°27.105) is reached by going to the Middle Torch Key causeway and continuing on the same road, jogging left and right for 5 miles to the end of the road. From the causeway there are 13 left and right turns in all, and at the 11th turn there is a little freshwater slough that is frequented by gators, frogs, and wading birds. At the end of the road there is excellent access to the western shoreline of Big Torch Key.

28. Little Torch Key

This launch is a small access point at the end of a road in a residential neighborhood. I polled a few of the neighbors, who thought that a single car with one or two kayaks wouldn't be too obtrusive. Use courtesy and common sense, as this is a neighborhood. At MM 28.5 on U.S. 1 coming from Big Pine, turn left onto Pirates Way, using the center turn lane in the highway. Follow Pirates Road to the end where it meets The Nature Conservancy's Torchwood Hammock Preserve gate. Take a left and follow Jolly Roger Drive to the end, and a small rocky beach will be on your right. Unload the boats here and park a ways up the street to keep the driveways clear.

29. Big Pine Lions Club

This is the last spot on the left off Key Deer Boulevard. Traveling from Key West on U.S. 1, you reach the first and only stoplight on Big Pine Key at MM 30.5. Take a left at the light, then bear left onto Key Deer Boulevard. Follow Key Deer Boulevard 4.5 miles, passing ballfields, subdivisions, the Blue Hole Alligator Observation Pond, and the Jack Watson Nature Trail. A few hundred feet up the road on the right past the Lions Club will be a small access trail that brings you to an old, sediment-filled canal. You can park on the roadside and portage your boat through the hardwoods, being cautious of the poisonwood that grows abundantly here.

30. Koehn Road Boat Ramp

This launch site on Big Pine Key can be reached by turning left at the only light on Big Pine Key as you travel from Key West. Immediately after your turn, bear right onto Key Deer Boulevard. Follow Key Deer Boulevard for about 2.9 miles, and you will see the parking lot for the Blue Hole Observation Pond on your left and Big Pine Street on your right. Take a right onto Big Pine Street and then take your second left onto Koehn Road. Follow Koehn Road all the way to the end to reach the boat ramp. Just before the boat ramp on both sides of the road are mangrove-fringed salt ponds that offer plenty of bird activity and great Key deer viewing.

31. No Name Key

This area has three great launches and is definitely off the beaten path. The No Name Pub is nearby and its slogan is "it's a nice place if you can find it." Traveling from Key West on US 1 turn left at the only light on Big Pine Key. Then bear right onto Wilder Drive and continue 1.2 miles to a stop sign. Take a left at the stop sign onto South Street. The road jogs to the right and continues down Avenue B until it merges with Watson Boulevard. Just after the merge you will cross over a little bridge on a boating canal. From that bridge continue one mile to the Old Wooden Bridge Fishing Camp. It is just before you reach the No Name Key Bridge (Bogie Channel Bridge). This is **No Name Key Launch A**. You can launch here for a nominal fee (or $3 if you mention the book), and they also have kayak rentals and guided tours (305 872-2241).

If the wind is blowing east and you would rather not cross the channel you can drive over the bridge and put in on the right side of the roadway where there are two rocky launch sites. This is known as **No Name Key Launch B** and gives great access to the lee shore of No Name Key during the strong easterly winds.

If you keep following this road onto No Name Key you will pass some wonderful pineland forests on both sides of the road. There is great deer viewing along this section and several hiking & biking trails on your right. It is 1.8 miles to the end of the road where you will arrive at **No Name Key Launch C**.

32. Long Beach

This site offers great access to the coral patch reefs and the shallows of Coupon Bight Aquatic Preserve. Traveling from Key West, pass almost all the way through Big Pine Key until you see a right-hand turning lane at MM 32.8. The Big Pine Fishing Lodge will be on your left as you start down Long Beach Road. If you follow this for about 0.5 mile, you will see a dirt road on your left. The road is a little rough, but short, and it delivers you to within a stone's throw to the ocean. There is room for several cars at **Long Beach site A** (GPS coordinates N 24°38.390, W 81°19.980), which is under the jurisdiction of the National Fish and Wildlife Refuge. You will see a yellow gate, which is the only thing that bars you from the ocean. If you continue another 0.5 mile down Long Beach Road, you will see two stone columns that mark the entrance to Long Beach Estates. At the roadside here there is room for one or two cars and a little opening in the mangroves, where you can launch a kayak. This is **Long Beach site B,** and the

GPS numbers are N 24°28.473, W 81°20.385. There is also room at the end of Long Beach Road to park and launch a small craft. This one can be quite muddy, but may be an alternative if the conditions warrant a more westerly launch site.

33. Spanish Harbor Boat Ramp

Leaving Big Pine and heading in the direction of the Seven Mile Bridge, you will quickly cross the Spanish Harbor Bridge. On the Marathon side of this bridge, on the bay side, is a boat ramp at MM 33.7. This is the Spanish Harbor Channel boat ramp, and may be used as a pickup point for a one-way, downwind trip from No Name Key. It is usually pretty active, with launching vessels and fishermen. The GPS coordinates for this site are N 24°38.966, W 81°19.043.

34. Bahia Honda Bridge

At the west end of the Bahia Honda Bridge, you can access the water on both the bay and ocean sides. The ocean side at MM 35 is an easy launch, as you can just about drive up to the tide pool-studded beach. Traveling from Key West, it is just 2 miles past Big Pine Key. Just before the divider in the highway, which usually has a speed-enforcement officer on duty, there will be a right turn that drops onto the shoreline adjacent to the bridge. The GPS numbers for this site are N 24°39.293, W 81°17.924. There is plenty of parking, and it may be a short portage to water deep enough for launching.

35. Bahia Honda State Park

This state park at MM 37 is a beautiful little treasure that was in the United States Top Ten Natural Beaches listing several years ago. The entry fee for the park is $4 per car and 50 cents per person. There is a concession building, which has great sandwiches and all the other amenities you might need. There are two launches easily accessed on the west side of the park. As you enter the park, you will encounter a STOP sign that allows you to pause and take in an incredible ocean-washed shore. This is where the cover photo for this book was shot. Take a right at the STOP sign and continue a short distance until you see a parking lot with a kayak rack in it.

This is where the launchings occur. The GPS numbers for this site are N 24°39.373, W 81°16.657. If the oceanside winds are too strong, you have the option of launching at the boat ramp, which is on the right just before the concessions building. Take a right and then continue for 100 feet and you will see the ramp.

36. Ohio Key

This launch site at Mile Marker 39 is also known as Sunshine Key Campground on the bay side of the highway. The ocean side of the highway was recently acquired by The National Wildlife Refuge and consists of an expansive salt pond adjacent to the ocean. The bridge on the southeast side of the island has a small area to park the car and a short walk to a sandy put-in. The GPS numbers for this shorebird paradise are N 24°40.378, W 81°14.653.

37. Little Duck Key

On the west side of the Seven Mile Bridge is a launch site that offers great access on either the bay or ocean side of the highway at MM 39.8. On the ocean side are picnic pavilions and an easy launch from the shoreline if the tide is not dead low. If the ocean side is crowded with beachgoers, the bay side has a small boat ramp and a large parking area. The restrooms are on the ocean side. This is known as Veterans Park, and the GPS coordinates are N 24°40.882, W 81°13.818.

38. Mile Marker 48.7 Public Ramp

This launch site is in Marathon at 33rd Street, next to the yacht club. The GPS coordinates are N 24°42.815, W 81°05.726. The kayak and boat launching ramp is located at the end of the boulevard. Coming from Key West, take a left at the stop light at 33rd Street across from the hospital. Follow this a short distance to the end of the road.

39. Sombrero Beach

Heading from Key West and about halfway through Marathon Key is a stoplight at MM 50. On your right will be Sombrero Beach Boulevard. Follow it to the end, about 2 miles, where you will find yourself looking at

Sisters Creek ahead of you. The Atlantic Ocean is on your left. This is Sombrero Beach, a jumping-off point for some major mangrove creek crawling.

40. The Island Boat Ramp

This launch site at MM 53.5 (GPS coordinates N 24°44.027, W 81°01.100), located at the east side of Marathon Key, gives access to Bamboo Key and wonderful sunset views over Florida Bay. It is a public boat ramp adjacent to The Island Restaurant and Tiki Bar.

41. Curry Hammock State Park

This site can be reached from Key West by heading up U.S. 1 to MM 56, ocean side. Take a right and follow the newly paved access road. You will travel over an old wooden bridge that smells of tar in the hot summer sun. Under this bridge is actually part of the park's loop trail. Next you will arrive at the honor-system entrance fee tube. The standard fee for state parks is $2.50 per person, and the beach is certainly worth it. I usually pull over to the right and try to find a shady spot under the buttonwood trees at the shoreline. The GPS coordinates are N 24°45.403, W 80°58.982.

42. Crawl Key North Sound

There is a borrow pit adjacent to Crawl Key North Sound at MM 57. This is a good access point to some wonderful, mangrove-pocked bays. Traveling from Key Largo, this pull-over on the right of U.S. 1 is at MM 57. You will cross a bike path and after 100 feet, look to your left to see a dirt road leading right down to the water's edge. The borrow pit was dug for hard coral rock that was used as fill for roadbeds and other construction. There is little mining still occurring in the Keys nowadays, as most of the needed fill is trucked down from the southern part of the Florida peninsula.

43. Tom's Harbor Keys

This launch site is right off U.S. 1 at MM 60.4. There is a nice pull-over on the ocean side of the highway that many use for fishing access. There is a slight embankment, but this levels out near the water's edge. The GPS numbers at this rocky put-in are N 24°46.518, W 80°55.674.

44. Long Key Bayside

This launch is a medium-sized pull-over that has a great little exposed shoreline that allows east access to Florida Bay. It is located on the bay side near Mile Marker 66.5. This access point is good for a quick trip out to watch the sunset or to try your luck fishing at Old Dan Bank. The shoreline that stretches out to your right is adjacent to the landfill and the solid waste transfer station. This shoreline is protected from the winter winds and makes a great lee shore for exploring the mangroves.

45. Long Key State Park

This launch site is easily reached from U.S. 1 at MM 67.5. Coming from Key Largo, take a left at the gumbo limbo tree-lined entrance. As you drive through the entrance, be sure to ask for a canoe trail map, as these are very informative and include some great natural history. After a short distance down this road it will intersect with a small creek that has a dock on the left side of the road. You can pull over and unload your craft and then park in the lot, up a bit on your left.

46. Long Key Bight

This site offers a wonderfully rich grass bight that features an incredible profusion of life. I really mean it—this is the most invertebrate-laden bottom in the entire Keys! The Channel 5 Bridge sweeps ocean and bay waters into this basin daily. The easiest access is on the ocean side of U.S. 1 along the causeway that leads up to the bridge. Coming from Key West, turn right off the highway at MM 70. The GPS numbers for this site are N 24°.50.454, W 80°.47.067.

47. Sea Oats Beach

This site is located on the 0.5-mile stretch of highway from MM 74.5 to MM 75. This shallow oceanside bank is frequented by wading fishermen and flats guide boats. The sandy shallows are a favorite feeding and resting area for permit, bonefish, and tarpon.

48. Lignumvitae State Park Launch

This site is adjacent to U.S. 1 at MM 77, bay side. Coming from Key Largo, the paved pull-over will be on your right. There is ample parking and a great launch at this location. The ramp usually has a number of big boats on trailers and there is an interpretive kiosk with park information nearby.

49. Indian Key Launch

This site is on the ocean side of the highway at MM 77. Coming from Key Largo, you have to turn left off U.S. 1 into a small roadside water access park. The launch here is easy, and it is a straight shot over to Indian Key.

50. Shell Key

This site is easily accessed from the Indian Key Causeway at MM 79.5. Coming from Key Largo, you will cross the bridge that connects Islamorada to the Indian Key Causeway. As soon as you travel over the bridge, pull over to the right. It is a bit rocky here and the traffic from the boats that gas up at the marina across the way can sometimes leave an awfully large wake. Once, as I was about to get into the boat at the shoreline, a 26-foot boat blasted by, leaving a tremendous wake. If I had been in the boat at the time it would have been quite an upset. The GPS coordinates for this launch are N 24°53.848, W 80°39.676.

51. Windley Key and Cotton Key

This is by far the most congested watercraft area in the entire Keys, with the possibility of hundreds of watercraft being encountered on a single day trip. There are several "no motor" zones set up for the wildlife, fishing boats, and paddlers, but the noise and constant traffic in season can be irksome and potentially dangerous. This area seems to be an experiment to see if wildlife can adjust to maximum human activity and still thrive! If you are staying in the area your hotel will probably have a ramp, but if not there is a rocky access site on the southwest side of the Whale Harbor Channel bridge at MM 83.7.

52. Snake Creek

At the end of the Windley Key area there is a little shoreside hotel called Smugglers Cove. You can launch here for $15 and have quick access to the shoreline of Windley Key Fossil Reef Geological Site. There are several endangered plants and some that grow nowhere else in the Keys along this shore. Because of the environmentally sensitive nature of the plants on this shoreline, no access or landing is allowed, but paddling near shore is allowed. These will probably be the least trafficked waters in this area.

53. Tavernier Creek

There may be a new launch facility at this location in the near future. The county is slated to install a paddlecraft launch site on the Key West side of the Tavernier Creek bridge at MM 90. This will provide easy access to the Cow Pens Keys, and also it can be used as the last leg of a one-way-with-the-wind trip to Bottle Key. There is a bit of boat traffic on the creek, but you can keep out of the way by hugging the right-hand shore as you travel.

54. Bottle Key Launch

This is a public boat ramp on the bayside of U.S. 1 at MM 92. Coming from Key Largo, take a right onto Jo-Jean Way. The launch is a short distance down this road. After unloading your craft, find an out-of-the-way place to park. This area is congested with small homes, and there is not that much street parking. GPS numbers at the launch site are N 25°00.808, W80°31.020.

55. Harry Harris County Park

This is a great launch site for the oceanside islands of Rodriguez Key, Tavernier Key, and Dove Creek. U.S. 1 is a divided highway at MM 93.5. Coming from Key Largo, take a left at the Circle K and cross the connector to Burton Drive. Follow the signs at each turn to the entrance of the county park. There is no admission fee for county residents; $5 for everyone else. Go through the gate and bear left as you continue down to the boat ramp. Unload your kayak, and then try to score a spot in the adjacent parking lot that will provide afternoon shade.

56. Sunset Park Launch

This is is a small park in a residential area that offers a great launching spot from which to explore the Swash Keys, Pigeon Key, Shell Key, and Nest Key areas. It is located in a subdivision right behind the Florida Keys National Marine Sanctuary building on U.S. 1 at Mile Marker 95.3. Driving from the Miami area down U.S. 1, take a right just past the Stone Ledge Motel onto Sunset Road. Follow this road a short distance, and as it curves around the corner look to your right to see the small park and boat launch.

57. Florida Bay Outfitters

You can't travel to the Keys to kayak and neglect to stop in at Florida Bay Outfitters at MM 104.5. Not only is this waterfront warehouse of paddle-craft a premier location for launching your manatee expedition, but also the staff is truly dedicated to the sport of paddling. Coming from Miami, turn right just after sighting the Caribbean Club. Park right in the lot, and get the lowdown on wildlife sightings in and around Dusenbery Creek. There is a slight fee charged to launch here, but if you purchase some-thing—which is highly likely considering the stock they have—you might get that waived. Ask about joining the Paradise Paddlers Club, which pub-lishes an excellent newsletter and all sorts of info on South Florida hap-penings. The phone number is 305-451-3018.

58. John Pennekamp State Park

This wonderful park is located on the ocean side of U.S. 1 at MM 102.5. Coming from Miami, the turnoff is on your left. Ask at the gate for a canoe trail map, which is thorough and up-to-date. The park has canoe and kayak rentals, and there are 47 campsites that can be reserved up to 11 months in advance by calling 1-800-326-3251.

59. Garden Cove Launch

This site is at the north side of Largo Sound. Coming from Key West on U.S. 1, bear right onto Card Sound Road and continue a short distance, then bear right onto Garden Cove Road. Follow this to just past Captain Slate's Dive Shop. On the right you will see a half dozen concrete barriers. This is a perfect place to start you trip to north Key Largo waters.

60. Mile Marker 111 Boat Ramp

This launch site is on the west side of the Overseas Highway. Coming from Miami, you will see the turnoff on the right, just before the Mile Marker

111 post. This launch has some heavy traffic, so use caution when loading and unloading your craft. The GPS numbers are N 24°12.856, W 80°25.548.

61. Little Manatee Bay

There is a little roadside creek at MM 114.2 with a small area that has sufficient room for a vehicle or two. The small creek that runs under a deep black water culvert connects Little Manatee Bay to more unnamed bays on the west side of the highway. This area seems to be a fishermen's paradise, as there is a ton of fishing paraphernalia around, as well as roadside litter. The GPS numbers are N 25°15.310, W 80°26.258. You can also access Short Key from here if the South Dade Marina is closed.

62. South Dade Marina

This launch site is located on the east side of U.S. 1 at Mile Marker 115. Open every day from 9:30 AM to 5 PM but closed Tuesdays and Wednesdays, this convenient launch location charges only $3 per kayak to put in and park. The marina also provides an excellently detailed chart of several paddling routes that notes the numbered PVC navigation markers in the area. The contact number for the South Dade Marina is 305-247-8730.

63. Steamboat Creek

This site is at the southern part of Card Sound Bridge Road. Leaving Key Largo and veering to the right on Card Sound Road, travel 9.2 miles to a stoplight. Card Sound Road continues to the left, and after about 1.7 miles you will cross the first of four small bridges that span the Steamboat Creek complex. The first bridge has a pull-over on the right as you pass over the bridge. This is a little rough, and usually it is quite full of trash. Be sure to lock up your valuables or bring them with you. There are several other launching spots along this stretch that give good access to the creeks that run through this area.

64. Card Sound Road Bridge

This site has room enough on either side to pull over and park. The launches may be a little rocky, but they provide instant access to the Card

Sound area. The Card Sound Road bridge is 12 miles from the junction that connects with U.S. 1 just south of Florida City.

65. Alabama Jack's

Alabama Jack's is a funky little bar and restaurant just to the north of Card Sound Road Bridge. You can check with the dockmaster here if you decide to drop in at this location. Exploring the funky live-aboards and rustic docks in this community can be a photographic gold mine.

66. Biscayne National Park

This site is at the northernmost island cluster in the long, graceful arc of the Florida Keys. The Dante Fascell Visitor Center has some great interpretive displays and a nice book selection. You can reach the park from the intersection of SW 328th Street and U.S. 1 in Homestead. The park entrance is 9 miles east of this intersection. If you are traveling down Florida's Turnpike, exit at Speedway Boulevard (exit 6), which is SW 137th Street. Follow this for 3.4 miles, and take a left onto SW 328th Street. From here it is another 5.2 miles to the park entrance. The phone number is 305-230-7275.

67. Herbert Hoover Park

This launch site is on the right at the entrance to the Biscayne National Park Visitor Center entrance. This Dade County–operated park has a swimming beach, showers, a 24-hour bait and tackle shop, motorboat launch, and overnight parking. If you plan to visit Elliot Key by ferrying your kayaks over by personal motorboat, you will have to use these facilities, because the National Park does not have facilities for launching a motorboat or parking the trailer overnight. There is a nominal fee for launching and overnight parking. The contact phone number is 305-230-3033.

PART IV
The Trips

THE TRIP INFORMATION that follows should give you a basic familiarity with each area and the suggested route. Other considerations, such as tides at the location, weather, your boat's design, and your physical abilities should always be factored into your trip plan.

All distances on the ocean are measured in nautical miles, which measure 6,000 feet, versus statute miles, which measure 5,280 feet. The overall average speed for a kayak on the water is approximately 3 nautical miles per hour, or 3 knots. You can calculate your trip's duration by using this as a starting point.

A good chart and simple compass will assist in any course corrections or route planning you may need to make, and a portable Global Positioning System (GPS) device makes a nice confirmation of your planned course. The GPS should not take the place of a good chart and basic compass, as I have had several GPS units fail me in the field.

There are 176 tide stations in the Keys. In some unique areas between the Atlantic waters and the Gulf and Florida Bay waters, there may be two or three different times for a particular high tide on an individual island. To assist you with your computations, there is a complete listing of the tidal differences and other constants in the Appendices. The web site www.saltwatertides.com is a quick resource for tide predictions.

The National Oceanic and Atmospheric Administration (NOAA) weather radio broadcasts weather updates for mariners on radio frequency 162.400 mHz in the Lower Keys and 162.450 mHz in the Upper Keys.

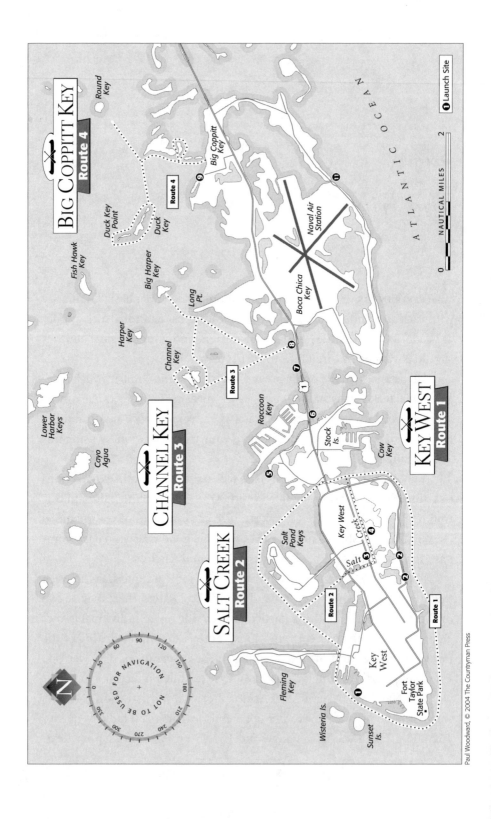

BIG COPPITT KEY
Route 4

Round
Key

Fish Hawk
Key

Duck Key
Point

Big Coppitt
Key

Duck
Key

Route 4

⑨

Big Harper Key

Long
Pt.

Harper
Key

Channel
Key

Route 3

⑧

CHANNEL KEY
Route 3

Lower
Harbor
Keys

Cayo
Agua

⑤

Raccoon
Key

⑦

1

⑥

Stock
Is.

Cow
Key

⑪

Naval Air
Station

Boca Chica Key

A T L A N T I C   O C E A N

KEY WEST
Route 1

Salt
Pond Keys

Key West
Creek

Salt

④

③

②

②

Route 1

SALT CREEK
Route 2

Route 2

Fleming
Key

Wisteria Is.

Sunset
Is.

Key West

Fort
Taylor
State Park

①

N

NOT TO BE USED FOR NAVIGATION

0 30 60 90 120 150 180 210 240 270 300 330

① Launch Site

0   NAUTICAL MILES   2

Paul Woodward, © 2004 The Countryman Press

Hourly updates, special warnings, and tidal information are given from a computer voice with a French accent. You can tap into this by buying a cheap weather radio or using a handheld VHF with a WX (weather channel) button.

All the trip information has been compiled to give you a basic idea of what to expect. The maps and other information have been made as accurately as possible. The trip descriptions and charts cannot be assumed to be exact, nor will they guarantee your arrival at any given point. You are about to embark on a wilderness adventure! Use sound judgment, common sense, and always tell someone on shore your float plan.

1. Circumnavigate Key West

Charts:
> Standard Mapping Services Aerial Photo Map #104
> TOPSPOT Key West Area #N209
> NOAA Chart #11447

Launch: Launch #1 and launch #2 provide easy access for this trip. You can use either of the two Key West launches, depending on the prevailing winds and tides. The winds usually blow from the east and southeast, so to take best advantage of a downwind run, the best starting point would be at Simonton Beach.

Habitats: Key West is built out almost entirely to its maximum capacity. There are private homes, condominiums, and commercial developments around the entire perimeter. Within the sights and sounds of the city there are abundant wildlife, clean waters, mooring fields full of sailboats, and lots of boat traffic. Turtle grass flats, patchy coral reefs, sponge flats, several miles of beach, and scattered mangrove shores comprise the circumnavigation.

Trip Length: The circumnavigation route is 10 nautical miles. There are optional launches to divide the route up.

Tides and Currents: The annual Swim Around Key West event is usually scheduled for a day or two after the full moon to take full advantage of the tidal currents. Departing from Smathers Beach at 8 AM the swimmers are usually swimming with the last of the incoming tide as they encounter the first half of the route and the outgoing tide as they come through Cow Key Channel.

Paddling Conditions: Key West Harbor is an active port with cruise ships, U.S. Navy and Coast Guard vessels, and scads of commercial and recreational boats. Use safe boating common sense, and keep clear of all boat traffic. Using a small bandana on a 6-foot pole will make your profile highly visible to boaters. Once past the port, the route is fairly tranquil until you reach the Cow Key Channel Bridge. The current under Fleming Key Bridge can be swift and dangerous in some conditions.

Featured Creatures: The big orange bill of the black skimmer looks so out of place on its streamlined body. There are large flocks of these unique birds in the Key West Channel area and the way they fly in a unified flock is poetry. The way they feed, with the longer lower bill slicing through the waters, can best be described as grace without effort.

Starting from launch #2 (Smathers Beach), you will head west and pass the White Street Pier, where you will probably encounter several anglers plying the waters with wet lines. After passing the Navy base radar dish, you will see the tall, wispy pines at Fort Zachary Taylor State Park. The bottom here is hard and pocked with sponges and small coral, which form a perfect habitat for the palolo worm hatch, an event that occurs in June. Keeping clear of the buoy-marked swimming areas of the park, you will pass several rocky groins, the last of which abuts Key West Channel. If the tide is in your favor you will feel the pull of the incoming tide as you pass the concrete seawalls that mark one of the cruise ship berths. This area is the most congested so paddle hard and keep your eye on the boat traffic.

As you pass the Pier House resort, you will see the Simonton Beach launch on your right. At this point you have covered about a third of the trip. From this point, the entrance to Fleming Key Channel is 0.5 mile away to the north. Your nose will tell you that it is close by when you pick up the aroma of the sewage treatment plant. After enjoying the view of the sailing vessel anchorage, you will be swept under the Fleming Key Bridge and will bear left about 45 degrees toward the Sigsbee Park Navy property. This shoreline is tranquil and usually out of the wind. The deeper part of this channel is a good spot to stop for a swim or snorkel if you have a dive flag, as the ledges provide great habitat for lobsters and grouper.

As you round Sigsbee Park, you will see the green roof of the newest condos in Key West, which are on Stock Island. Head toward these while keeping out of the main boating channel, and you will see the Cow Key Channel Bridge just past the jail on your left. Only 0.3 mile past the Cow Key Bridge on your right will be the entrance to Riviera Canal (launch #3), and beyond that lies the Atlantic Ocean and the beginning of your downwind trip home.

2.   Salt Creek Run

Charts:
> Standard Mapping Services Aerial Photo Map #104
> TOPSPOT Key West Area #N209
> NOAA Chart #11447

Launch: Little Hamaca City Park launch #4 and Riviera Canal launch #3 are the most convenient for this short trip.

Habitats: Mangrove creeks, residential canals, a concrete tunnel under Flagler Drive, and the salt ponds adjacent to the Key West Airport highlight this unusual trip.

Trip Length: Two nautical miles in length from one end of the linear route to the other end. Hurricane Hole Marina on Stock Island and the Hampton Inn in Key West are at each end.

Tides and Currents: Low tides can make passage tricky where the creek and the Riviera Canal join. This is a good trip to make when small craft warnings are posted.

Paddling Conditions: Protected residential canals and hidden mangrove creeks make this an easy adventure in the middle of the city.

Featured Creatures: Although the waters have an excellent array of marine creatures and birds, the four-legged canines are the most noticeable as they announce your presence. Much of this trip involves views of residential backyards, and these dogs are adamant about protecting the neighborhood from invasions of colorful kayaks.

When you put your boat in at the Riviera Canal ramp (launch #3) you are just about in the center of this linear trip. To the left are the Salt Ponds and

Black-bellied plovers winter on the coast and nest in the Arctic tundra.

Little Hamaca Park, and to the right the meandering backyard creeks and tunnel. The description of the trip will start at Hurricane Hole Marina and end at the gulf side of Key West. You can paddle right up to Hurricane Hole Marina, and it is a great spot for a bite to eat and a beverage. Leaving Hurricane Hole, you will enter Cow Key Channel and head left toward the Riviera Canal mouth, about 0.3 nautical mile away. As you pass under Route A1A within a short 0.5 nautical mile, you will encounter a small, mangrove-lined opening that canopies a small, shallow creek bed. This sandy creek is littered with shells and coral fragments, as well as many invertebrates dwelling in the rich currents that flow here. Paddling up the creek will take some navigation skill, and for a portion you will have to put the paddle away and pull yourself through with your hands. After a 10-minute journey you will find yourself at an opening to the Salt Ponds. Be sure to mark the creek with a visual aid, as it is a little tricky to find on the way back. Another trick is to turn around and study the route every so often so you will be familiar with its appearance on the way out. The Salt Ponds, really shallow inland seas, are rich with color and bird life. This is a good area to spot bald eagles, among other birds of prey. Back in the Riviera Canal, as you continue down toward the launch, you will see the Little Hamaca dock and adjacent trails about 0.3 nautical mile away. You can tie up here and stretch your legs on the hiking trails that meander through this hardwood scrub zone.

As you come to the end of the Riviera Canal, you will see that the water shallows and the stream becomes narrow and is completely lined with mangroves. This continues after a right turn to the Flagler Drive Tunnel. There is just enough room for a paddlecraft to sneak through here and come out on the other side, where you now seem to travel through many backyards.

After a short distance it will open up into a shallow lake known as Caroline's Pond, which can have a nice selection of wading birds. Not much farther on, you will pass TGI Fridays just before passing under the Roosevelt Boulevard bridge. The Hampton Inn will be on your right as you view the Gulf side of Key West, where there is a nice anchorage for vessels.

3. *Channel Key*

Charts:
> Standard Mapping Services Aerial Photo Map #104
> TOPSPOT Key West Area #N209
> NOAA Chart #11447

Launch: Launch #8 on the east side of Boca Chica Channel Bridge is recommended.

Habitats: These shallows near north Boca Chica Key are a mixture of sand and marl muds that are interspersed with sparse grass beds and sponge flats.

Trip Length: The route as shown is approximately 5 miles.

Tides and Currents: This area is shallow and it is best to coincide with a launch time that is three hours before high tide.

Paddling Conditions: Most of the trip can be made in the lee shore of Boca Chica Key. Wind would not be a factor until you jump over to Channel Key and even then it should be a tailwind.

Featured Creatures: The small sharks including lemon shark, bonnethead shark, and nurse shark are commonly seen on these shallow bright flats. The nurse shark is usually a solitary cruiser. If they are resting on the bottom in shade and current it is common for others to join them.

The east side of Boca Chica Bridge is usually not full of people like the west side, so there is plenty of parking and a great little ramp. Upon launching, you will head due north to a small unnamed island that has a ring of shallow flats around it. At most tides you can pass between it and Boca Chica, and this pass is a good shark highway. Stay with the shoreline edge and enjoy the windless zone, where you can really see into the water. As you round the first point, you will notice a canal entrance about 0.3 mile up this shore. This is an old series of canals that is surrounded by navy property and is sometimes used by locals to waterski in, but that is only on windy winter days. Following this shallow shoreline for another mile will put you at Long Point, where you can take in the view of the backcountry islands. From this point, if the wind is moderate and you are ready for another 0.5 mile of open-water paddling, you can choose to paddle to the Harper Keys.

The southernmost two of these three islands have some very nice mangrove fringe edges that harbor lots of fish and colorful invertebrates. Whichever way you go, the trip over to Channel Key should be a down-wind run from Long Point. As you depart Long Point, you will have to paddle under the power poles that stretch to Key West. These poles have a clearance of 30 feet under the wires, but on occasion an errant sailboater will tangle with them.

Drawing closer to Channel Key, there will be a marked increase in boat traffic, as all the boaters use the cuts in the banks north of the channel to travel to and from the backcountry. The deep creek that bisects Channel Key is about halfway up the shoreline and usually has a bit of water rippling at the entrance.

Once out of the wind, you can slowly meander and enjoy the greenery surrounding you. Look at the edges of the roots for tunicates, sponges, and pale anemones that filter plankton from the water. If you can hang out and sit still for a while, smaller mangrove snappers will be curious and nose right up under your boat's shadow. There is an osprey nest near the end of the creek that is utilized yearly, and in the future this part of the route may be closed to traffic during the winter nesting period. As you head back, you can island-hop to the first unnamed island, cruising along the shoal that connects it to Channel Key. These shoals are good for spotting the triangular fins of the stingray as they carve the surface in their underwater ballets.

The southern end of this island has a shoal extending south toward the bridge, but you should have no problem crossing it at high tide. From here it is only a little over a mile back to the launch, and if you are on an afternoon trip you will be able to enjoy the sunset over Boca Chica on the return trip.

4. Big Coppitt Key

Charts:
> Standard Mapping Services Aerial Photo Map #104
> TOPSPOT Key West Area #N209
> NOAA Chart #11447

Launch: Launch site #9 at Big Coppitt public ramp.

Habitats: The nearshore waters surrounding Halfmoon Key are shallow grass beds with scattered sponge flats. The light sandy-colored bottom there and on the way to Duck Key is full of sponges.

Trip Length: The circumnavigation of Halfmoon Key is approximately 2.3 nautical miles. The optional trip segments to Round Key and Crane Keys would add another 3-mile loop. The northwest option of exploring Duck Key and Fishhawk Key would be an additional 4.5-mile loop.

Tides and Currents: The currents in this back bay are negligible. The low tide can make approaches close to Duck Key difficult, but provide for great exposed sandy shallows.

Paddling Conditions: For the most part, this route is protected from strong easterly winds.

Featured Creatures: The large numbers of commercially valuable and other species of sponges make the bottom a delight to view as you paddle out to Duck Key.

Leaving from the Big Coppitt launch, head to the north, staying on the lee of the southernmost of the Halfmoon Keys. Less than 0.5 mile up the lee shore of this island, there will be an east–west cut between the islands that is a great passageway for stingrays and sharks. The island in the center of the passage holds abundant wading birds. Continuing on the lee shore of Halfmoon Key, 0.5 nautical mile up the shoreline, will bring you to the northernmost point of Halfmoon Key, called Jim Pent Point. There is a small bench that faces the sunset on the shoreline here and, after your trip to Duck Key or Round Key, this is a good resting point.

From Jim Pent Point you can choose to go either west or north, depending on the prevailing winds. If you go toward Round Key, it is better if the winds aren't too strong from the easterly direction. Round Key and Crane Keys are a series of small islands that have great habitat around the mangrove roots. Each of them also hosts specific birds that nest and roost during the winter months. Although it's a bit of a stretch to the first island on this route, it's easy to island-hop and fit in a rest behind each of the Crane Keys. This is where you usually see most of the wildlife on and in the water.

On the return trip, the wind should give you a little push back toward Jim Pent Point, and then you can work the lee shore back toward the launch.

If you opt to go to Duck Key and Fishhawk Key, be aware that you will be paddling upwind on the return. Duck Key is approximately 0.7 nautical mile in a westerly direction from Jim Pent Point. On the west shore of Duck Key there are isolated mangrove clumps with meandering trails through them. This is a good area to be on the lookout for the nonpoisonous mangrove water snake. It will either be laid up in the roots sunning itself, or submerged on the bottom, acting like a stick and waiting for a fish to swim by within striking distance. If you have the energy and you opt to extend the trip by heading west to Fishhawk Key, it will be approximately 0.7 nautical mile to the west side of the island. This backside of the island has a deep gutter that is frequented by mangrove snappers.

On the southeastern section of this deep gutter, you will find an entrance to the small creek that is completely enclosed by mangroves, and is the east–west shortcut through the island. Once inside this creek, you will have to put away your paddle and pull yourself through by the roots and branches. If you slow down and inspect the bottom, you will notice that it's rocky and has numerous sponges of diverse colors. Sea stars, anemones, and hordes of fishes make their homes here. The current can be pretty strong here, and that's why the bottom is scoured so clean. The best way to enjoy this experience is to just hang out for 5 or 10 minutes and watch the current sweep through this watery world.

The return trip from Fishhawk Key on a straight shot is approximately 2.5 nautical miles. If the winds are out of the east and strong, it makes good sense to island-hop to Duck Key and, from there, southeast to the Big Coppett shoreline. You can hug the shoreline all the way to the boat ramp, which is just 0.7 nautical mile away.

5. *Geiger Key*

Charts:
>Standard Mapping Services Aerial Photo Map #104
>TOPSPOT Key West Area #N209
>NOAA Chart #11447

Launch: Launch site #10.

Habitat: There is a diverse variety of oceanside flats and deeper channels that include large sponges, coral heads, and some great undercut mangrove edges.

Trip Length: This circular route can meander for a total of about 5 nautical miles.

Tides and Currents: Most of this trip can be accomplished on any tide, except for the last segment, which can get a little skinny on low tides.

Paddling Conditions: There are protected oceanside flats with lots of small islands to duck in behind if there is wind. The channel that cuts through Saddlebunch Harbor can sometimes be swift.

Featured Creatures: It is hard to imagine that a fish that looks like a minnow can grow to 150 pounds, but it is true in the case of the tarpon. The smallest tarpon I have ever seen was in the roots of a hidden creek in Saddlebunch Bight, the unnamed cove that is to the east of Saddlebunch Harbor. It was with a school of others that were 12-inch miniatures of their bigger brothers. Well hidden in this shady creek, they went about the daily business of being a fish by slamming silversides and causing cascading slices of silver to fly above the water.

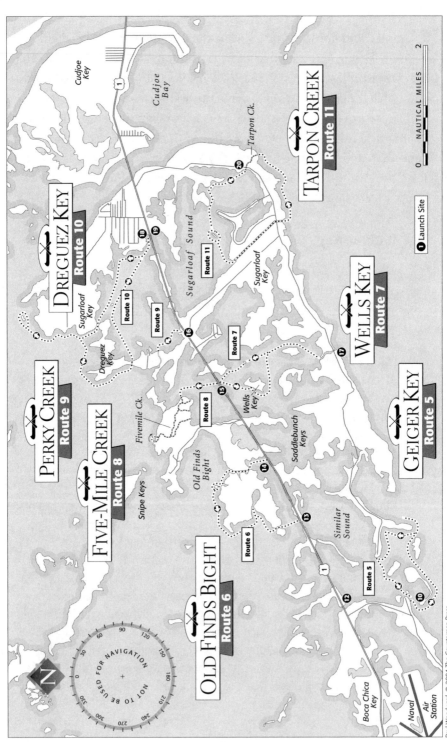

DREGUEZ KEY
Route 10

PERKY CREEK
Route 9

FIVE-MILE CREEK
Route 8

OLD FINDS BIGHT
Route 6

TARPON CREEK
Route 11

WELLS KEY
Route 7

GEIGER KEY
Route 5

① Launch Site

NAUTICAL MILES

0   1   2

Cudjoe
Key

Cudjoe
Bay

Tarpon Ck.

Sugarloaf
Sound

Sugarloaf
Key

Route 11

Route 10

Route 9

Route 7

Route 8

Wells
Key

Saddlebunch
Keys

Route 6

Similar
Sound

Route 5

Dreguez
Key

Sugarloaf
Key

Fivemile Ck.

Old Finds
Bight

Snipe Keys

Boca Chica
Key

Naval
Air
Station

N

NOT TO BE USED FOR NAVIGATION

30 60 90 120 150 180 210 240 270 300 330

Paul Woodward, © 2004 The Countryman Press

The Geiger Key Bar slogan is: "We are on the backside of paradise," and a watery paradise it is! The launch is a short walk from this waterfront bar and grill, and the trip route takes you right by it, so use caution and keep an eye out for wandering motorboats. From the launch, you can go right and travel down the canal until you see the waterfront bar. At this point you will see, off to the west, two markers that are on either end of a shoal. The sign reads DANGER, and the locals have dubbed it Danger Reef. It is a good place to hop in the water with a mask and see some of the biggest loggerhead sponges around and a prolific number of smaller conch that feed on the bottom here. If you are not ready to hop in the water yet, continue to your left toward the west end of Saddlehill Key.

As you approach Saddlehill, look for a small creek entrance that gives you access to the interior of this island. The creek parallels the north shore and pops you back out after a short trip. Continuing to curve around Saddlehill, you will be greeted by an uninterrupted span of blue ocean. The water is deep right up next to the island, and there are two blind corners, so if you hear a motorboat and it appears to be getting louder, be prepared for passing port to port as you round the bends. Some boaters will come in under full power, so it is wise to keep alert.

Once past the south tip, you can hug the shore and feast your eyes on the ocean's garbage strainer. The mangrove shores are full of debris that the winds blow in and buoys, trap lines, and lots of lumber litter the shoreline here.

The next island east will be Pelican Key, and the sandy flat here has a beautiful little colony of vase sponges growing on the sandy and rocky bottom. If the tide will allow, you can meander along the north side of Pelican through tightly clustered mangrove islets, where herons and egrets roost. Progressing another 0.5 mile east, you will be fetching the southwesternmost portion of Sugarloaf Key. If the tide is high, you can round this tip close to the land, but if not you will have to paddle some distance around the point to actually get into the bight. This stubby little finger of Sugarloaf has some excellent undercut edges on both the east and west sides, where mangrove snapper, parrotfish, grouper, grunts, and tarpon like to hide.

That secret little creek where the baby tarpon hide is 0.5 mile due east of here near the next point of Sugarloaf and impossible to reach at anything but high tide.

Backtracking to the point on southwest Sugarloaf, you can hug that western shoreline and cast for little mangrove snappers that hide in the root system. Following this cove for a mile, you will come to the old U.S. 1 highway that used to span this channel with a wooden bridge in the early 1900s. This is a good leg-stretching spot, and if the wind is east you will have a downwind paddle for the 1.2-nautical-mile journey home. The old highway bridge used to cross right over Bird Key, and there are some old piling remnants to be seen on the north end, but the south end has the creek and the undercut edge that holds the creatures. From the south end of Bird Key it is just about due west to the launch site. This section of the route has some rich, hard bottom and numerous golf ball coral, finger coral, and some rose coral littered about on the bottom.

6.   *Old Finds Bight*

Maps:
> TOPSPOT Middle keys area, #N208
> Standard Mapping Services #F104
> NOAA Chart #11445

Launch: Launch #13 is at Mile Marker 14.2.

Habitats: Very shallow sponge flats with a mixed bottom of rock and mud. Some rich turtle grass beds in Old Finds Bight.

Trip Length: Three miles as a circumnavigation. This is a good trip if you have two cars, but if not it is only a 1.5-mile walk back to the launch. Additional 2 miles if all creeks are explored.

Tides and Currents: Paddled on a 2.0 high or falling high tide with no water depth problems. Currents were less than one-knot outgoing.

Paddling Conditions: Shallow-water cruising with a bushwhacking creek at the beginning.

Facilities: Baby's Coffee 1 mile away at MM 15.

Featured Creatures: The shorebirds seem to love these low, scrubby mangroves. There are often many clustered flocks of mixed species that will sit and wait quietly until the boats are in close proximity, and then a low chattering can be heard. Sometimes this will be the first indication that they are nearby, as they are well

camouflaged among the mangrove roots. Willetts, plovers, sandpipers, and yellowlegs are roosters in these Everglades-like creeks.

The Antenna Farm is your constant companion on this semicircular trip, which takes full advantage of the east winds. The Antenna Farm is some sort of tracking and communications base that sprouts its prickly exterior to the skies. There is plenty of parking and nearby is one of the old Overseas Highway bridges, built in 1943. It is a great location to drink your cup of Baby's coffee while scouting the mangrove horizon.

Use caution on the rocky embankment under the new bridge, as portions of it are slippery. Once on the water, a nice little side trip is to go under the old bridge and check out Belle's Antique Shop. There will be a good current that flows through some culverts under the access road, and this is a good place to make any adjustments. Backtrack under the bridge and head toward the four tallest antennas.

About 0.25 mile across, there will be a tiny, narrow creek entrance (GPS coordinates N 24°37.728, W 81°36.443). Somewhere just south and west of the creek opening, the four tall radio towers line up together to provide an excellent navigation aid, which is good to keep in mind if no GPS is available. It is best to attempt this creek without a paddle by pulling with your arms on the crowded mangrove branches. A high tide and a narrow kayak are also necessary. It is a tight corridor and at any moment you think that it will narrow down to impassable, but persevere. The 0.125-mile creek opens into stream #1 at GPS coordinates N 24°37.803, W 81°36.460.

Stream #1 has some great bottom, and the fish life is plentiful. This one appears to be a dead end that has two strainers at the terminus. Nurse sharks and little green turtles are likely nearby. Sailing downwind, you can now head to creek #2 at GPS coordinates N 24°38.088, W 81°36.705, just 0.25 mile away. This seems to be the most substantial and has many roosting shorebirds as well as several great blue herons. If you don't stare at the birds and move slowly with your paddle held low, they will not spook as easily and you can really see some great behaviors.

There is a small, unnamed mangrove island to the north that has a great undercut ledge and is "holding." "Holding" is a local term used to denote habitat that has potential for fishability, and this island certainly has it. Three- to 5-foot depths and some severe undercuts make this island a unique haven for finfish, fire sponge, mangrove oysters, and anemones.

From here it a short hop to the entrance of creek #3 at GPS coordinates N 24°38.138, W 81°36.882. This one may meander and connect to #2, but I was so entranced with all the shorebirds coming in to roost that I never made it to the terminus. Backtracking and heading west toward a cluster of five islands, you may notice that the outermost island has mostly dead branches. A solitary osprey gives a series of peeps and flies off. I imagine that it has probably lost its mate and that is what accounts for the empty nest on the deadwood island. Maybe next year it will be active again.

As you head toward the point and look out to the west, there are five islands that look like a giant's stepping stones on the horizon, equally sized and spaced apart. These are the Crane Keys, Waltz Key, and Round Key. This area has a good number of lemon sharks during the falling tide, and they blend in well with the marl and mud bottom. After rounding the point and heading south, you can pick out what appears to be a beach on the shoreline.

This marks the pass (GPS N 24°37.157, W 81°37.527) that gives you quick access to the highway. If you have time you can explore the eastern inner bight of this island complex or head over to the "beach," which is an ancient wood platform that makes a good picnic spot. The pass has some big sharks cruising at the exits, and once there were three or four good splashes as I went through it near sunset. A short run over a healthy sponge bottom, and you will be at the Saddlebunch #5 bridge. It seems to be easier to exit the kayak next to the shoreline under the new bridge and portage the gear up between the new and old bridges. From here it is a short, 1.5-mile hike back to the car at the original launch.

7. *Wells Key*

Maps:
TOPSPOT Middle Keys #N208
Standard Mapping Services #F104
NOAA Chart #11445

Mangrove roots support a rich variety of fish and colorful invertebrate life.

Launch: Launch #15, which is Mile Marker 16 on the bay side. There is a significantly larger section of cable in the lower power lines that indicates the launch site.

Habitats: Shallow, soft mud sponge flats with some sandy shores and beaches.

Trip Length: This 5-nautical-mile loop includes the Sugarloaf Creek area, also known as Sammy's Creek. The creek was christened with this local name because of the Sammy residence, which is at the creek's exit to the ocean, adjacent to the bridge.

Tides and Currents: Low tides allow for more beach, and the currents can be strong in Sammy's Creek.

Paddling Conditions: Protected island-hopping over shallow mud flats.

Featured Creatures: Sea cucumbers by the dozen guard the sandy entrance to Sammy's Creek. This is a perfect habitat for them. They graze the nutrient-rich, algae-laden sediment, which gets scoured daily by the tides.

This route has three small beaches on the islands nearby, where you can while away the time before sunset. Departing from Mile Marker 16, you will head south 0.5 nautical mile to Wells Key.

The west shore of Wells Key is a mixture of hard rock and grass that is home to scores of baby barracuda. You can count a dozen at any given time, and the pack of youngsters will actually follow you as you pass, apparently thinking that there may be some opportunity for prey in your wake. Halfway down the island's shore, you will come across an old, rustic dock that allows good access to the small bit of dry land on the island. Sea purslane lines the short trails, and there is a small, dry spot where you can stretch you legs and enjoy the sun. The rocky shore is littered with ram's horn snails and various other small mollusks that graze here.

As you round the southwest tip of Wells Key, a small island will come into sight. This little bird island (GPS coordinates N 24°37.471, W 81°34.348) features a diverse collection of flying creatures, and the undercut edges hold numerous mangrove snappers. On the south side of this island, you will be able to look to the south and see some of the white PVC markers, about 0.5 mile away, that mark the route to the creek entrance.

To the north are two small islands that have secluded little sandy beaches on their western shores. You will usually have the first of these exotic little beaches (located at GPS coordinates N 24°37.761, W 81°34.517) all to yourself, for a sublime sunset vista at trip's end.

On my most recent visit, there was an old Jet Ski on the left as you enter the bay that narrows into the creek. Although it had been there since the hurricane of 1998, it may not be a good landmark in the future. The PVC markers will always be there, though, and they will snake you through to the right of the island, into the back bay, and lead you to one of several courses that connect to the ocean. This entrance is a little confusing, but if you follow the tidewaters almost all the tributaries will bring you to the sea eventually. The farther west you go in this maze of creeks, the more convoluted the creeks become.

A word of caution: The GPS signal weakens as you enter the canopied creeks, so take note of any unusual tree growths where the creeks intersect so that you can find your way around in the labyrinth. The bridge that spans the creek near the outfall to the ocean (GPS coordinates N 24°36.207, W 81°34.259) is frequented by fishermen and is part of the old highway that used to bring traffic into Key West. After taking in the ocean view and daydreaming of Cuba on the horizon—just 90 miles away—you can backtrack through the creeks and head for the pocket-sized sandy beach islet, which is only about a mile away.

8. *Five-Mile Creek*

Charts:
> Standard Mapping Services Aerial Photo Map #F103
> TOPSPOT Middle Keys Area #N208
> NOAA Chart #11445

Launch: Launch #15, which is at Mile Marker 16 on the bay side. There is a significantly larger section of cable in the lower power lines that will help you locate the launch site from quite a distance on the water.

Habitats: Although it is really only about 1 nautical mile long, if you count all the tributaries, parallel routes, and dead ends, the total extent of these creeks may amount to about 5 miles.

Trip Length: The trip can be about 3 to 5 miles in length, depending on how much of the feeder creeks you decide to explore.

Tides and Currents: The water depth is always sufficient, but the currents can get strong at new and full-moon tides.

Paddling Conditions: This route consists of wind-protected, mangrove-lined creeks that are sometimes used by powerboaters traveling from the backcountry. The numerous little feeder creeks are heavily overgrown by mangrove branches. Going with the current is advisable, because it's difficult to use the paddle in some of the smaller creeks.

Featured Creatures: Spiders spin their webs daily. Some of the smaller feeder creeks will be completely covered with webs from the crab spider, the silver argiope, and the golden orb weaver. The golden orb weaver spins the biggest web, and its strands have a higher tensile strength than steel of the same diameter. Because of its rustproof nature, it was used as gun sight crosshair material during World War II.

Departing from the Center of the Universe of Kayaking (MM 16), you will head due north approximately 0.6 nautical mile. You will find the main entrance to the southern end of Five Mile Creek at N 24°38.805, W 81°35.115. If you don't have a GPS, just follow the currents and read the bottom as you approach the island.

There's also a white PVC marker at the entrance. On your transit across, there is a good chance that you will see the colorful parachutes of the many skydivers who depart from the Sugarloaf airport a short 0.25 mile away from the creek entrance. On the east shore you will also notice the trapezoidal, shingle-covered structure known as the Bat Tower. This was built in the early 1900s to house mosquito-eating bats. However, the locals say the mosquitoes ate the bats.

Paddling up the creek, you will be surrounded by deep, current-undercut mangrove ledges that are covered with sponges and other invertebrates. Just a short distance up the main creek there is a feeder creek that is a dead end, and the next feeder creek on the left traverses the island and exits at the island's southernmost point.

At the beginning of this second creek there is a jog to the left, which is another dead end. If you bear to the right and continue about 0.25 mile, you will wind up close to the outflow, where there is a sunken boat at 24°38.654 N, 81°35.179 W. This boat has numerous large mangrove snappers living in and around it. The boat may not be visible during outgoing tides.

Back in the main creek, continuing toward the north, you will run across two more main arteries that jog off to the left. When I was there in 2003, there were some handmade signs at each of these trail junctures. The first (at 24°38.850 N, 81°35.332 W) is called Clyde's Corner. It seems to be a memorial for Clyde, whose favorite spot on the earth must have been here. Carolyn's Way is the next marked jog on the left (N 24°38.981, W 81°35.814). It also runs south for about 0.5 mile until it outflows on the southern edge of Five Mile Creek Island. I lost my Birkenstock in there, so if you see it, it's a size 9, left!

Once you reach the northern exit of Five Mile Creek, you can head in a northwesterly direction to the inner narrows of Snipe Keys. It's 0.5 nautical mile to Snipe Key, and on the lee shorelines here are shallow turtle grass beds where it's common to see bonefish and smallish permit.

9.   *Perky Creek*

Charts:
> Standard Mapping Services Aerial Photo Map #F103
> TOPSPOT Middle Keys Area #N208
> NOAA Chart #11445

Launch: Launch #16, Sugarloaf Marina.

Habitats: This route features mangrove-lined creeks and shallow mud and grass flats. There are also rich sponge flats that are festooned with various types of algae.

Trip Length: This loop trip is about 3 nautical miles in length.

Tides and Currents: Low tides can make some of the back bays shallow but not impassable. Currents are strong in the tidal creeks, but can be avoided by paddling in the smaller feeder creeks.

Paddling Conditions: The 0.5-mile crossing to get to the creeks can be difficult on the return trip if there is a strong east wind. The main marked creek that runs through Sugarloaf Key is heavily

> trafficked by large motorboats. Most of the time, they will slow down to minimal wake speeds, but sometimes they will not. It is best to adhere to the rules of the road and stay on the right side of the channel.
>
> **Featured Creatures:** Lettuce-leaf slugs graze upon animal and plant material that grows on the long turtle grass blades near the shallow areas of the creek. These 2-inch-long members of the mollusk family have a remnant shell on the interior of the dorsal side. They have the remarkable ability to consume jellyfish and then extrude the jellyfish's undischarged stingers out of their outer perimeter, thus arming themselves.

Departing from Sugarloaf Creek Marina, head north-northwest for about 0.6 nautical mile to the entrance of the southernmost creek. During this transit, you will see the Bat Tower on your left, when you are about halfway through the trip. It's easy to overlook this southernmost entrance, because it's not well marked, and the white PVC markers that mark the main channel through the island may confuse you. If you hug the shore, you will have no trouble finding the 10-foot-wide entrance.

As soon as you pop into this deep creek, you will notice that the roots are completely covered, especially with fire sponges. The creek meanders for approximately 0.25 mile, and its terminus is quite narrow and constricted. This narrow, constricted portion may be difficult to paddle during a full-moon current.

As you paddle into the first bay, be on the lookout for shark fins and great wading birds on both shorelines. From this bay you will be able to see approaching motorboats that enter the main portion of the creek, and you will also be able to view the backcountry islands of Johnston and Marvin Keys. Continuing north along the shoreline of Sugarloaf Key, 0.25 mile past the main boating channel, there will be a small, shallow gap in the island that will let you access Upper Sugarloaf Sound. From here you can head due south back toward the marina, which will be approximately 1 nautical mile away.

10. *Dreguez Key*

Charts:
> Standard Mapping Services Aerial Photo Map #F103
> TOPSPOT Middle Keys Area #N208
> NOAA Chart #11445

Launch: Launch #18, Upper Sugarloaf Sound (northeast).

Habitats: Soft mud bottoms and grass patches alternate with hard bottom in the channels. Several creeks nearby that are largely unexplored and hold lots of fish.

Trip Length: The trip is 4 nautical miles in a straight line to and from North Dreguez Key.

Tides and Currents: There is one shallow spot in the cut between Sugarloaf and Dreguez, which may present problems at lower tides. Gentle currents sweep through this same channel.

Paddling Conditions: The protected waters of this sound make it an easy trip. The creeks are overgrown and have several dead ends that are not easy to back out of.

Featured Creatures: Large schools of mullet inhabit the milky white patches of water that are found commonly throughout this sound. For 20 years I've been driving by and witnessing these mullet muds. There is some controversy as to whether or not these muds are produced by the mullet or by certain unique chemical conditions that are found in this specific area. Bioturbation is the term used to describe this "blender" effect in the water.

Departing from Launch #18, head due north and work the lee shoreline of Sugarloaf Key. In the evenings, it's common to see "sun-worshiping" great white herons along the shoreline. The birds face the sun and turn their wings almost inside out, it appears, and receive direct sunlight on the undersides of their wings. The theory is that the herons are trying to get rid of parasites that live in the shadows under their wings, by subjecting them to intense ultraviolet rays. The little unnamed island east of Dreguez Key is your first stopping point. It is approximately 1.2 nautical miles from the launch site. This little island has numerous pigeons and doves that nest on it during the summertime.

The back (west) side of the island has an army of small red mangrove

Anemone on blade of turtle grass

seedlings sweeping off to the north. They are rooted in soft, sedimentary mud that has an incredible consistency, very much like clay. I think these muds were the ones that Henry Flagler preferred when he was dredging for sediments on which to build his railroad, because of their adhesion and drying characteristics.

Heading northeast between Dreguez Key and the Sugarloaf Key, you will encounter a winding cut that has little deep pockets mixed among turtle grass beds. As you pass the small island to your right, in the narrow section of this pass, directly to the west will be access to the small creeks that are hidden within Dreguez Key. Because of all of the bioturbation in this specific area, the visibility in the creeks and some of the nearshore waters is reduced to zero. However, there are still numerous fishes in this turbid creek that splash and crash amongst the roots.

From this point, as you paddle into the bay north of Dreguez Key, you can head north along Sugarloaf Key and explore the mangrove-studded north point of the island. This island has incredible shallows and a scattering of mangrove islets where there are many shorebirds and barracuda. It is about a 3-mile round trip to the northernmost point of the island and back to the Dreguez Key Pass.

Another option from Dreguez Key Pass is to head west and circumnavigate Dreguez Key. This circumnavigation will add another 3 miles to the overall trip length and will also utilize the small cut that is found in the middle portion of Dreguez Key.

11. *Tarpon Creek*

Charts:
> Standard Mapping Services Aerial Photo Map #F103
> TOPSPOT Middle Keys Area #N208
> NOAA Chart #11445

Launch: Launch #20 is a particularly rough road that requires a vehicle with good ground clearance, as there are some fairly deep potholes in this old, abandoned stretch of U.S. 1.

Habitats: Oceanside flats with rich sea grass sponges and small coral heads are connected by a mangrove creek to shallow interior bays. These bays are composed of turtlegrass and soft muds, which are a favorite feeding ground for the reddish egret.

Trip Length: The circular loop trail is slightly more than 5 nautical miles.

Tides and Currents: The currents that run through Tarpon Creek and the canal on Sugarloaf Key can be strong and tiresome. It is best to time your route so that you are paddling with the current on the incoming or the outgoing tides at these two particular creeks. The suggested route would have you paddling counterclockwise, with the peak of the high tide occurring when you are paddling the interior of Sugarloaf Key Sound.

Paddling Conditions: The paddling here is in protected and wind-sheltered bays, with 0.5 mile of mangrove-lined creek and 2 miles of canal.

Featured Creatures: The clarity of Tarpon Creek varies with the wind speed and direction. Toward the end of the creek you will find shallow, sandy banks that are festooned with sea stars. They move slowly on their tube feet over the sandy bottom, distending their stomachs and digesting material from the sand and grass and occasionally running across a clam. The undercut edges of the mangroves on the south end of the creek have a nice scouring current that keeps the ledges clean. These ledges are home to a resident green moray eel named Charlie.

If you're reading this, you've just traveled down the roughest road in the Florida Keys. And now you'll be viewing a burned-out bridge that overlooks Tarpon Creek to the left and in front of you, and Sugarloaf Sound will be to your right. At this point you will be able to judge the current and tidal situation. Ideally, the tide will be coming in and sweeping to the right, and you will be able to put your boat in on the right-hand side of the burned-out bridge.

Entering Tarpon Creek and heading to the right, after a short distance you will pop out onto Sugarloaf Sound, at which point you will be able to follow the marked channel northward into the sound. The right-hand shore is easy to explore while still keeping the channel markers in sight, and as you pass through the narrow gap where the red marker #8 is located, you will see, just to the left of the channel markers, a small mangrove island that is your destination.

Taking a quick break at this small, unnamed island, you'll probably notice the small flock of the yellow-crowned night herons that winter here. Heading just south of due west, you'll come to the shoreline of Sugarloaf Key, and you will follow that as it curves around to the left and enters the canal. This canal is 1.5 nautical miles in length and has just a handful of homes along its shoreline.

At about the 1-mile mark down this canal is an abandoned bridge that the locals use as a swimming hole. You can pull your boats out here and have a walk around some of the old dirt and paved roadways in the area. As you finish paddling down the canal, you will be greeted by the Atlantic Ocean. Come out of the canal, go left, and proceed up the shoreline for 1.7 nautical miles. As you approach the entrance to Tarpon Creek, you'll see some white PVC markers and you will scoot in to the left and follow the meandering creek northward.

Most of the life is in the scoured bottom near this southernmost portion of the creek. Moray eels, sea stars, and mangrove snappers all find refuge in these protected creek waters. As you paddle up the creek you will notice little dead-end creeks that branch off to the left and right. These are fun to explore, but they usually leave your boat full of twigs, leaves, and debris. The entire length of Tarpon Creek is only 0.5 nautical mile and will connect with the main boating channel just before you reached the burned-out bridge.

12. Cudjoe Key

Charts:
 Standard Mapping Services Aerial Photo Map #F103
 TOPSPOT Middle Keys Area #N208
 NOAA Chart #11445
Launch: Launch #22, at the end of Blimp Road.
Habitats: The shoreline that takes you by the blimps is rich with vase sponges and loggerhead sponges. The most constricted portion of the mangrove creek has an incredible diversity of small fish, including enough small jewfish to form a soccer team.
Trip Length: This 4-mile loop covers some really interesting backcountry areas.

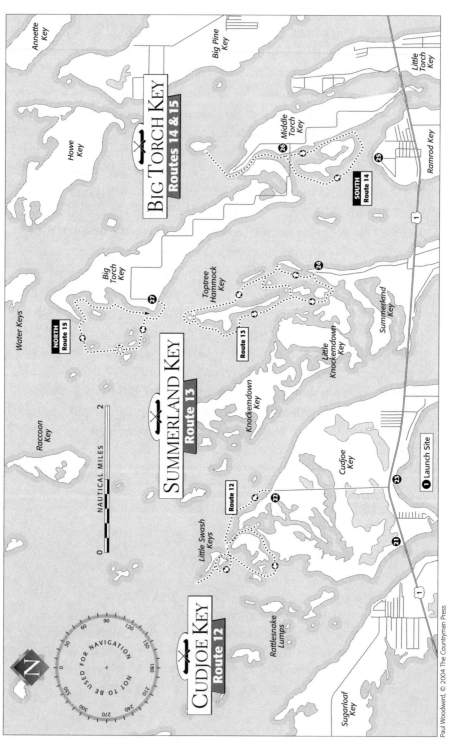

CUDJOE KEY
Route 12

SUMMERLAND KEY
Route 13

BIG TORCH KEY
Routes 14 & 15

NORTH
Route 15

SOUTH
Route 14

Route 13

Route 12

N

NOT TO BE USED FOR NAVIGATION

0   30   60   90   120   150   180   210   240   270   300   330

NAUTICAL MILES

0   2

Annette Key

Big Pine Key

Little Torch Key

Howe Key

Middle Torch Key

26

25

Ramrod Key

1

Water Keys

Big Torch Key

27

Toptree Hammock Key

24

Summerland Key

Raccoon Key

Little Knockemdown Key

Knockemdown Key

Cudjoe Key

23

1 Launch Site

Little Swash Keys

22

21

Rattlesnake Lumps

Sugarloaf Key

1

Paul Woodward, © 2004 The Countryman Press

Tides and Currents: There is plenty of water at all tidal phases, and the currents are minimal.

Paddling Conditions: Almost all of the route is protected from the east winds, and the only windward section is on the last 0.5 mile of the return leg.

Featured Creatures: The jewfish population has made a comeback, and these members of the grouper family are quite noticeable in many of the shallow areas of the backcountry. It was surprising to see so many jewfish laid up in the current of the outgoing tide, waiting for prey to float downstream into their voluminous mouths. The multitude of black spots on the front half of the fish's body and the rounded and spotted tailfin enable easy identification.

Depart from the Cudjoe Blimp Base boat ramp and head northwest along the shoreline. Fat Albert, which is an aerial surveillance balloon, will be your constant companion. Just 0.5 nautical mile down the shoreline, and you will see the last of the NO TRESPASSING signs. Bear left around the mangrove island and hug the shoreline on your right to enter the inner lakes of Cudjoe.

As you explore these inner lakes, bear to the right and follow that shoreline until it narrows and constricts into a rocky, sponge-covered channel. This channel is where all the wildlife is concentrated. Mangrove snappers, sharks, jewfish, and scads of baitfish hang out under the cover of the prolific mangrove roots.

Peering down among the rocks at the bottom of the channel, you will see anemones and the whiplike antennae of juvenile lobsters. Passing through the creek, heading west and bearing right, you will soon encounter a small forest of miniature mangrove islets. Weave your way through these in a northerly direction, heading toward the Little Swash Keys. The Little Swash Keys have lots of soft sediments surrounding the islands. These are the favorite habitat of the southern stingray. You'll spot the rays feeding on the bottom or possibly covered by the bottom sediments so that only their eyes and spiracles can be seen above the sediment. They feed on the numerous mud-dwelling mollusks that are common in this area.

From the eastern side of Little Swash Keys, it is a short, 0.75-nautical-mile paddle over to the Budd Keys. These isolated mangrove islands are a great roosting habitat for large numbers of cormorants. On the west shore of the southernmost Budd Key are a cabin and dock from the 1960s, at GPS coordinates N 24°42.668, W 81°30.075. There is a rocky beach shoreline on the south of this island with old dock posts jutting out of the water.

You can beach your kayak on this rocky shoreline and take a short walk among the sea purslane and ox-eye daisy plants. A short walk brings you to the "estate of disrepair." This dream home consists of three completely trashed trailers at the edge of an old borrow pit. In the borrow pit is a floating dock with several decrepit old lawn chairs. Australian pine, palm trees, and one Norfolk Island pine mark this section of the island.

Another optional leg of exploration from the Cudjoe Blimp Area is Knockemdown Bay, at GPS coordinates N 24°41.952, W 81°29.210. This is about 1 nautical mile from the blimp base launch. The western sides of these islands usually have deeper cuts and channels parallel to the shore, where nurse sharks and barracuda patrol. The inner reaches of the Knockemdown Bay area have many isolated little mangrove islands surrounded by sand banks. If you explore this area at the peak high tide, it's possible to run into a school of bonefish that are resting in the innermost shallows. Permit will also lay up and sunbathe on these sandy flats at the peak of the high tide. They do this by floating at the surface with their backs barely exposed. Their tailfins sweep slowly above the surface as if waving to passing kayaks.

Traveling from Knockemdown back to the blimp base is approximately a due-west course. Just 0.5 nautical mile into this route you will encounter a small island with a prolific diversity of wading birds. In the winter, roseate spoonbills, cormorants, herons, and egrets all share this island as a nighttime roost. The Cudjoe Ramp is about 0.3 nautical mile west of this little island.

13. Summerland Key

Charts:
> Standard Mapping Services Aerial Photo Map #F103
> TOPSPOT Middle Keys Area #N208
> NOAA Chart #11445

Launch: Launch #24.

Habitats: This route features a shallow, rocky bottom with clusters of mangrove islands scattered throughout. Extensive grass flats are at the north end of Wahoo Key.

Trip Length: This is a circular route of approximately 5 nautical miles.

Tides and Currents: At low tide, some portions of this trip are not floatable, especially near the launch site and at the cluster of islands in the middle. The currents are negligible.

Paddling Conditions: These are protected, shallow bay waters with lots of island-hopping along the route.

Featured Creatures: At the north end of Wahoo Key, in the grass flats, there are numerous pink-tipped anemones. These soft-bodied creatures wave their tentacles in the currents, searching for small plankton to capture and consume. If it's glass-calm and you can look closely at these anemones, you may see a small shrimp with long white antennae living among the tentacles. This is a symbiotic creature that keeps the tentacles clean from debris and occasionally steals a food particle or two. The small island in the middle of the route has a world-class anemone in the center of its creek. It is the biggest anemone that I've ever seen in the wild.

Departing from the launch and heading in a northerly direction, you can hug the shoreline of Wahoo Key until you reach the northern end about 0.5 nautical mile away. There is a little swimming hole next to a mangrove clump. This is deep and often has small jewfish living in the ledges. Heading in a northwesterly direction for 0.3 nautical mile, you will come across a small mangrove island that is undercut on the backside and has tons of baitfish living in its shaded edges.

From here, if the conditions are good, you can head north for approximately 1.2 nautical miles to the little island on the northern tip of Top Tree Hammock Key. This little island (GPS coordinates N 24°42.835, W 81°27.394) has a deep, sandy bottom on the north shore that is frequented by barracuda and smaller yellow-spotted stingrays. There are numerous stands of sargassum weed that are buoyed to the surface by small floats that make up its leaf structure. Mask and snorkel is a great way to explore this forest under the sea.

Heading south and west from this little island, you will see Knockemdown Key due west, and you can follow the lee shore of Top Tree Hammock

Alligators can be found in the freshwater areas of the Keys.

Key for some 1.5 miles to the southernmost point. From here you'll see a cluster of small islands to the south, and one small island off to your left at about 15 degrees. This island has the small cut in it with the gigantic anemone. After exploring the small island, head south for about 0.5 mile on the lee shore of the cluster of islands. Just off the southwestern tip of this centralized cluster of islands is a small bomb crater that makes a great little swimming hole. The swimming hole has soft mud and grass around the perimeter and an 8-foot-deep section in the center. From the swimming hole, head south and east until you see a pass on your left, where you will paddle a short 0.25 mile to the launch site.

14. Big Torch Key (South)

Charts:
> Standard Mapping Services Aerial Photo Map #F103
> TOPSPOT Middle Keys Area #N208
> NOAA Chart #11445

Launch: Launch #26.

Habitats: This route takes you along shallow inland seas with soft sand sediments. There are a large number of smaller mangrove islands that wading birds utilize for roosting and nesting.

Trip Length: This loop trail around Middle Torch Key is approximately 3 nautical miles.

Tides and Currents: This trip is difficult near the full- and new-moon tides because of the exposed shallows near the launch site. Currents are nonexistent except near the culverts that are under the causeway.

Paddling Conditions: This is a perfectly protected route in high winds and is a relatively easy paddle.

Featured Creatures: The stone crab is a common inhabitant of these rocky, shallow flats. This crab can grow to large size, and its burrows can be located on the bottom by looking for a swath of small stones that appear to have been brushed away with a tiny bulldozer. The crabs' claws are broken off their bodies and sold in restaurants throughout South Florida. The crab is put back in the water, where it will shed and grow legal-sized claws in about two years' time.

The Middle Torch Key causeway affords a wonderful view to the south, where you can see the Niles Channel Bridge about 2 miles away. The locals frequently use the culverts that go under this causeway for swimming. At the southern edge of the culverts there is usually a deep, Jacuzzi-like swimming hole. When the tide runs out hard, you can jump in the water at the north end of the culvert and be swooshed through at the Jacuzzi end.

You can depart from the westernmost culvert and head toward the Niles Channel Bridge. A short paddle will bring you right to the mangrove shoreline of Middle Torch Key. This island is only about 1 mile in length. Working slowly along its western shore, you're likely to see bonefish, sharks, stingrays, and other inhabitants on this sponge flat. Following the shoreline in the southerly direction as you reach the southernmost point, you'll be looking at Ramrod Key to the south.

This entire bay is fun to explore, as it is made up of large patches of turtle grass with shallow, meandering channels. If you were to continue south toward Ramrod Key, you would come across the Ramrod Key swimming hole, launch #25. As you follow the southern shoreline of Middle Torch Key, the mangrove walls will close in, and you'll be traveling northward in a shallow tidal creek. It gets quite narrow, and at the lower stages of the tides it is a challenge to pass through here, but the seclusion of this little creek provides numerous wading birds with wintertime roosts.

The creek itself is only 0.5 nautical mile long, and soon you will sight the causeway with the culverts. If the tides are high and you want to continue exploring, you can portage your boats to the north side of the causeway. This narrow bay is approximately 1 mile in length and opens up to the north with a wide-angle view of the backcountry. From the last point of land on your right on Middle Torch Key, looking to the northeast you will see a small, unnamed mangrove island. This little island is undercut on its western shore, and is one of the few places in the backcountry where you might see a mangrove terrapin, a unique species of turtle found in the Keys.

15. *Big Torch Key (North)*

Charts:
  Standard Mapping Services Aerial Photo Map #F103
  TOPSPOT Middle Keys Area #N208
  NOAA Chart #11445
Launch: Launch #27 is at the end of the road.
Habitats: This route features beautiful views of the true backcountry islands that include miles of shimmering, brilliant sponge flats, rich turtle grass flats, and exposed, algae-strewn rocky shallows. Great bird islands dot this trip, and the creek has a secret sunken boat in it.
Trip Length: The circular loop trail will cover 3.5 nautical miles of backcountry.
Tides and Currents: No problems with this route at any tide, although you may have to skirt a few shallows if it is a full-moon tidal phase.
Paddling Conditions: This is protected island-hopping at the gateway to the backcountry areas. The lee shore of Big Torch Key has a few permit that travel the inner reaches.
Featured Creatures: Clapper rails are abundant on these isolated mangrove islands. They will usually give the "clappering" call all

day long. Near the end of the day and especially at sunset, they seem to communicate as a flock, calling to other flocks on neighboring islands with a chorus of "clappering."

When leaving this launch, use caution, as it's not an easy entrance to find upon return. Oftentimes there will be a piece of surveyor's tape or other material on the outer mangrove trees to alert you to the entrance. As you come out of the narrow entrance, head right up the shoreline of Big Torch Key to the very westernmost portion of the island. There are several small clusters of mangrove islands there that are frequented by barracuda and other fish as the tides sweep by. This is a good spot to see needlefish and silversides bursting from the surface.

Heading toward the west-northwest, you will see a cluster of small islands. All of these have great rocky substrates that hold many invertebrates and other marine creatures. The largest island has a rich sponge flat on the south that is full of juvenile lobster living in large numbers around the bases of the sponges. As you round this island, there will be a small mangrove island in the middle of the grass flat. This island has a small creek in the middle, in which a 15-foot boat is sunk. It is crowded with mangrove snappers, smaller groupers, and parrotfish. Take your time to sit there a while and enjoy the antics of the fish as they come up to investigate, because all fish are curious. From here you can head north and east about a mile to a small mangrove isle that sits amongst the sponge flats. This island (GPS coordinates N 24°43.785, W 81°27.841) has numerous birds that roost around the perimeter, and I've seen hundreds of cormorants and frigate birds. The flats surrounding these islands are also home to many permit and bonefish, but this flat is impassable during full-moon low tides. Heading northeast to the north end of the Big Torch Key, you can work close to the island in the lee, where there are scattered mangrove pockets full of baitfish, shrimp, and crabs. This is a good spot to coast slowly down the shoreline making little noise and watching the surface for the fins, wakes, and tails of hunting predatory fish. Cruising back along this shoreline, you will notice one house on your left with a big white roof. Pass this on your left and follow the shoreline until it turns to the left, and a short stretch down this shoreline will be your launch point.

16. *Big Pine Key*

Charts:
>   Standard Mapping Services Aerial Photo Map #F103
>   TOPSPOT Middle Keys Area #N208
>   NOAA Chart #11445

Launch: Launch #29 at the end of Key Deer Boulevard.

Habitats: Along this route you will see grass flats interspersed with sponge areas and a short series of tidal creeks that cut through Howe Key.

Trip Length: The main loop trail is nearly 5.5 nautical miles in length.

Tides and Currents: The low tides make the inner creeks a little shallow, but rarely are they impassable.

Paddling Conditions: This can be a rather long trip, and if the east winds are strong they can wear you down on the return trip.

Featured Creatures: This is one of the few places where I have seen the giant land crab female actually out in the sea grass beds as she is about to shed her eggs. This is a spring occurrence, and in some areas thousands of these crabs cross roads and highways to travel back to the sea to spawn.

Departing from a small dead-end canal and heading north, you will progress up the shoreline of Big Pine Key. The shoreline has several small schools of baby tarpon in the 20-pound range. After 0.5 nautical mile going up the shoreline, there will be a deep gutter right next to the shoreline of Big Pine Key. This little gutter acts as a highway for many fish, including sharks, barracuda, and stingrays. Rounding the northeast point of Big Pine Key, you will see Howe Key to your left, Cutoe Key straight ahead, and Annette Key on your right. All three of these islands have wonderful shorelines to explore, but we will continue to the west to explore Howe Key.

About halfway down the shoreline of Howe Key, you'll see a large hunk of sun-bleached driftwood. This marks the entrance to Howe Key Creek. This short creek opens up into a small pond, which then narrows down again to a small opening that allows you to enter another small, sea cucumber-laden pond. At the northernmost reach of this little pond is the deeper creek that feeds these ponds. This creek is only wide enough for

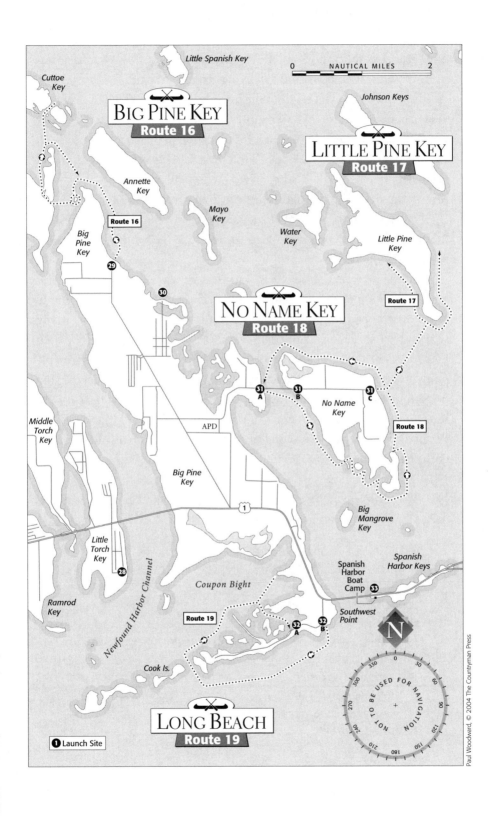

Little Spanish Key

Cuttoe
Key

NAUTICAL MILES

BIG PINE KEY
Route 16

Johnson Keys

LITTLE PINE KEY
Route 17

Annette
Key

Mayo
Key

Water
Key

Little Pine
Key

Big
Pine
Key

Route 16

Route 17

29

30

NO NAME KEY
Route 18

31
A

31
B

31
C

No Name
Key

Route 18

Middle
Torch
Key

APD

Big Pine
Key

Big
Mangrove
Key

1

Little
Torch
Key

28

Spanish
Harbor
Boat
Camp

Spanish
Harbor Keys

33

Ramrod
Key

Coupon Bight

Newfound Harbor Channel

Southwest
Point

Route 19

32
A

32
B

N

NOT TO BE USED FOR NAVIGATION

Cook Is.

LONG BEACH
Route 19

1 Launch Site

Paul Woodward, © 2004 The Countryman Press

one kayak, but the bottom and the mangrove roots of this creek have colorful sponges, anemones, and fish living amongst them.

This creek pops you out into the inner bay of Howe Key. This bay provides a panoramic vista of backcountry islands. The small clusters of mangrove islets commonly have shorebirds roosting in them during nearly all tides. Willets, plovers, and terns all use these islands as a resting spot and can be approached rather close. Staying within 30 or 40 feet of the shoreline on the right, you'll progress due north toward Cutoe Key.

As you reach the point of Howe Key, you can choose to travel another 0.5 nautical mile to Cutoe Key Creeks or round to the south and head back toward Big Pine Key.

Another option, a good one in a strong east wind, is to head northeast across the channel about 1 nautical mile. This will bring you to Annette Key, and you can hug the lee shoreline for miles. This area has many sharks, barracuda, and some snook that stalk the shoreline. The area known as The Grasses can support a wide variety of creatures from dolphins and turtles to lobsters and anemones. This is due to the fact that the bottom in these protected waters is primarily grass beds, but the beds are interspersed with deep channels that provide habitat for large creatures. When done exploring this shoreline, you can catch a downwind run back to the launch site.

17. Little Pine Key

Charts:
 Standard Mapping Services Aerial Photo Map #F103
 TOPSPOT Middle Keys Area #N208
 NOAA chart #11448
Launch: No Name Key Launch #31C.
Habitats: This route features an open water passage on 12-foot-deep waters, culminating with a pristine, mangrove-fringed, pine-studded island.
Trip Length: The distance across open water is 1.8 miles one way. Total trip can be about 7 miles, depending on how much of the shoreline you explore.
Tides and Currents: Tidal flow is a concern, but can be used to your

benefit if the initial trip over open water coincides with an incoming tide. The wind will be fatiguing if blowing more than 12 knots from the east on the way out, but a tailwind will assist you on the way back.

Paddling Conditions: It is best to be experienced and in good shape for this moderately strenuous journey.

Featured Creature: Alligators.

Departing from that old ferry landing always gives me a sense of just how much ocean there is between these islands and the rest of the world. This trip is a bit of a paddle, but worth the journey because Little Pine Key has some great wildlife living on it. During the summer, when there is more rainfall, the young male gators will move around quite a bit, and we often see them in the saltwater habitats. This occurs off the southernmost tip of the island about 1,500 feet up the western shoreline, where there is a little nook in the shoreline. The alligators are quite shy and will usually slink away slowly into the depths until you pass.

At almost any time of year you can see or hear the bald eagle as it calls to the ospreys. The summer thermals can carry both these species as they rise under the towering cumulus clouds.

There were five homesteads on Little Pine in the early 1900s, and all of the pioneers who built them were engaged in farming, sponging, and fishing. This farming was so extensive that nearly half the island was cleared for agriculture. Storms, mosquitoes, and the difficulties of making do with few resources eventually whittled the population down to only one family. This family consisted of Captain Tom Key, his wife Emma, and nine children, who still hung on after losing everything but their lives during the hurricane of 1919. Finally they tired of this unique life and moved back to Key West in 1923. So this island has had some 80 years to cast off the mark of man and really revert back to its natural state.

All the artifacts on these islands are national treasures, and until recently public visitation was prohibited. Today some of these backcountry islands are open for visitation; to confirm which ones, contact the Refuge headquarters on Big Pine Key at 305-872-0774.

Twenty years ago there were still feral hogs living on the island, but they have all been relocated at this time. Only the endemic species are there now, including the Key bunny, Key deer, alligator, and the bald eagle. It is believed that at one time bobcats may have existed here, but today the only evidence of bobcats you might find is probably buried underground or in the bottom of the sources of fresh water. It has been claimed that there are crocodile nesting areas on the island, and some have tried to find these nests, without success.

The crossing is the most difficult part of this journey, and it would be wise to have a rudder and some waterline on your boat. Remember, it is not the destination but the journey that counts.

18. No Name Key

Charts:
Standard Mapping Services Aerial Photo Map #F103
TOPSPOT Middle Keys Area #N208
NOAA chart #11448
Launch: No Name Key Launch #31A, B, or C.
Habitats: On this route you will see a beautiful, pine-studded, mangrove-fringed backcountry island.
Trip length: The circumnavigation covers 8 nautical miles.
Tides and Currents: A low tide can make the southern tip of the key impassable.
Paddling Conditions: You can always stay within 100 feet of the islands shoreline.
Featured Creature: Key deer.

By all rights this 1 x 3 mile island should have been named Middle Pine Key, because she sits right between Big Pine Key and Little Pine Key and is covered with pine trees. Somehow this little jewel was christened No Name Key. There is some great history here that involves the ferry docks, a hermit Russian farmer, and a secret stash of gold. During various early years in the Keys, there was only one way to get to the Lower Keys and Key West, and that was by ferry from Marathon or Grassy Key. Model A Fords were transported across the ocean and dropped off on No Name Key, where they continued the final 8-hour driving leg to Key West (that is at

Red mangrove–lined creeks fascinate the imagination.

about 3.2 miles per hour).

Nicholas Matcovich was the hermit farmer. He excelled at growing fruit trees and is rumored to have hidden a cache of gold he acquired by assisting the Cuban revolutionaries in the 1880s and 1890s.

Departing from The Old Wooden Bridge Fishing Camp, head east across the channel, making sure to give a wide berth to any boat traffic and people fishing from the bridge. Keep an eye out for turtles and dolphins as you cross the deeper channel. Look for a white PVC marker that denotes the small channel where you can cut through to No Name's western shore. This shoreline can afford an excellent lee throughout every season but summer.

About 1.5 miles down this shoreline you will see an abandoned dock that juts out into the water. This is in fairly rough shape, but allows access to the interior for some excellent birding. In the next mile you will encounter a small opening to a bay where, upon entering, you will notice a distinct browse line on the red mangroves from the local deer. Continuing forward you will reach the southwest tip of No Name Key and will have a clear view of the Bahia Honda Bridge. The island that is 100 yards due west of this point has several little creeks in it that are full of mangrove snappers, grunts, and even several parrotfish. As you head north into the inner bay, the nearshore edges hold a lot of baby sharks, barracuda, and the occasional permit. If the tide is high you can really get into the inner reaches, where old stone docks jut out into the shallows and piles of ancient conch shells litter the bottom.

Heading south out of the bay, you will encounter another small island at the eastern end of the mouth. The western edge of this island has an undercut edge that holds snook, snappers, and other finfish. A short distance to the east, rounding the next point will bring you into Bird Bay, where the wintertime birding is raucously noisy at low tides. As you continue the circumnavigation, you will now be at the southeasternmost point of the island and probably heading into the east wind.

Almost all of the 2.5 miles of the eastern shore shows some signs of being storm tossed from previous hurricane winds. There will also be an awful lot of floating debris from Bahia Honda Channel on this shore, and this makes for good sea bean hunting. About 2 miles up this shore you will encounter a stake in the shallows that marks the old ferry landing spit. It was dredged away in the early 1980s and is now a shallow-water hazard. Rays can be seen feeding on this flat, and there are some great artifacts in the channel next to it, which used to serve as a ferry canal.

Just 0.5 mile up from here you will round the northeast corner of No Name Key; this is a great spot for sharks, baby tarpon, and permit. The waters along the next 2 miles of this shore are clean and clear, although the shore itself has quite a layer of decomposing sea grass. This entire shoreline has good deer viewing potential. A little over 1 mile down this section you will encounter the canal access for the residents of No Name Key. These two parallel canals will sometimes hold tarpon and alligators.

Before you round the next point, take in the wonderful vista of sea and sky that marks the gateway to the Great White Heron National Wildlife Refuge backcountry areas. As you round the next point, you will see the Bogie Channel bridge and your circumnavigation will be complete.

19. Long Beach

Charts:
Standard Mapping Services Aerial Photo Map #F103
TOPSPOT Middle Keys Area #N208
NOAA chart #11448

Launch: Use launch #32A for oceanside explorations and launch #32B for Coupon Bight Aquatic Preserve trips.

Habitats: Oceanside rocky sponge flats are interspersed with small clusters of coral heads. The second half of the trip inside Coupon Bight Aquatic Preserve is mostly over shallow grass banks and through a maze of mangrove islands.

Trip Length: This 3.5-nautical-mile loop trip can easily be divided into two separate excursions.

Tides and Currents: Currents are negligible, but the lower tides might make the grass bank crossing a challenge.

Paddling Conditions: This trip can be customized to take advantage of any excessive winds by hiding on the lee shore of Long Beach. Coupon Bight is protected from nearly all winds, but the oceanside portion of the paddle can be rough if the southeast winds are strong.

GPS Coordinates for Patch Reef Snorkeling Adventures:
Third set of coral heads: N 24°37.145, W 81°22.826.
Last house heads: N 24°37.581, W 81°21.267.
Cooks Cut Patch: N 24°37.581, W 81°21.267.

Featured Creatures: This is the area where you begin to see more of the colorful tropical reef species of fish. In the soft coral forests you will encounter entire shoals of blue-striped grunts and porkfish. Big, burly porcupine fish hide in the shelter of hollowed-out coral mounds, and angel fish will escort you to their coral homes. Moon jellies and migrating mackerel appear out of the clear green waters to pass by you and continue onward. This is only a small sampler of what the coral reef offshore holds.

The first portion of the trip is all about snorkeling and exploring these shallow coral seas. A sit-on-top kayak is the preferred type of craft, because it is much easier to get in and out of while wearing snorkeling gear. A dive flag, anchor and line, and waterproof dry bag are essentials for your waterborne excursion.

Traveling south and west, you will be entranced with the variety and color of the bottom structures. The soft coral gardens and isolated coral heads are usually growing in the rocky bottom shallows. As you progress out deeper to the 9- to 12-foot-deep waters, you will encounter the larger colonies of boulder corals. You can use the GPS coordinates above or just float with your kayak tethered to you and wander westward.

Some of the most interesting coral colonies are the smaller ones that are often overlooked. At a depth of about 12 feet you will notice a discernible sandy edge that parallels the shoreline. This was the shoreline when sea levels were lower than they are today, and this edge has the most consistent coral structure about 10 to 50 feet north of it.

The Coupon Bight portion of this trip is predominantly shallow grass flats that are interspersed with sponge flats and rocky bottoms. The portion of the trip that is near Long Beach Launch #2 consists of meandering lakes and open creeks that flow into the shallows on the south shore of Coupon Bight Aquatic Preserve. The outflows at this edge are gathering points for travelling fish such as sharks, bonefish, and stingrays.

A nice sandy beach can be found on the inside of Coupon Bight on a spit of land that juts out from the eastern shore. This beach is only one nautical mile from launch #2. Half of the route is across open water, and the other half a winding trail through a stunted mangrove forest. Although this area is confusing, the maps are accurate and you can see the power poles lining the road where launch #2 is located. This area is famous for large numbers of tarpon in the spring, and there is a good possibility that several flats guides will be poling their skiffs in the shallows.

20. *Bahia Honda State Park*

Charts:
> Standard Mapping Services Aerial Photo Map #F103
> TOPSPOT Middle Keys Area #N208
> NOAA chart #11448

Launch: Launch #35 is in the state park.

Habitats: The deep channel on the western side of this island brings in big fish, turtles, and a major march of lobster. This is the major channel between the ocean and the backcountry waters. The

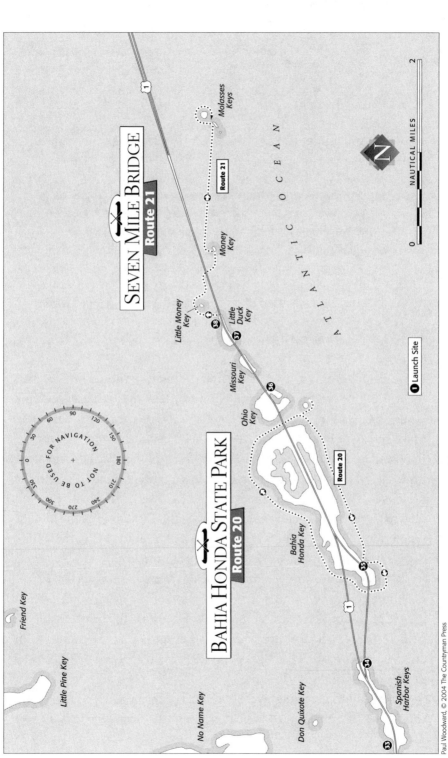

SEVEN MILE BRIDGE
Route 21

BAHIA HONDA STATE PARK
Route 20

Molasses Keys

Route 21

Money Key

Little Money Key

Little Duck Key

Missouri Key

Ohio Key

Bahia Honda Key

Route 20

Friend Key

Little Pine Key

No Name Key

Don Quixote Key

Spanish Harbor Keys

ATLANTIC OCEAN

USED FOR NAVIGATION
NOT TO BE
0 30 60 90 120 150 180 210 240 270 300 330

N

NAUTICAL MILES
0 2

Launch Site

Paul Woodward, © 2004 The Countryman Press

beaches that ring the island have been ranked among America's top ten natural beaches and the shorebirds that frequent them are numerous.

Trip Length: A circumnavigation of this island covers close to 4.5 nautical miles.

Tides and Currents: Bahia Honda Channel can have some swift currents, and the low tides provide exposed beach on the northern side of the island.

Paddling Conditions: If the winds are strong the surf can be rough, because there is no offshore coral reef to slow the waves. Keep to the lee shores if strong winds are blowing.

Featured Creatures: Sea turtles use this beach for nesting during the spring and summer. On calm days you might be fortunate enough to have a huge loggerhead turtle surface and breathe near your boat. The south wind of summer can drive in numerous jellyfish, and we once watched as one small green turtle chomped one after another in a single-file line.

If you launch from the park, your first destination should be the small rocky islet that is 0.5 nautical mile from the launch site. This islet has a sandy beach on the northwest corner, where it is easy to beach your vessel. Make sure your boat is secure, and then you can make your way around the island on foot or by snorkeling. The shores of these islands are sometimes closed to protect the birds, but you can always snorkel around the perimeter. The wave-washed rocky island has a series of small caves and blowholes that have been eroded by wave action, as well as by the urchins that festoon the limestone walls. It is like a natural Jacuzzi in these little caves as the surge washes all the inhabitants to and fro.

As you continue your circumnavigation, you will travel north 0.5 nautical mile and paddle under the old portion of the bridge that used to carry cars to Key West back in the 1960s. Nowadays the bridge is a footpath for people who would like the best view of Lower Keys waters from an aerial perspective. From this point it is 1 mile up the shoreline to the sandy beaches of the north shore.

Peering into the mangroves shoreward of the beaches, you will see a small creek that is shrouded in shadow. This little creek used to bring you into the inner lakes of eastern Bahia Honda, but since the hurricane the latter portion of this creek is not passable because of the branches and tree limbs that have fallen in and blocked the route. All the branches below water level here are colonized with sticky sea cucumbers that are about 2 inches in length. This interior creek usually has a resident school of baby tarpon that roll on the surface of its dark brown waters.

After spending some time on the beaches, you will head to the east along the rocky shore. This shore offers an excellent vista of the mangrove transition zone, as red, black, and white mangroves grow adjacent to one another. The fossilized coral shoreline is sharp but has some smaller tide pools and sandy areas where you can look for colorful invertebrates. Some of the mangrove trees are stunted by the extremely harsh growing conditions, and they seem to be perfect replicas of the larger trees that grow on nearby islands.

The last 0.5 mile before you round the east shore of the island will be shallow mud and grass, and you may have to stay off the shoreline a bit for this section. As you head south along the eastern shore, you will paddle under the old and new bridges of U.S. 1. The pilings are home to large fish like jacks, tarpon, and snapper.

As you head out to the limitless horizon of the Atlantic Ocean, there is a small island on your left to explore. This island is the gateway to the ocean side of Ohio Key, which is a great rocky shore that sees little public use and has lots of wildlife. Heading west along the beach, you will travel 2 nautical miles back to your launch site.

21. *Seven Mile Bridge*

Charts:
Standard Mapping Services Aerial Photo Map #F112
TOPSPOT Middle Keys #208
NOAA Chart #11453
Launch: Launch #37, Little Duck Key.
Habitats: This route takes you across open water with deep channels and oceanside flats. Turtle grass shoals and a few rocky shoals make the shallow-water habitats rich with creatures. There are also two beautiful offshore islands with sandy beaches that you

can island-hop to make this an enjoyable paddle.

Trip Length: Round trip is about 4.5 nautical miles.

Tides and Currents: This trip is possible at all tide levels, although some flats may be exposed during the lowest tides. The full and new moon currents that move through Money Key Channel and Molasses Key Channel should be considered, as well as strong winds, which can make the trip bumpy in these channels.

Paddling Conditions: Although the route goes across open water, if the winds and tides are moderate it is an easy island-hopping expedition with a downwind run on the way back to the launch.

Featured Creatures: The rocky shorelines of these islands are littered with the black horn snail. This 0.5-inch spire of black mollusk is so dense in population that it rings the perimeter of these keys with a black halo in the intertidal areas.

From an airplane, the Seven Mile Bridge appears to be a thin ribbon of concrete stretching into an unending ocean of blue. When you paddle under it you get the feeling of something solid, earthbound, and magnificent. In the past we used to time the slack tide in the channel and free-dive some of the more than 500 bridge pilings, looking for lobsters and other tasty creatures. These old concrete spans are full of living coral and other invertebrates living in the luxury of their underwater condominium. The old bridge was finished and put in service for the railroad in 1912, but in 1935 it was put out of commission by the Labor Day hurricane. Soon after that, it was converted to an automobile thoroughfare. Today it is probably the world's longest fishing pier.

Departing from the launch on the bay side of the bridge you will see Little Money Key on the left. This small island has an old guano-encrusted dock and a small cabin in the interior. Please respect this piece of private property, but be aware that there are some great snorkeling flats to the north of the dock.

The hard-bottom sponge flats are full of life here, and the shallow waters make the sunlight sparkle on the bottom. A short 0.5-mile paddle will bring you to a good area to cross under the bridge. If the winds are strong and you decide to use the lee of the bridge to travel, be aware that some boaters will not slow down as they approach the bridge pilings, and you

Looking east toward Marathon, the Seven Mile Bridge links the lower Keys to the rest of the world.

could be obscured from their line of sight by the pilings. These currents can produce eddies near the pilings and make for tricky navigation. From Little Money to Money Key is a short 0.6 nautical mile, and you can be digging your toes in the sun-baked sands in a matter of minutes. Rest and enjoy the small trip that leads to big adventure.

Heading out into the wind you will brace yourself for the 1.5-nautical-mile trip slightly north of east. The extensive sand flats are enchanting as you approach the islands, and you can search for the shadows of rays and sharks as you pull toward the sandy shore. The island is a completely rocky shoreline on the Atlantic side with sand flats on the bay side. There is an old stone wall left from a homestead from the early 1900s and a stunted gumbo limbo tree that looks like it might be from the same time period. The rocky beach is home to flocks of shorebirds, and the neighboring island is a roosting area for cormorants, frigates, and pelicans.

The beachcombing is intriguing on this wind-blown shore, and some of the ocean's treasures have been made into a makeshift table and chairs for plush, yet rustic dining. Relax on the beach, knowing that your return travel is with the wind. This would be a good segment of the trip on which to utilize a small sail to practice and perfect your downwind travels.

22. Boot Key

Charts:
Standard Mapping Services Aerial Photo Map #F112
TOPSPOT Middle Keys #208
NOAA Chart #11453

Launch: Launch #39, Sombrero Beach.

Habitats: The winding mangrove-lined channels on this route seem worlds away from the bustling city of Marathon Key. The inner reaches and salt ponds are extraordinary, and the bird life can be plentiful in the winter.

Trip Length: The loop trip around the interior of Boot Key and a short side trip into Boot Key Harbor will total about 3 nautical miles.

Tides and Currents: Full-moon low tides can make the inner reaches of Boot Key impassable. The current that flows through Sister Creek is minimal and will barely affect any transit.

Paddling Conditions: Protected in any weather conditions, this route is perfect for beginners and advanced paddlers alike because of the diversity of habitats and unmarked channels.

Featured Creatures: Mangrove tree crabs are plentiful in these creeks. They hide on the backsides of the branches and roots as you pass, but if you sit tight long enough they will come out of the woods to show their spiderlike movements. If you would like to catch one, wrap your hand on a branch with a crab nearby and scare it onto your wrapped hand with your free hand. It will cautiously crawl onto your skin and try to make its way up your arm. If it happens to drop off into the water watch the unique way these crabs swim.

Sombrero Beach has a little sandy beach that makes a great launch to Sister Creek. Heading north up Sister Creek, you will no doubt notice that the shoreline on the right is completely covered with man-made structures, while the shoreline on the left is all natural. The rocky spit on the right is a good place to see black skimmers, and a little farther down the shore you can usually see some green iguanas sunning themselves.

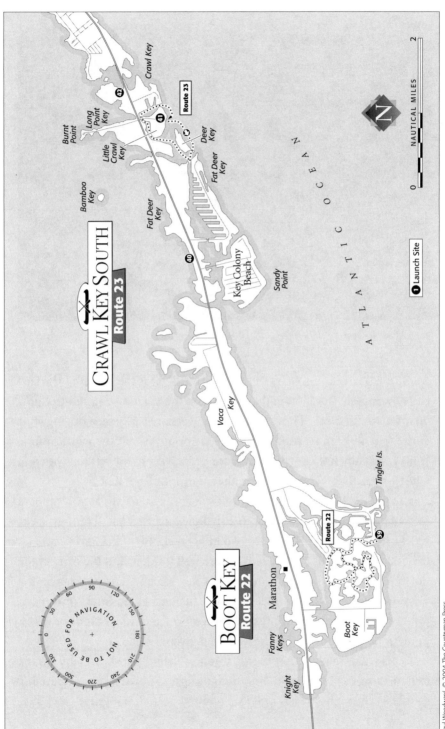

CRAWL KEY SOUTH
Route 23

BOOT KEY
Route 22

Route 23

Route 22

Crawl Key

Long Point Key

Burnt Point

Little Crawl Key

Deer Key

Fat Deer Key

Bamboo Key

Fat Deer Key

Key Colony Beach

Sandy Point

ATLANTIC OCEAN

Vaca Key

Tingler Is.

Marathon

Fanny Keys

Knight Key

Boot Key

NOT TO BE USED FOR NAVIGATION

N

NAUTICAL MILES

0   1   2

🅞 Launch Site

Paul Woodward, © 2004 The Countryman Press

Manatees have a safe haven in Dusenberry Creek.

Just 0.3 nautical mile up the creek you will be at the shores of the federal government installation that broadcasts the Voice of America to Cuba, 90 miles to the south. These four radio towers are easily seen during your entire trip and can be used as a reference point. About 0.5 nautical mile from your launch there will be a major branch off to the left that you will take to enter the hidden creeks on the interior of Boot Key.

As you paddle down this section, watch for manatees as you prepare to take the second right turn into a shallow enclosed bay. This bay is excellent for wading birds and has two little creeks that feed into it, besides the one you have just traveled. Both are well hidden, and the one on the north of this bay will bring you to Boot Key Marina. The other is on the west side of the bay and will lead you to the enchanted interior. You can follow the watercourse for most of this section and not get too confused, but if in doubt always go to the left when given the choice.

This will pop you out into the largest of the interior bays, which has a rich turtle grass bottom with hundreds of upside-down jellyfish. Traveling southeast through this bay will lead you to another mangrove creek that is off on the right of the innermost bay. Follow this to a smaller bay, where you will find the last section of creek on the left (north) side of this small lagoon. When you exit this mangrove creek into the larger river you will see the radio towers, and you can hug the right-hand shore for the 0.25 nautical mile back to the main channel of Sister Creek. This is a great little loop trail where you will hear airplanes, boats, and cars but still feel as if you could get lost in the wilderness.

23. *Crawl Key South*

Charts:
> Standard Mapping Services Aerial Photo Map #F112
> Top Spot Middle Keys #208
> NOAA Chart #11453

Launch: Use launch #41, Curry Hammock State Park.

Habitats: This trip has shallow oceanside flats with soft sand and mixed grass bottoms. There are three small mangrove creeks to explore. Undercut mangrove islands provide good habitat for fish and birds.

Trip Length: This 2-mile loop trail has several small creeks to explore at the west and east ends, as well as a nice beach to relax on pre or post trip.

Tides and Currents: The full-moon low tides could present a problem, but current and wind concerns are nonexistent.

Paddling Conditions: This route is excellent for beginners and families.

Featured Creatures: The fall migration of about 30,000 raptors makes this a wonderful place to lie in your boat and watch the birds go by. You can call the Refuge at 305-872-0774 for current information on the Florida Keys Birding and Wildlife Festival.

It does not seem like it was ten years ago that I served as the official photographer for The Nature Conservancy's dedication ceremony of this parkland. I had no idea what incredible bird migration phenomena this parcel of land would witness. The small oceanfront beach is alive with raptors and other birds in October as they migrate to warmer climes. The annual birding festival is centered at this park, and up to 200 peregrine falcons have been counted in one day.

After finding a spot to park and launch, check the beach for unique and watchable shorebirds. I pulled up once and was able to watch a pair of black-bellied plovers forage in the weedy shoreline right from my launch site.

After an easy beach launch, head southwest to the mangrove island known as Deer Key. On the ocean side of this island are great roosting areas for frigate birds and cormorants. As you approach the western edge you will notice that the island has an undercut edge and there are numerous fish in this protected habitat. There is a spot where you can peek into the interior of the island and see some vegetation that is great butterfly and songbird habitat. The little island west of Deer Key is also undercut and holds numerous fish. The oceanside flats to the south have sharks, bonefish, and rays that ripple the waters as they search the shallows.

Turning northwest from this mangrove key you will encounter the main boat channel, which provides access to the larger boats going into the Cocoplum Beach subdivision. Bear right around the small mangrove finger that borders the canal and follow this to the narrow entrance of a red mangrove creek. The shade and water depth in this dead-end creek will usually attract mangrove snappers, grunts, and masses of baitfish. The roots lining this creek hold colorful invertebrate life as well, and dozens of tree crabs.

There is enough room for a 12-foot boat to turn around and make its way out to continue along the mangrove-fringed shore of Long Point Key. The rich grass bottom varies in depth from 1 to 3 feet and always appears to be too shallow in front of you, but this is an optical illusion. This habitat is good for baby lemon and bonnethead sharks, as well as hundreds of Cassiopeia sunbathing in the shallow seas.

Follow the cove and wend your way along the left-hand side. It will finally constrict to creek size, and you will find yourself in a sandy-bottomed creek that has mangrove snappers, parrotfish, barracuda, and mojarras enjoying the current. The aftermath of Hurricane George is apparent in the stripped and sun-bleached deadwood lining the creek.

As you go under the access road bridge, look for barracuda hanging out near the tarred columns. The creek deposits you in the east bay off

Bottlenose dolphin pods can be found throughout the Florida Keys.

Little Crawl Key, and the eastern shore of this bay has a nice mangrove edge with a small dead-end creek in it. The mouths of these creeks always have a diverse abundance of life and the most prolific here seem to be the big orange clusters of mangrove tunicate.

Making your way down the shore, you will run by the Valhalla Resort with its tiny sandy beach and hidden harbor. As you coast the shoreline on your last stretch of the loop, search for shorebirds and small rays on the shoal grass flats.

24. *Tom's Harbor Keys*

Charts:
Standard Mapping Services Aerial Photo Map #F112
Top Spot Middle Keys #208
NOAA Chart #11453
Launch: Launch #43.
Habitats: This route takes you along a deep, grassy channel that leads to a secluded sandy island beach that is crowded with land hermit

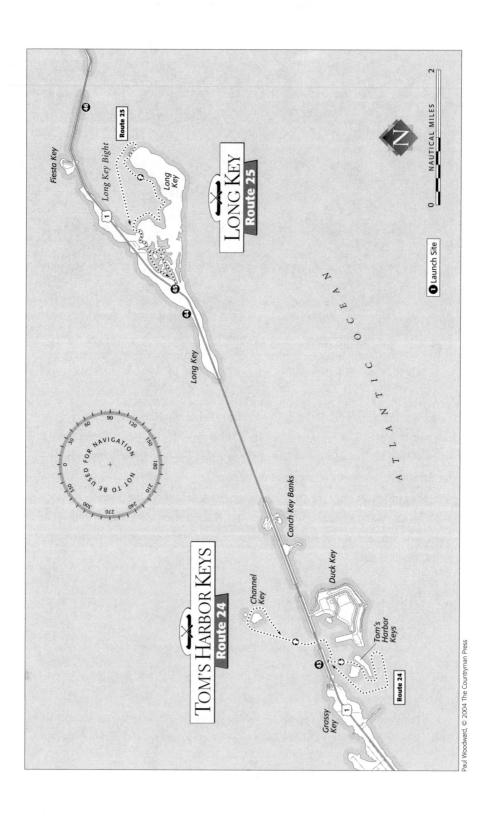

TOM'S HARBOR KEYS
Route 24

LONG KEY
Route 25

Grassy Key

Channel Key

Route 24

Tom's Harbor Keys

Duck Key

Conch Key Banks

Long Key

Long Key

Long Key Bight

Fiesta Key

Route 25

NOT TO BE USED FOR NAVIGATION

ATLANTIC OCEAN

N

NAUTICAL MILES

0   2

Launch Site

Paul Woodward, © 2004 The Countryman Press

crabs. On the south side of the main island are many tide pools and rocky shorelines.

Trip Length: The trip is slightly more than 2 nautical miles. If the weather conditions are favorable you can paddle out into the bay for a circumnavigation of Channel Key on the north side of Duck Key. This leg would add an additional 3 nautical miles.

Tides and Currents: Low tides make for great tide pools and sandy bars where the birds like to forage. Currents have a negligible effect except where you cross under any bridges.

Paddling Conditions: This route is excellent for beginners and families.

Featured Creatures: Land hermit crabs are plentiful and provide comic relief with their daily antics. The sands are laced with their tracks from foraging travels. Put an empty shell in the path of one, and there is a 90 percent chance that the crab will stop, size it up, and try it on.

Departing from the roadside launch, you will have to carry your kayaks over several small coral boulders. The knee-deep water right next to the boulders is shallow enough for you to stand in. Looking south you'll see the two islands that make up Tom's Harbor Keys. Head for the left-hand island, and as you make the short crossing you'll see the cut between the two islands. The island on the left has a sandy shoal that extends northward and is full of sea cucumbers. The shallows usually have wading birds and gulls.

Following the gap between the two islands, you'll hear birds calling from the interior. About halfway down the island you can get close to the edge and peer down into the undercut mangroves. As you progress in a southwesterly direction, you will round the point where a small beach can be seen. The beach is shallow, and you can paddle right up and beach your craft. A short walk on the island will allow you to encounter dozens of trails that are left by the land hermit crabs. There are several little campfire circles along this stretch, and you can follow the trail as it winds south and then west along the rocky shoreline.

The shoreline is a good place to see small tide pools and all the invertebrates that are associated with this habitat. The trail peters out, with lots of deadwood and branches blocking the way, but if you persevere, you can continue down for quite a stretch of windblown shoreline. Ospreys frequently use the tall Australian pine as a perch from which to watch for small barracuda and needlefish.

Hopping back into your kayak, you can paddle out toward the southwest and find some shallow rocky substrate that exposes more tide pools at low tide. Little sharks, stingrays, and cowfish are common on these rocky flats. From here you can choose to return by the eastern or western sides of the islands. The western side has less boat traffic and more channel-laced flats. It's a short return trip from this point.

25. *Long Key*

Charts:
>   Standard Mapping Services Aerial Photo Map #F105
>   Top Spot Upper Keys and Florida Bay #207
>   NOAA Chart #11449

Launch: Use launch #45, Long Key State Park or launch #46, Long Key Bight.

Habitats: Lush turtle grass meadows and mangrove-lined creeks that feed some of the richest shallow bay environments in the Keys.

Trip Length: The standard canoe loop trail is about 1.4 nautical miles. A trip that includes a loop around Long Key Bight will add 3.4 miles.

Tides and Currents: A low tide can make the launch in the park a bit muddy but will attract the wading birds. The congregation of birds on the right-hand side of the road across from the launch is sometimes wildly alive with waders busting up the baitfish. Long Key Bight also has a few inside areas that will present a problem if it is low water. The benefit of these low tides is that the fish are easier to spot tailing and leaving wakes. There could be a slight tidal current in Zane Grey Creek.

Paddling Conditions: Protected shallow waters and easy navigation make this a good trip for beginners and families.

Featured Creatures: The invertebrates steal the show here. The bottom here seems to have no growth-limiting factors, and the burrowing anemones, sea stars, Cassiopeia, and a city full of chicken liver sponge colonies are among the long list of creatures that abound here.

If departing from the park canoe dock, you will have one of the park maps in your hand. This map denotes markers that will guide you through the maze of inland mangrove islands. After about marker 5 and 6 it really starts to get interesting, with a little more current sweeping the bottom and providing food and shelter for many species.

There are several little bays that jut off to the right and are quite untouched and not on the marked trail. These have great wading bird viewing areas, and the wakes of small barracuda and mangrove snapper zip near the mangrove edges. About halfway through the loop you can connect to Zane Grey Creek. One of the first and finest fishing lodges in the Keys was located near this rich creek, and Zane Grey was a frequent visitor in the 1950s.

Grey was a famous author of both Westerns and fishing books, who wrote about "vanishing America" and how we should start to respect and

Exploring the mangroves of Dusenberry Creek

become better stewards of our natural resources. He challenged the millions of sportsmen to teach their kids the value of respecting the environment. His views catalyzed the sportsmen of his day and have led us to our modern "catch-and-release" standards. It is a fitting tribute that this fecund creek bears his name.

Halfway down the creek there was a perched osprey tearing into the head of a still-wriggling mullet. I shipped the paddle and did not stir a muscle as the current slowly brought me by the scene. The yellow eye froze on me for a few seconds and then the bird continued dining. Giving ospreys a sideways glance doesn't threaten them, and they will usually go on about their normal behavior.

I took up the paddle after I rounded the corner and headed out into the bight. It was a glass calm day and only one bonefish skiff in sight. Taking a moment to determine his direction of travel, I then plotted my course to paddle in behind his route so as not to disturb his fishing. Crossing the bight hugging the south edge there were dozens of wakes slicing the surface. The tall dorsals of bonnetheads, the double dorsals of lemon sharks, and the clear gray tails of bonefish were working that shore for the entire mile and a half.

Poking around the point gives an unobstructed view of Hawks Channel and the Gulf Stream beyond. If the wind is from the east-southeast it will be of great assistance on your return. A course due west for about 1 mile will bring you right back to the green day markers that mark the boat channel to Zane Grey Creek.

26. *Lignumvitae Key*

Charts:
Standard Mapping Services Aerial Photo Map #F105
Top Spot Upper Keys and Florida Bay #207
NOAA Chart #11449
Launch: Launch #48.
Habitats: This route takes you along deep channels coursing through sea grass beds. Lignumvitae Key is a beautiful, mangrove-fringed island with a pristine hardwood hammock in its interior.
Trip Length: The route is 1 nautical mile to the edge of this island,

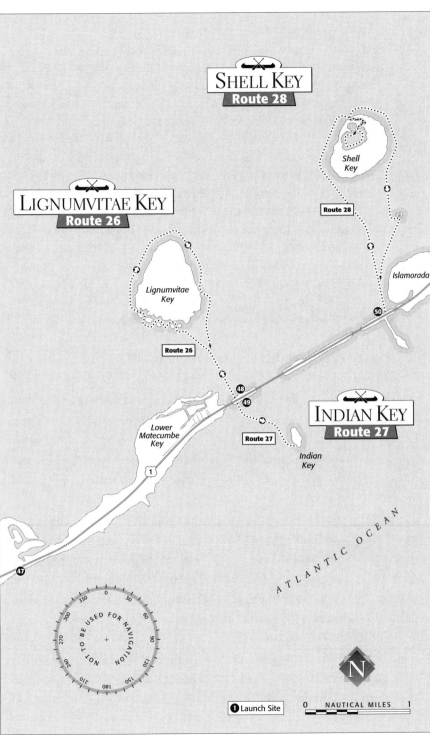

SHELL KEY
Route 28

LIGNUMVITAE KEY
Route 26

Shell
Key

Route 28

Lignumvitae
Key

Islamorada

Route 28

Route 26

50

INDIAN KEY
Route 27

48

49

Lower
Matecumbe
Key

Route 27

Indian
Key

1

47

ATLANTIC OCEAN

NOT TO BE USED FOR NAVIGATION

300 350 0 30 60 90 120 150 180 210 240 270

N

1 Launch Site

0   NAUTICAL MILES   1

Paul Woodward, © 2004 The Countryman Press

which has a 2.5-nautical-mile perimeter.

Tides and Currents: Tides can be strong in the channels.

Paddling Conditions: Lots of boat traffic and confusing channels will cause the motorboaters to do strange things. The short open-water crossing has lots of traffic, so use due caution.

Featured Creatures: "Tree of life" is a literal translation of the island's Spanish name, Lignumvitae. This slow-growing tropical hardwood has so many medicinal and industrial applications that it is hard to begin to list them all. From curing arthritis to self-lubricating ball bearings for submarines, this wood has been put to many uses, and this is why it was almost completely clear-cut everywhere it occurs. The lignumvitae is native to South Florida, the Keys, and the West Indies. In the United States it is listed as endangered and is protected by law. The tree's unique properties can be attributed to the fact that nearly 30 percent of its weight is in its valuable resin. The wood is so dense that it will not float in water. The tree has small dark blue flowers that open in March and April.

Departing from the launch it is about 1 nautical mile at 320 degrees across shallow, fish-filled flats and deeper S-shaped channels. Looking off to the left you will notice a kind of picket fence structure, perhaps with perching birds. The structure marks previous groundings by motorized vessels and the current attempt to recolonize the propeller scars with natural sea grass. The markers actually keep other boaters out of the area as well as providing the cormorants a perch from which they can fertilize the young grass beds.

As you progress toward the island, you will want to bear right if you intend to dock and join on one of the ranger-led talks. The two-hour tours usually start at 10 AM and 2 PM. Cost is $1 per person. Be sure to bring bug repellent, as there isn't any aerial spraying conducted on this key and the bugs can be fierce. After the tour of the island, which includes orchids, night-blooming cactus, gumbo limbo trees, and the Matheson family home built in 1919, you can continue on a circumnavigation of the key. The 2.5-mile route follows the shore with no real breaks until you reach the southern tip, where you can pull inside the small mangrove-fringed lagoons and escape from all the traffic outside. Enjoy your solitude and

*High tides triggered by the moon's phase urge horseshoe crabs to lay
eggs in the surf zone.*

maybe scout for a bonefish or two before heading back along the short mile to the launch.

27. *Indian Key*

Charts:
> Standard Mapping Services Aerial Photo Map #F105
> TOPSPOT Upper Keys and Florida Bay #207
> NOAA Chart #11449

Launch: Launch #49, Indian Key Launch.

Habitats: This trip features rich turtle grass beds and an iron shore island with a long and colorful history.

Trip Length: This route is a 1.5-mile round trip. The island is worth spending a few hours on, especially if the Indian Key Festival is in full swing.

Tides and Currents: The only thing to impede you on this trip will be the lowest of low tides and/or high winds with small craft warnings.

Paddling Conditions: There is a short open water crossing over shallow grass flats.

Featured Creatures: The Bahama sea star or cushion star is one of the largest invertebrate inhabitants of the turtle grass beds, reaching up to 14 inches across and 3 inches thick. It moves slowly with its tube feet across the grass blades, scouring them clean of bacteria and small animals. It envelops the grass with its distended stomach and leaves a trail of clean green grass. It is a big, beautiful animal and was kept as a souvenir in the past, but is protected by law from harvest now.

It is difficult to imagine what an island's history might be as you stare at it from a distant shore. Indian Key has a colorful past that includes shipwreck salvage, Indian attacks, and a once-thriving settlement.

There is a channel that runs parallel to the road and is used by motorboaters, so use common sense as you depart. The course is southeast, and the distance is 0.5 nautical mile. Your destination is a dock on the southwest side of the island, where there is room for several kayaks. If this spot is full, double back along the shoreline and look for some small sandy areas in the shade of the mangroves to beach your boats. There are some soft mud areas along this shore, so unless you want to lose a shoe to the mud's suction, stay in the boat until you are near the hard-packed sandy shore. There are a number of hiking trails, open fields, and an observation tower that can keep one occupied for some time. Shade trees, old brick cisterns, and foundations of structures, including the main hotel (which even had a bowling alley) are scattered about the island. A replica of the gravestone of the famed and wealthy salvor Jacob Housman makes history come alive in your imagination as you envision yourself living in the days of pirates and cargo salvage.

On the east shore there is a little bench that lets you contemplate the royal purple colors of the nearby ocean waters. Check with the park (305-664-4815) about the interpretive talks that are scheduled in the winter.

28. *Shell Key*

Charts:
Standard Mapping Services Aerial Photo Map #F105
TOPSPOT Upper Keys and Florida Bay #207
NOAA Chart #11449

Launch: Use launch #50, Shell Key, from the Indian Key fill causeway.

Habitats: This trip takes you along deep meandering channels flanked by grass flats, shoals of finger coral, and soft mud bottoms. There is a lot of boat traffic and many flats fishermen in this area, and they seem to come at you from all directions. Keep out of the channels, or at the least minimize your time in them.

Trip Length: From the causeway to the northeast corner of Shell Key is about 1.5 miles. Continuing on the north shore of Shell Key for 0.5 mile will bring you to the creek entrance. The return trip from the east side of Shell Key to the causeway is about 2 miles.

Tides and Currents: A spring low tide might cause a bit of a problem on the northeast corner, but if you hug the shore it is just a bit deeper. Currents can be strong near the causeway bridges.

Paddling Conditions: This trip can be a bit confusing with the various markers and channels, as the channels do seem to snake around quite a bit. The operators of most big boats are courteous and slow down to limit their wake size. Always attempt to cross a wake

at a 40- to 70-degree angle so as not to upset your vessel.
Featured Creatures: The sport fish are numerous here. Redfish,
snook, bonefish, permit, and many sharks love to feed on the flats
and hide in the deeper channels.

One of my favorite places in the Keys is not on them but a hundred feet
over them. With the back door of the Piper Tripacer left behind, I had an
unobstructed head-to-toe view of the glassine ocean surface below. The
stall speed on this plane is about 45 miles per hour, and flying low and
slow lets an aerial photographer get great results. My assignment was to
document the sea grass restoration project. It had been another year since
the T-shaped PVC posts had been planted. The posts not only cautioned
against running aground there but also provided a perch for the fertilizers.
Cormorants gave their daily best to increase nutrient levels to assist the
grass seedlings in recolonizing the prop scars. From my vantage point it
seemed to be working. There was no doubt that the fish were numerous
here. I counted over 200 large shadows, with some schools of permit numbering a dozen fish. The black diamond shadows of rays floated over the
flats between Lignumvitae and Shell Keys. I couldn't wait to paddle here.

The short 1.5 miles to Shell Key has you looking down at the diverse
bottom more than looking ahead. There are tremendous numbers of
finger corals (*Porites* sp.) growing in the grass flats, and in these coral
structures are hundreds of crabs and shrimp. This structured bottom
holds all the food a hungry sport fish might desire. Anemones burst forth
in slow-motion dances on the bottom and shark fins wake the surface.

As you approach the shoreline the sloped snouts of snook often poke
out of the shadows to investigate. At random they will charge the silversides and send shiny slivers skyward.

Rounding the northeast corner, you will pass a big sign on a sandy
area of shoreline, and about 200 feet farther another sign that reads Shell
Key State Preserve. Just 30 to 40 feet from this sign is the creek entrance.
It meanders for 300 or 400 feet and carries you to a small sandy pond with
scads of Cassiopeia undulating on the sun-drenched bottom. Follow this
pond, bearing right, and you will enter a creek that barely allows an 18-
foot kayak with rudder. After spooking hundreds of mangrove snappers

Shore birds are plentiful at Bahia Honda State Park.

that are often found among the roots, you pop out onto the inner lakes. There is a beautiful, eerie silence that envelops you as you make the first couple of paddle strokes, and then the splashes begin. Redfish are zooming after baits, and kingfishers are chattering away as they dive-bomb the fingerlings. At this point make sure to turn around and memorize your exit. You may want to leave something in the trees to mark this well-hidden creek.

After enjoying the big bowl of blue sky overhead and the lush green of the surrounding mangroves, you will backtrack out of the lakes and continue your route around the island. The shallow, hard bottom around the east side is a great feeding ground for stingrays, whose triangular black fins wave at the surface. As you progress along the eastern shore, a small island will come into view as you look south. This is Channel Key, and this area was a dredging area for the fill that was used to create the railroad bed in the early 1900s. Henry Flagler sought a specific type of marl mud that held together like cement when drained of water, and this was one of his mud quarries. It is a short trip of less than 1 mile and a nice respite from the winds to duck in behind this island. The birds roost and sunbathe on this mangrove clump, and the deep waters nearby hold large numbers of fish.

Leaving Channel Key and heading south, you will run into the shoreline of Upper Matecumbe and follow this to Papa Joe's Marina. At the marina entrance there is a canal that stretches into the woods for about 1,500 feet. As you paddle back in time you will notice the wreckage of the old Papa Joe's fishing camp on the left, and under the surface ghostly boat wrecks loom toward the surface. Close to the end of this canal, where the baby tarpon are rolling, you will see a rocky shore on your left, where you can exit your boat and jump into the protected waters for a swim.

If it is near sunset and you want a refreshing libation, pull on up to the tower bar at Papa Joe's for a beautiful sunset view and some fish stories. From here it is a short trip across the Shell Key Channel to your launch site.

29. *Bottle Key*

Charts:
   Standard Mapping Services Aerial Photo Map #F109
   TOPSPOT Upper Keys and Florida Bay #207
   NOAA Chart #11463

Launch: Launch #54 can be recognized on the return from Bottle Key by the large off-white condo on the shoreline and the nearby antenna tower.

Habitats: This trip takes you across open water, shallow grass, and mud banks. The mud banks are rich with diverse algal growth.

Trip Length: This paddle covers about 9 nautical miles round trip.

Tides and Currents: It is a difficult circumnavigation of the island if the tides are low, due to the extensive shallow banks surrounding the island. Upper Cross Bank can also be difficult to cross if the tides are low.

Paddling Conditions: The open water crossing makes this a strenuous trip in strong winds. A performance boat with a good waterline and a rudder will make this trip more pleasant. There are no rest stops, so be sure to stretch out all your paddling muscles before departure and bring an anchor in case you need a break.

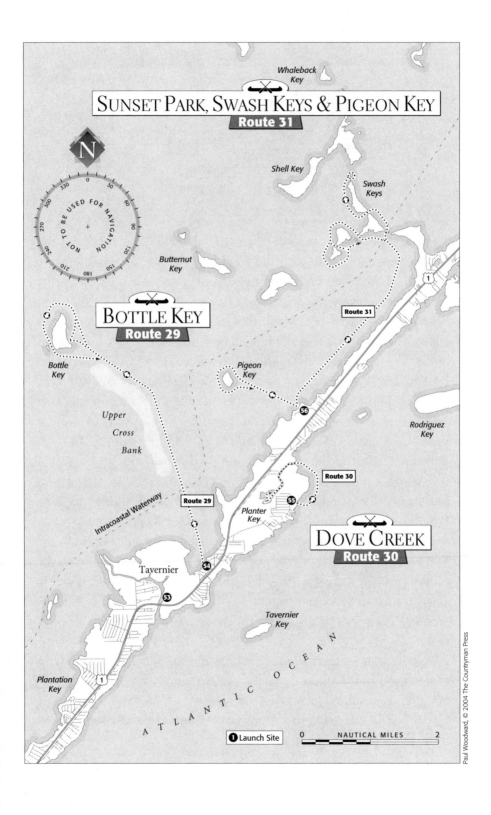

SUNSET PARK, SWASH KEYS & PIGEON KEY
Route 31

Whaleback
Key

N
NOT TO BE USED FOR NAVIGATION

Shell Key

Swash
Keys

Route 31

1

Butternut
Key

BOTTLE KEY
Route 29

Bottle
Key

Pigeon
Key

Upper
Cross
Bank

56

Rodriguez
Key

Route 30

Route 29

Intracoastal Waterway

Planter
Key

55

DOVE CREEK
Route 30

Tavernier

54

53

Tavernier
Key

Plantation
Key

1

ATLANTIC OCEAN

1 Launch Site

0   NAUTICAL MILES   2

Paul Woodward, © 2004 The Countryman Press

Featured Creatures: Spoonbills are the highlight. These pink birds really stand out from the crowds. During the height of the breeding season it is wise to stay clear of the nesting adults, because disturbances that cause the adults to leave the nest can cause heat-related death to the unprotected eggs in a short time. The birds have a limey green head and a distinctive spoon-shaped bill. The spoon is waved from side to side in the water, straining out small shrimp and other crustaceans. Most pink-plumaged birds have a diet rich in shrimp.

This is the greatest open water distance of all these half-day trips. It can also be the most tiring if the wind is working against you. Make sure the conditions are favorable for you and your particular boat. From the launch, a bearing of 326 degrees will let you skirt most of Upper Cross Bank on the western side, which should be a little more protected from wind-driven waves. I always enjoy hugging the bank's edge looking for wakes, fins, and tails of fish in the skinny water. There is a portion of the bank that juts out to the west for a solid 0.5 mile that may give you some trouble at low tide. You can avoid this by starting your trip on a course of 340 degrees and skirting the bank on the eastern side, crossing the bank at the narrow section (GPS coordinates N 24° 03.219, W 80° 32.140) 1.5 miles to the north of the marked navigation channel.

As you approach Bottle Key there will be a cluster of mangrove islets to the east of the island that is worth ducking into. Primitive-looking horseshoe crabs are usually bulldozing the sandy flats in search of worms and other edibles. As you cross over these shallows heading toward Bottle Key, you will come across a deeper area with a small sandy beach on the southwest tip. If there is no possibility of disturbing nesting birds, this is a nice little area to stretch your legs. The interior of the island has numerous shallow salt ponds, which the spoonbills seem to prefer for their nesting islands.

Continuing your circumnavigation, you will round the northern tip of the island and continue down the western shore, where the sandy bottoms hide the cautious bonefish. As you make your way to the south shore, you should be able to scan the southern horizon and get a fix on the radio tower that will lead you home.

30. *Dove Creek*

Charts:
> Standard Mapping Services Aerial Photo Map #F109
> TOPSPOT Upper Keys and Florida Bay #207
> NOAA Chart #11463

Launch: Use launch #55, Harry Harris County Park.

Habitats: This trip takes you along a rocky shoreline that leads to a mangrove-lined creek. Dove Creek has a few homes on it, but the majority of it is natural shoreline and it culminates in a no-motor zone.

Trip Length: Round trip is under 2 nautical miles.

Tides and Currents: Tides and currents are not a concern, except for the location where the creek "T-bones" into the canal section. On an outgoing tide the water really has some force and it can be a challenge to make the turn and beat the current.

Paddling Conditions: This is a short, protected paddle, good for beginners, families, and those who want a great adventure in a short timeframe.

Featured Creatures: In March the ragged sea hares come to the shorelines to form mating clusters referred to as daisy chains. Most mollusks are hermaphrodites and can link up in such a way that they can perform the male and female functions simultaneously. The rocky shores along this route are a common gathering area for this full-moon event. At first you might think they are the ubiquitous upside-down jellyfish, but as you peer closer you will be able to make out the fat sluglike appearance of the ragged sea hares.

Pulling out from your launch, you will head left down the rocky shoreline. This short section of island is a catchall for debris from the ocean, and you will see trap buoys and other floating objects that ended their journeys here. The rocky pools near shore are the waters where the ragged sea hares come when the March full moon signals the spawning event. As you round the eastern point, you will notice several large rafts of sargassum. These seaweeds are attached to the bottom and provide a rich underwater forest for creatures such as seahorses and pipefish. They camouflage well in this floating forest, and a trained eye with a mask and snorkel can usually spot them. As you head up the shoreline toward the channel markers, you will see Snapper Annies, a local restaurant and waterfront bar, where it is easy to dock your craft and get a bite. The creek entrance is wide and the edges are scoured clean by the currents.

A snorkel and mask are not necessary to look into the water and view dozens of fire sponges, hundreds of mangrove snappers, and tunicates by the thousands at every corner in this creek. Soon a few homes will appear on your right, and you will encounter the area that branches off to the left. The NO MOTOR ZONE signs will be just a short distance up this canal, and thereafter the shoreline is dominated by mangroves. The first branch to the left is a dead end, but all the other branches just hook around and join the main route after 50 to 70 feet or so. Not far up this creek, you will encounter Dove Lake. This interior salt lake has a thick undulating grass bottom and many upside-down jellyfish. A quick circle around the lake and you should encounter a dozen different birds before you head back, retracing your route.

31. *Sunset Park, Swash Keys, and Pigeon Key*

Charts:
  Standard Mapping Services Aerial Photo Map #F109
  TOPSPOT Upper Keys and Florida Bay #207
  NOAA Chart #11463

Launch: Launch #56 is located at MM 95.3. There may be a closer launch, but I just haven't been able to find it.

Habitats: This trip takes you around twisted and tortuous mangrove islands surrounded by marl mud flats interspersed with scattered beds of sea grasses.

Trip Length: It takes about 2.5 nautical miles to get to the lee shore of the southernmost of the Swash Keys. To circumnavigate the Swash Keys it is an additional 3 to 4 miles. The trip would be a total of 9 miles in its entirety.

Tides and Currents: Currents are negligible, and some of the lower tides will expose some great flats on the eastern side of the westernmost Swash Key.

Paddling Conditions: The first portion of the trip is open water and probably against the wind, but once inside the protection of the Swash Keys it is a very enjoyable paddle.

Featured Attraction: Sunsets are wonderful and privately viewed a short distance away at Pigeon Key. Pigeon Key is about 1 mile at a 280-degree compass bearing from the launch site.

The 2.5 nautical miles are parallel to the shoreline of Key Largo. Once you reach the peninsula of Key Largo that juts out to the north, you will travel across Baker Cut to reach the Swash Keys. These islands are a great habitat for wading birds, which roost in the treetops and feed on the shallows that surround these islands. The convoluted shorelines are pocked with little lagoons, rivers, cuts, and tufted mangrove islands where you can meander and explore, knowing that every corner you come around will hold some interesting marine or airborne animal. Because of the convoluted nature of the perimeter of these islands, if you were to hug the shoreline as you circumnavigate it, you would probably wind up paddling 6 miles instead of 3.

32. *Dusenberry Creek*

Charts:
Standard Mapping Services Aerial Photo Map #F109
TOPSPOT Upper Keys and Florida Bay #207
NOAA Chart #11463

Launch: Launch #57 is behind Florida Bay Outfitters—the best source for all your paddlecraft needs.

Habitats: This route takes you along deep, protected mangrove creeks inhabited by large fish and even larger mammals. Shallow grass beds are extensive in Tarpon Basin.

Trip Length: This route is about 5.5 nautical miles.

Tides and Currents: Currents can be strong in the Dusenberry Creek area, but the tides are of little consequence.

Paddling Conditions: There is open water for 1.5 nautical miles, and then you will be in completely enclosed creeks that run parallel to Dusenberry Creek. Some boat traffic can be encountered in the main portion of the creek.

Featured Creatures: Manatees are commonly sighted in this series of creeks. The creeks are deep and protected from motorboat traffic by their constricted and overgrown nature.

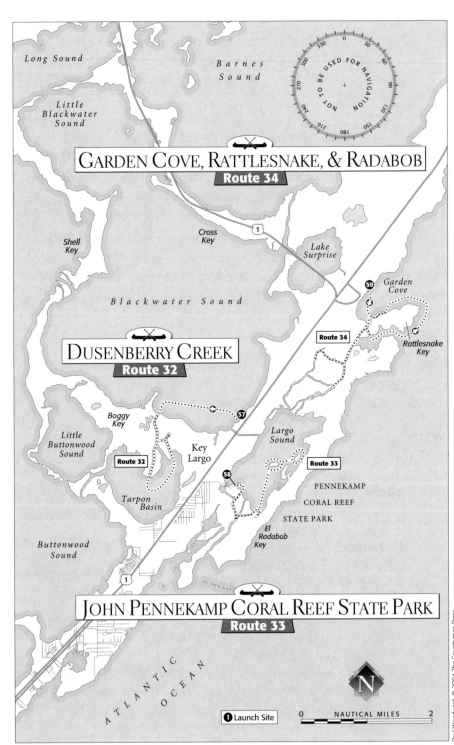

Long Sound

Barnes
Sound

Little
Blackwater
Sound

NOT TO BE USED FOR NAVIGATION

GARDEN COVE, RATTLESNAKE, & RADABOB
Route 34

Shell
Key

Cross
Key

Lake
Surprise

Garden
Cove

59

Blackwater Sound

Route 34

Rattlesnake
Key

DUSENBERRY CREEK
Route 32

57

Boggy
Key

Largo
Sound

Little
Buttonwood
Sound

Key
Largo

Route 33

Route 32

PENNEKAMP

58

CORAL REEF

Tarpon
Basin

STATE PARK

El
Radabob
Key

Buttonwood
Sound

JOHN PENNEKAMP CORAL REEF STATE PARK
Route 33

ATLANTIC

OCEAN

N

1 Launch Site

0   NAUTICAL MILES   2

Paul Woodward, © 2004 The Countryman Press

The 1.5 nautical mile open water crossing is the most strenuous part of this trip. As you cross, take note of the buildings adjacent to your launch on the shoreline so that on your return trip you will have a good landmark. You'll probably see some boat traffic coming in and out of the creek, as this is the major thoroughfare between Blackwater Sound and Tarpon Basin.

Just 0.5 mile after you enter the creek, you will see smaller creeks that jut off to the left and right. All of these are great little expeditions and it's easy to get turned around in some of them because of their convoluted nature. Bearing off toward the right-hand creek, you can follow this as it progresses along 0.3 mile or more. Some of these creeks are up to 8 feet deep and the clear, slightly amber water is home to some very large mangrove snappers near some of the more substantial underwater root systems. Manatees are commonly seen at the junctures of these interior creeks where it's a little deeper. These junctures also collect rafts of sea grasses and red mangrove seedlings, which are great food for grazing manatees. The manatees move slowly under the surface, raising their head and nostrils to breathe occasionally. It is when they break the surface that they can be spotted easily, or when they are feeding on the rafts of floating salad. Upon exiting this section of the creek, you can head left and pass by marker #46 and then head to marker #43, where you will find another creek entrance just a short distance up the shoreline. Follow this creek up into the interior. After about 0.25 mile it jogs to the left and comes out to the main portion of Dusenberry Creek. From here you can head back to Florida Bay Outfitters by taking a right and following the Dusenberry Creek back out to Blackwater Sound.

33. *John Pennekamp Coral Reef State Park*

Charts:
>   Standard Mapping Services Aerial Photo Map #F109
>   TOPSPOT Upper Keys and Florida Bay #207
>   NOAA Chart #11463

Launch: Launch #58 is located within John Pennekamp State Park. There is an entrance fee.

Habitats: This route features mangrove creeks and open bays with seagrass flats.

Trip Length: This trip covers 3 nautical miles, round trip.

Tides and Currents: The currents that run out of Largo Sound can be strong.

Paddling Conditions: This route is in mostly protected waters with some boating channels to cross. Winds and tides are not usually a factor.

Featured Creatures: Red mangrove seedlings are sprouted in the summertime by the parent tree. The little yellow flower soon gives way to an almond-shaped seed. From this seed sprouts the green, bean-shaped seedling, which has a brown root tip. You can see them by the hundreds on certain red mangrove trees during the peak of the summer. It is at this time of year that it is most advantageous for the seedlings to drop, because hurricanes and summer storms can disperse them widely. Look for big rafts of weeds that have scores of red mangrove seedlings woven into them, and see if you can find any that have started to send out their root tips.

An osprey rose slowly in a spiral, circling me three times. With each spiral I could see the frantic fish clasped in its talons and hear the victorious calls of the bird as it flew off into the morning sun. This happened first thing in the morning, when there wasn't much human activity on any of these creeks and channels.

As the day progresses the story changes. This is a heavily traveled area, and it is fortunate that a well-marked canoe trail is available for peace and tranquility on the water. If you like solitude, avoid this route on holiday weekends, but if you like protected mangrove bays with a raised wooden platform for bird watching, check this out on weekday mornings.

34. Garden Cove, Rattlesnake Key, and Radabob Key

Charts:
Standard Mapping Services Aerial Photo Map #F109
TOPSPOT Upper Keys and Florida Bay #207
NOAA Chart #11463

Launch: Use launch #59, Garden Cove.

Habitats: This route takes you over grass flats and along deep channels with mangrove creeks that weave for miles.

Trip Length: There is a 2.5-nautical-mile circumnavigation of
Rattlesnake Key and many more miles of North Sound Creek,
which leads to Largo Sound.

Tides and Currents: Low tides can make the bay between El Radabob
and Rattlesnake impassable but the wading birds are numerous at
that time.

Paddling Conditions: This route consists of protected bays and mangrove channels. Some major boating channels need to be
navigated, and motorboats use many of these creeks.

Featured Creatures: The nickname of the reddish egret used by many
birders is the "drunken sailor." This active feeder will dance and
sway in the most extravagant manner as it chases small fish on the
flats. It will spread out its wings as if in flight, shuffle its feet like a
tap dancer, and strike 20 to 40 times at the water for every fish it
captures. This bird is one of the easiest to identify without binoculars because its behavior gives it away. The slate gray body and
reddish head and neck complement its pinkish bill with a black tip.

From the launch site, strike out east and cross the busy boating channel
first. If you watch for a while you can determine what the traffic is like
and when to depart so there won't be too many boats. As you cross, keep
Rattlesnake Key straight off your bow at 170 degrees and soon you will
enter a no motor zone. From here you can head into the channel that
runs through the interior of Rattlesnake. This deep water seems perfectly
suited for manatees or possibly an errant crocodile, but all we saw on our
last trip were mullet cascading over one another to pass the time of day.
Mullet seem to like to jump just to have a look around or maybe to feel
gravity for a moment. They will jump out of necessity to escape a
predator, but often it seems that they jump just for fun. This creek will let
you out in short order, and you can continue east on your circumnavigation of Rattlesnake Key. As Radabob Key comes into view there will be a
shallow bay on your right where it is possible to see a good number of
waders on every low tide. Another little creek will be on your right after
about 0.5 mile of paddling in this bay. This creek has some sand-washed
bottoms and some great undercut edges and will exit into North Sound

Creek. From here you can head right back toward the launch or travel to the left and spend hours meandering through the creeks that wind their way toward Largo Sound. There are over a dozen sections to this system, and every time I go I discover new, smaller feeder creeks. This system of creeks, even though it has some boat traffic, is sure to enliven your appreciation of the natural world.

35. *Steamboat Creek and Cormorant Point*

Charts:
> Standard Mapping Services Aerial Photo Map #F109
> TOPSPOT Upper Keys and Florida Bay #207
> NOAA Chart #11463

Launch: Use launch #61, Little Manatee Bay.

Habitats: You will travel along mangrove-lined tidal creeks with rich sea grass beds at their mouths.

Trip Length: A 3-nautical-mile loop lets you explore the main creeks, and the others could add an additional 3 nautical miles.

Tides and Currents: The tidal waters flow swiftly, but usually to your advantage for half the trip. In the shallow bay areas the currents are negligible.

Paddling Conditions: This trip is through protected creeks and backwaters.

Featured Creatures: Sea eggs are common on the grass flats just outside the creek mouths and adjacent shorelines. These urchins are covered with 0.5-inch-long white spines and graze on the algae and turtle grass blades. They cover themselves with bits of debris from the bottom for camouflage from predators. The entire interior of the shell is used to produce and store eggs, which can number in the hundreds of thousands and are shed when ripe. The eggs are considered a delicacy in Japan, Greece, and Barbados. People in California and the West Indies believe they exhibit powerful aphrodisiac qualities.

These creeks are numerous and full of big fish, crashing the waters. Almost any route can be planned that will take advantage of current weather conditions, since the access points are numerous in this location. The loop

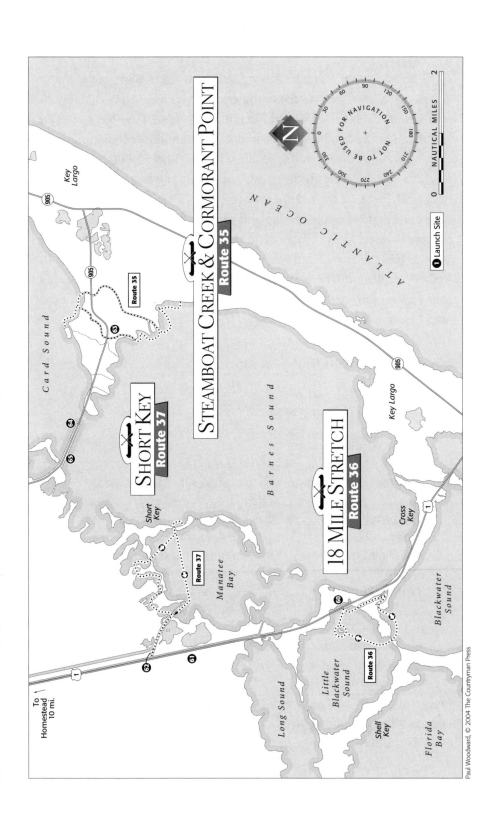

STEAMBOAT CREEK & CORMORANT POINT
Route 35

SHORT KEY
Route 37

18 MILE STRETCH
Route 36

Route 35

Route 37

Route 36

Key Largo

Card Sound

Barnes Sound

Key Largo

Short Key

Manatee Bay

Cross Key

Long Sound

Little Blackwater Sound

Blackwater Sound

Shell Key

Florida Bay

ATLANTIC OCEAN

N

NOT TO BE USED FOR NAVIGATION

30
60
90
120
150
180
210
240
270
300
330
0

NAUTICAL MILES

0
2

① Launch Site

To Homestead 10 mi.

905

905

64

65

1

Paul Woodward, © 2004 The Countryman Press

route leaves from the first bridge at Steamboat Creek and goes with the current. If this takes you to the south you will have a mile or so of creek to meander through before you run into Barnes Sound. From here you can exit through the left-hand creek and hug the shoreline looking for sea eggs, baby nurse sharks, and crocodiles. Cormorants and other birds use this little cove for roosting. Retracing your route you will come across the next creek just past the next point going west. This creek has numerous dead ends that branch to the left and right and are worth exploring just because you feel like the first one in there. About 0.25 mile up the creek you will pass under the Card Sound Road and continue north to its mouth in Card Sound. From here you can opt to visit Cormorant Point about 0.5 mile west or journey back to Steamboat Creek and be back to your car after less than 0.5 mile of paddling.

36. *18 Mile Stretch*

Charts:
   Standard Mapping Services Aerial Photo Map #F109
   TOPSPOT Upper Keys and Florida Bay #207
   NOAA Chart #11463

Launch: On U.S. 1, launch #60 is at Mile Marker 111.

Habitats: This route takes you through Florida Bay backwaters consisting primarily of soft mud, oyster bars, and sea grass flats.

Trip Length: The loop trail covers about 3 nautical miles.

Tides and Currents: Low tides can make some areas a struggle.

Paddling Conditions: This trip goes through relatively calm, protected shallows.

Featured Creatures: White ibis are found in great numbers inside the old railroad ruins. These white birds sport a pink recurved bill that sucks up crustaceans like a soda straw. The white ibises are common and can be seen feeding in the wild, on golf courses, and even in your backyard.

From the launch, head left and follow the shoreline looking for the sizable opening that gets you into the protected ruins areas. One of the first things you will notice is that some of these old pilings have a crocodile-like sil-

Darya Key, in the Barracuda Keys, has vibrant, sandy channels to snorkel through.

houette. Keep a sharp eye out though, because these reptiles have been spotted here.

Winding your way through these backwaters you can really see how fast mangroves can take over, as these little islands of mangrove in the middle were fill piles topped with rail tracks in the 1930s. Less than 0.5 mile through this section you will notice a switchback on your right. This switchback is the route out of and into Blackwater Sound, where you will paddle west for 0.5 mile to reach Blackwater Pass. The red mangrove shore here will have snook, redfish, and blue crabs all eking out an existence in the ocean. As you go through the pass there will be some deep water on the right that has a bundle of baitfish feeding on the plankton that gets carried through the pass. Heading north you will see a small island on the far side of Little Blackwater Sound. This island is a good rookery and has a tidal station on the north side. From here it is a short trip east to the launch at Mile Marker 111.

37. *Short Key*

Charts:
   Standard Mapping Services Aerial Photo Map #F109
   Top Spot Upper Keys and Florida Bay #207
   NOAA Chart #11463
   South Dade Marina custom canoe trail map

Launch: Launch #61 is on the side of the road, but it is a good alternative when launch #62 (South Dade Marina) is closed on Tuesdays and Wednesdays.

Habitats: These habitats are at the edge of the Everglades, and this is the zone where the fresh waters mix with the ocean. Turtle grass, mangroves, and sponge flats are interspersed throughout the area.

Trip Length: This one is about 4 nautical miles round trip if you have good weather and take the open water route. The protected route adds 1.2 nautical miles, making for a 7-mile round trip.

Tides and Currents: In moderate winds, the open bay can be a challenge. There are moderate currents as well, and the low tides can mean some struggling.

Paddling Conditions: The protected route has little boat traffic, while the canal and open water areas have considerable traffic on weekends.

Featured Creatures: Redfish love these shallow muddy back bays, and one morning when it was glass calm there was a school of them that fed so vigorously that it seemed to be a pod of dolphin. The redfish net ban has been one of the major success stories in fisheries conservation. Brought to the brink of collapse during the blackened redfish culinary craze in the 1980s, these fish were harvested by the ton. They were fished during the breeding months, when they congregate en masse, and hardly any escaped the netting. Now they are a recreational fish only in Florida, with strict size limits and fishing seasons.

A can of sardines for Thanksgiving dinner was all I had to share with the thousands of unwanted guests at my tent screen. The mosquitoes had chased me inside, and all I desired was a good night's rest. Earplugs helped me obtain this because, apart from the bites, the whine of a thousand

Fossil remains of horseshoe crab date back 360 million years.

mosquitoes is intolerable. In the summer there are a lot of insects on this route, so be prepared.

The South Dade Marina is a great location to launch from, and you will paddle about 0.75 nautical mile before you reach the open waters of Glades Cove. The protected portion of the trail is in a northerly direction 0.25 nautical mile away. As you approach the shoreline you will see marker #1. This leads you through a great little creek, and at marker #2 you will have entered Ellis Lake. The next marker is behind the mangrove island in front of you, and from #3 you will head southwest toward #4. This jogs to the right around a little island, where you come out with Jim Smith Creek on your right and marker 5 on your left. If you follow Jim Smith Creek out to the point, there is a fine little sand beach to stretch your legs on. Continuing east and then north through Krome Lake will lead you to markers #6 and #7, which mark the cut into Halfway Pond. The next markers, #9 & #10, lead you into Brookshire Pond. Paddling due south will bring you to the open water leg to Short Key. Paddling around inside Brookshire Pond will give you great encounters with redfish, black drum, and plenty of bird life. These muddy bottoms are the rich estuaries needed for the marine food chain to exist.

From Brookshire Lake to the cut on the north side of Short Key is 0.6 mile. Passing through the cut, you can hug the shore and beach anywhere it looks inviting. If you have an east wind and are up for the crossing you can shorten the trip back by heading west 260 degrees to Flat Point at Glades Cove. This will save about 1 mile and will take full advantage of the winds.

There are two smaller branches to this area that are good to explore if you have the time. The northern branch brings you into a wild mangrove creek that offers good fishing. The southern branch has a rocky beach at Pine Point and access to Sarge Lake via Sarge Creek. Sarge Lake has a soft mud bottom that redfish love, and this lake is also easy to access from launch #60.

The Backcountry Islands and Beyond Paddling Tours

Ten-nautical-mile trips out over the backcountry waters of the Keys will definitely challenge you. Most of the following trips are 10 nautical miles or more, and as discussed before a nautical mile is 6,000 feet vs. the 5,280 feet of a statute mile. Although this will not mean a big difference with the shorter trips, it will add considerably to these backcountry trips.

These longer trips take careful preparation and planning. You will want to make sure you are up to the rigors of an open water crossing, where the wind can actually wear you down and cause you to lose ground every time you stop to consult a chart.

Touring boats with a long waterline and a rudder will allow you to make an energy-efficient journey. Smaller boats, canoe-like doubles and flat-bottomed craft are not efficient vessels for these extended journeys.

The routes here are briefly described and outlined, but your preparation should be thorough. A complete checklist of essential items to carry along is in the chapter on orientation.

38. *Content Keys*

Charts:
> Standard Mapping Services Aerial Photo Map #F103
> TOPSPOT Middle Keys Area #N208
> NOAA chart #11448

Launch: Launch #27 is at the end of Big Torch Key.

Habitats: This trip takes you through miles of shallow backcountry waters rarely traversed by others. Grass and sponge flats dominate the transit portion of the trip, and sandy mangrove creeks lace the interiors of these islands.

Trip Length: This trip covers 10 nautical miles, and several additional miles if you want to explore the many creeks.

Tides and Currents: The proximity of these islands to the deeper waters of Florida Bay and the Gulf increases the volume of tidal waters that flow over the shallows. Currents can be strong, and low tides may induce you to take a less direct route to your particular

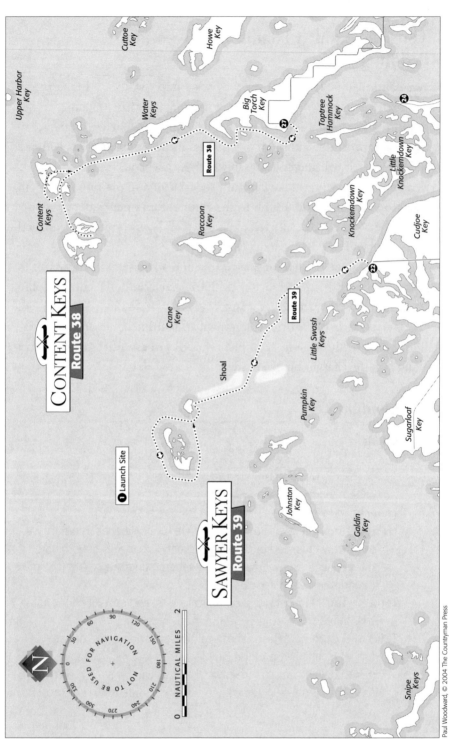

CONTENT KEYS
Route 38

SAWYER KEYS
Route 39

❶ Launch Site

NAUTICAL MILES

Cuttoe Key

Upper Harbor Key

Howe Key

Water Keys

Big Torch Key

Toptree Hammock Key

Content Keys

Route 38

Raccoon Key

Little Knockemdown Key

Knockemdown Key

Cudjoe Key

Crane Key

Route 39

Shoal

Little Swash Keys

Pumpkin Key

Sugarloaf Key

Johnston Key

Galdin Key

Snipe Keys

NOT TO BE USED FOR NAVIGATION

N

30 60 90 120 150 180 210 240 270 300 330

Paul Woodward, © 2004 The Countryman Press

destination. There is always enough water in the passages between the islands to journey home.

Paddling Conditions: All backcountry trips require planning, good supplies and safety equipment, and the stamina for a full-day trip.

The little beach on the inside passage of West Content Key is located at 24°47.399 N, 81°29.071 W and will make a nice destination for this trip. The creeks in these islands are numerous, and almost all have wonderful sand bottoms. Sharks, spotted eagle rays, tarpon, and scores of baitfish make these creeks come alive with shadows and splashes. Roseate spoonbills are commonly seen in the east cluster of islands, and the rocky ridge that parallels the north shore has all kinds of marine creatures entrenched in the wave-washed rock. One of the more unique aspects of this out island paradise is the soft sounds of crashing surf heard on the north shore. There are not many places to hear the surf (albeit miniature) in the Keys, but this is one.

39. *Sawyer Keys*

Charts:
> Standard Mapping Services Aerial Photo Map #F103
> Top Spot Middle Keys Area #N208
> NOAA chart #11448

Launch: Use launch #22 on Cudjoe Key at the blimp base.

Habitats: Most of this route runs along the deep waters of Cudjoe Channel, which is flanked by grass flats and coral-studded rocky shallows. The islands themselves are mostly red mangroves with a rocky shore on the north. There is a small patch of sandy beach on the northeast section of the island.

Trip Length: This is a 10-nautical-mile round trip in open water conditions. Tarpon Belly Keys can provide a good halfway stopping point or an alternative destination if the first portion of the trip wears you down.

Tides and Currents: Cudjoe Channel can have some of the strongest currents in this area, but you can avoid most of it by limiting your time in the deepest sections of the channel.

Paddling Conditions: All backcountry trips require planning, good supplies and safety equipment, and the stamina for a full-day trip.

Grunts and smaller baitfish swarm the shallow seas.

The Tarpon Belly Keys are home to an abandoned shrimp hatchery that was started in 1967 and relocated the same year. There are two dredged canals that cut through the island, and the spoil banks from this dredging make for some high and dry land. Many locals use this area for picnicking, and it has a rocky beach on the western shore at GPS coordinates N 24°43.636, W 81°31.140. The island stands out from the rest nearby because of the Australian pine trees that give it a forested look. Riding Key is at the southernmost point of the Sawyer Key complex, at GPS coordinates N 24°45.059, W 81°33.056. This set of mangrove islands has some interior creeks that are closed to all boating. This was enacted to give the nesting birds a sanctuary where human disturbance could be kept to a minimum. The perimeter of Sawyer Key has some of the more unique habitats you will encounter in these islands. As you progress counterclockwise, you will pass the rocky shorelines that are adjacent to the Cudjoe Channel outflow. These shores have some great tide pools and offer good scouting perches for ospreys and eagles. Traveling on the north shore, you will encounter the sandy shorelines that give way to the tidal creeks that feed the interior bays of the island. At one time there were several small homes on Sawyer Key, and the posts that were to become a dock still stand guard at the ocean's edge. Continuing to the western shore you will encounter smooth sand and rock tidal flats that are home to sharks, rays, and migrating tarpon that feed with the tidal currents that wash over this bright bottom. As you round the southwest edge there will be a few small, mangrove-lined creeks that usually harbor barracuda and mangrove snappers. You should be able to see Riding Key and far to the south the tethered weather balloons of Cudjoe Key. Meandering toward Riding Key, keep searching the flats for tailing bonefish, permit, and the baby bonnethead sharks that frequent this flat. From the southern tip of Riding Key it is about a 4.5-nautical-mile journey home. If the current is with you, travel on the Cudjoe Channel side of the flat. If not, travel on the west side of the flat.

40. *Barracuda Keys*

Charts:
  Standard Mapping Services Aerial Photo Map #104
  TOPSPOT Middle Keys Area #N208
  NOAA Chart #11447
Launch: Use launch #16, Sugarloaf Marina.
Habitats: Outer islands that number in the high teens with sand-scoured channels sum up the Barracuda Keys. The grass flats are rich and extensive, and the bird life is diverse.
Trip Length: This is an 11-nautical-mile round trip from Sugarloaf Key Marina.
Tides and Currents: Currents can be strong in these constricted channels.
Paddling Conditions: All backcountry trips require planning, good supplies and safety equipment, and the stamina for a full-day trip.

Use GPS coordinates N 24°43.106, W 81°36.797 for the creek inside the largest island in the easternmost cluster of the Barracuda Keys. The trip is made a bit less tiresome if you take the opportunity to island-hop from Bill Finds Key to Marjoe Key to a major rest at Galdin Key. Galdin Key has a nice undercut edge on the northernmost of this cluster of islands. From

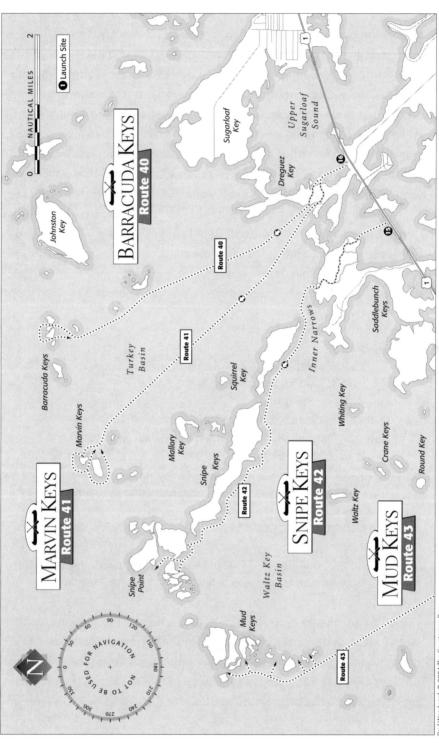

NAUTICAL MILES

0   2

1 Launch Site

BARRACUDA KEYS
Route 40

MARVIN KEYS
Route 41

SNIPE KEYS
Route 42

MUD KEYS
Route 43

Route 40

Route 41

Route 42

Route 43

Johnston Key

Barracuda Keys

Marvin Keys

Turkey Basin

Mallory Key

Snipe Keys

Squirrel Key

Snipe Point

Waltz Key Basin

Mud Keys

Waltz Key

Whiting Key

Inner Narrows

Crane Keys

Round Key

Saddlebunch Keys

Dreguez Key

Sugarloaf Key

Upper Sugarloaf Sound

16

15

1

1

N

NOT TO BE USED FOR NAVIGATION

30 60 90 120 150 180 210 240 270 300 330

Paul Woodward, © 2004 The Countryman Press

Galdin Key you can break behind Pigeon Key and look for bald eagles. Northeast of Pigeon Key by about 0.7 nautical mile is a small island that looks like a boomerang on the chart. This island marks the entry to your explorations in the Barracuda Keys.

41. *Marvin Keys*

Charts:
> Standard Mapping Services Aerial Photo Map #104
> TOPSPOT Middle Keys Area #N208
> NOAA Chart #11447

Launch: Use launch #16, Sugarloaf Marina.

Habitats: Lots of exposed sand flats and good motorboating access make this area the people's playground. Volleyball nets, cookouts, family pets, and scores of beached boats overrun this area on the weekends. Weekdays provide a transition to the remarkable wilderness that it can be.

Trip Length: This is a 12-mile round trip from Sugarloaf Marina

Tides and Currents: Backcountry channels can have strong currents. There is always water enough to float a kayak.

Paddling Conditions: All backcountry trips require planning, good supplies and safety equipment, and the stamina for a full-day trip.

The cone marker south of Marvin at GPS coordinates N 24°42.366, W 81°37.841 marks the entrance to a deep channel that runs right into the beach. The beach at Marvin Keys is at 24°42.690 N, 81°28.764 W and has a perfect sunrise view. This island complex is enchanting to circumnavigate, and the sand flats at high tide hold schools of sleeping bonefish.

42. *Snipe Keys*

Charts:
> Standard Mapping Services Aerial Photo Map #104
> Top Spot Middle Keys Area #N208
> NOAA Chart #11447

Launch: Use launch #15, at Mile Marker 16.

Habitats: The Snipe Keys are the most extensive and convoluted of all

Marvin Key sand flats are a spectacular spot for shorebirds at low tide.

of the backcountry mangrove clusters. It was because of their primitive nature that some of the BBC's *Walking With Dinosaurs* televison special was filmed here. The creeks here are so complex and contorted that you could easily be confused in this amazing maze.

Trip Length: It is a 10-nautical-mile round trip from the north end of Five Mile Creek. An additional 3 nautical miles should be added for the round trip through Five Mile Creek.

Tides and Currents: Considerable currents can sweep through Five Mile Creek. The creeks in the interior of the Snipe Keys can also be strong.

Paddling Conditions: All backcountry trips require planning, good supplies and safety equipment, and the stamina for a full-day trip.

The wonderful sandbanks the Snipe Keys are known for are located just off the main channel at N 24° 41.626 N, 81°40.404 W. There are usually quite a few boats in this area. With a kayak and all the adjacent no-motor-zone channels, you can easily find your own little piece of private beach.

43. *Mud Keys*

Charts:
> Standard Mapping Services Aerial Photo Map #104
> Top Spot Middle Keys Area #N208 and #N209
> NOAA Chart #11447

Launch: Use launch #9 at Big Coppitt Key.

Habitats: Most of these mangrove channels run from east to west and provide some sandbank interiors to idle in. The extensive flats on · the western side are full of sea cucumbers and scattered grass. Several of the smaller tidal creeks are closed to all boats.

Trip Length: It is a 9-nautical-mile round trip from the Big Coppitt launch.

Tides and Currents: At low tides the western side of this island complex is primarily damp sand. The currents in the channels are moderately strong.

Paddling Conditions: All backcountry trips require planning, good supplies and safety equipment, and the stamina for a full-day trip.

The central creek of the Mud Keys is at GPS coordinates N 24°40.376, W 81°41.503. The best beach is at the terminus of this central creek. This trip is best accomplished by island hopping. From Big Coppitt to the west end of Duck Key is about 2 nautical miles. Traveling from Duck Key to Fish Hawk Key is about 1.5 nautical miles. Fish Hawk Key has some great narrow tidal creeks to get in out of the sun and take a break. From the western side of Fish Hawk it is a short 1.6 nautical miles to the southernmost of the Mud Keys. To plan your navigation at this point, take into account the wind direction so you can have the best possible lee shore on all these little island clusters.

44. *Lower Harbor Keys*

Charts:
> Standard Mapping Services Aerial Photo Map #104
> TOPSPOT Middle Keys Area #N208 and #N209
> NOAA Chart #11447

Launch: The most direct route is from launch #5 at the Florida Keys

A nurse shark rests on the North Little Pine Key sponge flat.

Community College. An alternate route that is more protected and allows island hopping can be taken from Boca Chica Key at launch #8. This route will add 2 nautical miles, but provides rest stops that offer protection from the winds.

Habitats: This is typical backcountry with idyllic, twisty creeks running through emerald islands. The shallow sandy seas all expose themselves at low tide so you may beachcomb for egg cases, cast-off shells, and other marine treasures.

Trip Length: The round trip is 9 nautical miles from launch #8 on Boca Chica Key.

Tides and Currents: Low tides produce extensive sand flats, and the tides coming in from the Gulf can be strong in the channels.

Paddling Conditions: All backcountry trips require planning, good supplies and safety equipment, and the stamina for a full-day trip.

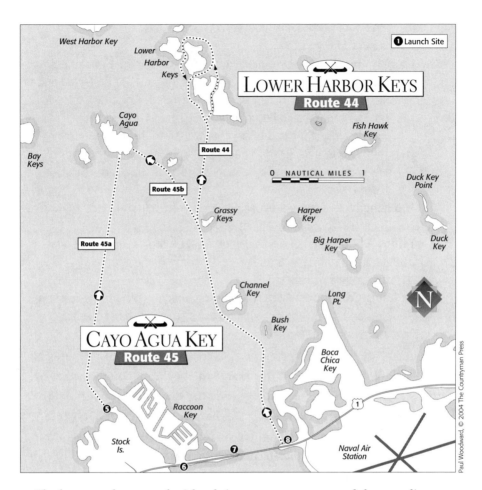

The large gap between the islands is a no-motor zone and the coordinates for this section of the Lower Harbor Keys are 24°30.610 N, 81°43.797 W. There are few motorboats in this area due to the shallow seas. The boaters you do encounter will probably be bonefish guides, who stalk the flats silently from the poling platforms on their high-tech boats. They will add to the surreal auditory nothingness your ears will encounter in this unique backcountry environment.

45. *Cayo Agua Key*

Charts:
   Standard Mapping Services Aerial Photo Map #104

Top Spot Middle Keys Area #N208 and #N209
NOAA Chart #11447

Launch: The most direct route is from launch #5 at the Florida Keys Community College. An alternate route that is more protected and allows island hopping can be taken from Boca Chica Key at launch #8. This route would be an additional 2 nautical miles, but provides rest stops that offer protection from the winds.

Habitats: This is an isolated mangrove island that has skinny-water flats surrounding it and a network of deep channels that crisscross the island.

Trip Length: This trip is 6 nautical miles in length from launch #5 and 8 nautical miles from launch #8.

Tides and Currents: Currents can be swift on the interior of the tidal creeks, and the low tides can make some of the southern approaches difficult.

Paddling Conditions: All backcountry trips require planning, good supplies and safety equipment, and the stamina for a full-day trip.

The southeast tip of Cayo Agua Key is located at GPS coordinates N 24°37.829, W 81°44.539, and this marks the beginning of a world away from Key West. The deep channels inside the island are wonderful. Protected from the outside elements, these channels offer a great opportunity to snorkel and explore many hidden mangrove passes. The trees appear old and gnarled here, weather-beaten sentinels left on the outskirts of the major island chain.

The flats that surround the island are mostly exposed white sand beaches at low tide and provide you with temporary real estate where you can park it for a while. Tailing bones and the dorsal fins of sharks cruise on these bright-bottomed flats. You may share your bit of beach with shorebirds or gulls that also know where a good rest stop can be found.

46. *Dry Tortugas National Park*

Charts:
One of the best charts for this trip is the brochure distributed by the National Park Service.

Launch: From Key West there are several concessions that will ferry you and your kayak to the Dry Tortugas about 70 miles west of Key West. Sunny Days Catamarans offers transportation to the park for about $100 plus an additional fee for camping gear and kayak transport. Call them at 305-292-6100. Overnight camping is at a temporary hold in 2003 because of infrastructure problems, which should be brought up to date soon. Call the park for current information at 305-242-7700 or visit the park's web site at www.nps.gov/drto.

Habitats: President Franklin D. Roosevelt set these islands and the surrounding waters aside in 1935 as a national monument. In 1992 it was designated as a National Park, and 100 square miles of ocean and islands were brought under the protection of the National Park Service and The Florida Keys National Marine Sanctuary. The central core of this park consists of seven coral rubble isles. Three are accessible by kayak from the main island of Garden Key, where Fort Jefferson is located. Sandy beaches, grass flats, and coral reefs are all within a short paddling distance.

Trip Length: Garden Key, Bush Key, and Long Key comprise a 2-nautical-mile circumnavigation. Loggerhead Key is due east from Fort Jefferson, and makes for a 5-nautical-mile round trip.

Tides and Currents: The return trip from Loggerhead Key is usually upwind, and the winds are stronger in the afternoon. Kayak decks can easily be washed with waves in the deeper areas of the channel.

Paddling Conditions: The snorkeling, bird watching, and quiet solitude of these outermost islands are enhanced by the excellent paddling conditions found close by at Bush and Long Keys. Loggerhead Key is an open water journey, but the isolated sandy beach and corals growing within a stone's throw of the shoreline make it worth the trip.

The birds that nest here are numerous and unique. Frigate birds, sooty terns, and noddy terns have their peak nesting season in the months of

DRY TORTUGAS NATIONAL PARK
Route 46

Gulf of Mexico

Loggerhead Key

Bush Key

Long Key

Fort Jefferson

Garden Key

Bird Key Bank

Straits of Florida

N

NOT TO BE USED FOR NAVIGATION

0 30 60 90 120 150 180 210 240 270 300 330

NAUTICAL MILES

0   1

March and April. Estimates of the number of birds using this area for nesting run as high as 100,000. The nearby islands of Bush Key and Long Key are closed from February through the middle of summer, or until the nesting activity has ceased.

47. *Key Biscayne National Park*

Charts:
Standard Mapping Services Aerial Photo Map #F109
TOPSPOT Upper Keys and Florida Bay #207
NOAA Chart #11463 and Chart #11451
Launch: Use launch #63 if taking the park ferry, or launch #64 if taking your own motorboat with kayaks.
Habitats: This trip takes you through miles of wilderness that encompass coral reefs, protected bays, and tidal creeks.
Trip Length: From the campground on Elliot Key you can paddle north 4 nautical miles to reach Boca Chica Key or south 4 nautical miles to reach Adams Key on Caesar Creek, the jumping-off spot for exploring the shallow protected bay and creeks of Jones Lagoon on Old Rhodes Key.
Tides and Currents: Currents can run strong through Caesar Creek, but it is a short distance to travel across its width.
Paddling Conditions: The conditions on this trip are protected in all but the north winds. This area is in close proximity to Miami, and this means lots of recreational motorboat activity, especially on weekends. Use the kayak to its best advantage by staying in the skinny nearshore waters and shallow protected bays of Jones Lagoon, where there will be minimal motorized traffic.
Featured Creatures: Schuas swallowtail butterfly has its stronghold on these islands in the northernmost keys. This is primarily due to the fact that there has been little done in the way of mosquito control on the islands over the years. This rare butterfly and many other insects are some of the innocent bystanders that are exterminated along with mosquitoes when insecticide that is not species-specific is used for mosquito eradication. On the other side of the coin is the fact that the mosquitoes can be thick on these islands, and the summers are particularly unbearable because the quantity of the blood-sucking critters is extremely high.

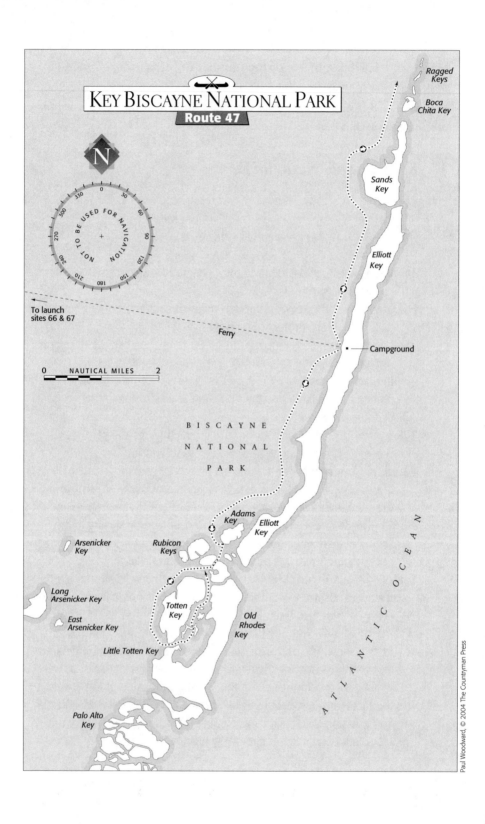

KEY BISCAYNE NATIONAL PARK
Route 47

N

NOT TO BE USED FOR NAVIGATION

0
30
60
90
120
150
180
210
240
270
300
330

To launch
sites 66 & 67

Ferry

0 NAUTICAL MILES 2

BISCAYNE

NATIONAL

PARK

Ragged
Keys

Boca
Chita Key

Sands
Key

Elliott
Key

Campground

Adams
Key

Elliott
Key

Arsenicker
Key

Rubicon
Keys

Long
Arsenicker Key

Totten
Key

Old
Rhodes
Key

East
Arsenicker Key

Little Totten Key

Palo Alto
Key

ATLANTIC OCEAN

Paul Woodward, © 2004 The Countryman Press

Lighthouses like this one at American Shoals were built in the late 1800s.

Biscayne National Park is the largest marine park in the United States. It is comprised of shallow bays, oceanside reefs, and a stretch of islands that add up to about 182,000 acres in size. The island portions outlined in the trip consist of a stretch of islands some 12 miles in length and about 8 miles offshore from the launch site. If you are a strong paddler, you can elect to travel the 8 nautical miles from the mainland to Elliot Key. If not, you have the option of the ferry, which runs from November through May, and will portage you and your kayak across. The cost is about $40 for you and the kayak, but this is well worth the money, as the paddle across cuts into time better spent exploring the nearshore waters of the park. Biscayne National Underwater Park, Inc. runs the ferry concession and recommends reservations. Contact them at 305-230-1100.

Appendices

I. Parks, Preserves, and Refuges

Florida Keys National Marine Sanctuary
Upper Keys office: 305-852-7717
Middle Keys office: 305-743-2437
Key West office: 305-292-0311

Florida Keys National Wildlife Refuges
Visitor Center: 305-872-0774 (Includes Crocodile Lakes National
Wildlife Refuge, Great White Heron National Wildlife Refuge, National
Key Deer Refuge, and Key West National Wildlife Refuge.)

Florida State Lands
Biscayne Bay/Card Sound Aquatic Preserve: 305-372-6583
Key Largo Hammocks Botanical State Park: 305-451-1202
John Pennekamp Coral Reef State Park: 305-451-1202
Windley Key Fossil Reef Geological State Park: 305-664-2540
Lignumvitae Key Botanical State Park: 305-664-2540
Indian Key Historic State Park: 305-664-2540
San Pedro Underwater Archaeological Preserve State Park: 305-664-2540
Long Key State Park: 305-664-4815
Curry Hammock State Park: 305-664-4815
Bahia Honda State Park: 305-872-2353
Coupon Bight Aquatic Preserve: 305-292-0311
Fort Zachary Taylor State Park: 305-292-6713

National Parks
Dry Tortugas National Park
P.O. Box 6208
Key West, FL 33041 www.nps.gov/drto

Key Biscayne National Park
9700 SW 328th Street
Homestead, FL 33033 www.nps.gov/bisc

Everglades National Park
305-242-7700
www.nps.gov/ever

II. Outfitters and Guides

Florida Bay Outfitters, MM 104, 305-451-3018
Frank and Monica have put together the most complete selection of
gear, boats, and other stuff you need while on the water. This place reminds me of the early days of L.L. Bean when I was traveling to and
from Maine. I hardly ever pass the store without stopping in to buy
something or catch up on the wildlife and kayak events. They also
offer guided tours and rentals.

Florida Keys Kayak and Sail, MM 77.5, 305-664-4878
Located at Robbies Marina, which is famous for its resident herd of
watchable tarpon, this establishment offers tours and rentals with excellent access to Lignumvitae Key and Indian Key State Parks.

Marathon Kayak Resource, MM 50, 305-743-0561
Located at Sombrero Resort in Marathon, this location offers great access to the Boot Key area of Marathon. Rentals and tours available.

Big Pine Kayak Adventures, MM 30, 877-595-2925 or
305-872-7474; www.keyskayaktours.com
Captain Bill Keogh offers daily trips to the Great White Heron and
Key Deer National Wildlife Refuges by kayak, charter boat, or a

combination of the two. Rentals, tours, and custom charters available. Trips are offered throughout the Middle and Lower Keys, and boats are available at Parmers Place (305-872-2157) and The Old Wooden Bridge Fishing Camp (305-872-2241).

Scarlet Ibis Tours, MM 21, 305-872-0032
Captain Markus conducts kayak tours from the Cudjoe Gardens Marina and offers trips to the Cudjoe Key area. Rentals and tours available.

Mosquito Coast Kayak Tours, MM 0, 305-294-7178
One of the first to offer trips in Key West. They run daily kayak trips from the Key West area.

Raft Voyageurs, 305-743-0887
Offers multiday adventures aboard their custom-built catamarans. They are able to explore and really soak up the tranquility of the Florida Keys backcountry and the Everglades. State-of-the-art equipment and a knowledgeable crew make your adventure unique.

Potomac Paddle Sports, 1-877-KAYAKH2O
Offers weeklong land-based excursions to the Florida Keys. ACA-certified instructors and local naturalist-guides introduce participants to the best the Keys have to offer in terms of accommodations, dining, sightseeing, and nature trekking.

III. Clubs, Groups, and Organizations

Paradise Paddlers
PO Box 1657
Key Largo, Florida 33037
This is the Florida Keys canoe and kayak club dedicated to education, environment, and paddling fun. Monica from Florida Bay Outfitters is the chairperson and produces the informative newsletter.

The Nature Conservancy, Florida Keys Office: 305-745-8402

The Ocean Conservancy, Florida Keys Office: 305-295-3370

World Wildlife Fund, Florida Keys Office: 305-289-1010

Reef Relief, Key West: 305-294-3100

Friends and Volunteers of the Refuges: 305-872-0645

Florida Keys Wild Bird Center (rehabilitation of sick and injured birds): 305-852-4486

IV. Suggested Reading

Alden, Peter. *National Audubon Society Guide to Florida.* New York: Alfred Knopf, 1998.

Brookfield, Charles M. and Griswold, Oliver. *They All Called It Tropical: True Tales of the Romantic Everglades, Cape Sable, and the Florida Keys.* Miami, Florida: Historical Association of Southern Florida, 1985.

Brothers, Betty. *Wreckers and Workers of Old Key West.* Big Pine Key, Florida: Betty Brothers, 1985.

Day, John A., and Vincent J. Schaefer. *Peterson First Guide to Clouds and Weather.* Boston: Houghton Mifflin, 1991.

Dunaway, Vic. *Sport Fish of Florida.* Miami: Wickstrom Publishers, 1998.

Gallagher, Dan, ed. *The Florida Keys Environmental Story.* Big Pine Key, Florida: Seacamp Association, 1997.

Gilpin, Vincent. *Cruise of the Seminole Among the Florida Keys.* Homestead, Florida: Florida National Parks & Monuments Association, 1905.

Glassberg, Jeffrey. *Butterflies Through Binoculars: The East.* New York: Oxford University Press, 1999.

Humann, Paul, and Ned DeLoach. *Reef Creature Identification, Florida, Caribbean, Bahamas.* Jacksonville, Florida: New World Publications, 2002.
(One of a must-have trilogy of reef dweller books. A little light on the shallow bay creatures but fully comprehensive on the reef creatures.)

Humann, Paul, and Ned DeLoach. *Snorkeling Guide to Marine Life, Florida, Caribbean, Bahamas.* Jacksonville, Florida: New World Publications, 1995.

Humann, Paul, and Ned DeLoach. *Reef Coral Identification, Florida, Caribbean, Bahamas.* Jacksonville, Florida: New World Publications, 2002.

Humann, Paul, and Ned DeLoach. *Reef Fish Identification, Florida, Caribbean, Bahamas.* Jacksonville, Florida: New World Publications, Inc., 2002.

Kale, H. W., and D. S. Maehr. *Florida's Birds.* Sarasota, Florida: Pineapple Press, 1990.
(A comprehensive bird guide with seasonal occurrences, species description, and habitat on one page and a narrative of life history in a reference section.)

Kaplan, Eugene H. *Peterson Guide to Southeastern and Caribbean Seashores.* Boston: Houghton Mifflin, 1988.

Lazell, James D. *Wildlife of the Florida Keys: A Natural History.* Washington, D.C.: Island Press, 1989.
(This book covers many of the creatures that can be found in the Florida Keys in a scientific and informative way. It is a bit heavy on the scientific side, but has some great natural history facts.)

Littler, Diane Scullion. *Marine Plants of the Caribbean.* Shrewsbury, England: Airlife Publishing, 1989.

Meinkoth, Norman A. *National Audubon Society Field Guide to North American Seashore Creatures.* New York: Alfred A. Knopf, 2002.

Munroe, Ralph, and Vincent Gilpin. *The Commodore's Story.* Miami: Historical Association of Southern Florida, 1990.

Pasachoff, Jay M. *Peterson First Guide to Astronomy.* Boston: Houghton Mifflin, 1988.

Patton, Kathleen. *Kayaking the Keys: 50 Great Adventures in Florida's Southernmost Archipelago.* Gainesville, Florida: University Press of Florida, 2002.

Ripple, Jeff. *Sea Turtles.* Stillwater, Minnesota: Voyageur Press, 1996.

Ripple, Jeff. *The Florida Keys: The Natural Wonders of an Island Paradise.* Stillwater, Minnesota: Voyageur Press, 1995.

Robins, R. C., and C. C. Ray. *A Field Guide to Atlantic Coast Fishes of North America.* Boston: Houghton Mifflin, 1986.

Scurlock, Paul J. *Native Trees and Shrubs of the Florida Keys.* Lower Sugarloaf Key, Florida: Laurel & Herbert, 1996.

Sibley, David Allen. *National Audubon Society, The Sibley Guide to Birds.* New York: Alfred A. Knopf, 2000.

Stevenson, George B. *Key Guide to Key West and the Florida Keys.* 1970. Privately published.

Voss, Gilbert L. *Seashore Life of Florida and the Caribbean.* Miami: Banyan Books, 1976.

Wachob, Bruce. *Sea Kayaking in the Florida Keys.* Sarasota, Florida: Pineapple Press, 1997.
(Great book with natural history chapters and 13 detailed trips in the Lower Keys.)

V. Bird List

This bird list is adapted from U.S. Fish and Wildlife Service publication #RF-41580, published in 1994. It was produced with the expertise of Marge Brown, Wayne Hoffman, and the staff of the Florida Keys National Wildlife Refuges.

KEY

SP Spring: March, April, and May
S Summer: June, July, and August
F Fall: September, October, and November
W Winter: December, January, and February

C Common
U Uncommon
r rare
O Occasional, sighted fewer than 10 times
* Confirmed breeding in area

Tropical Audubon Bird Hotline: 305-667-PEEP
Key West Bird Hotline: 305-294-3438

	SP	S	F	W
Loons				
Red-throated loon	O		O	O
Common loon	U		U	U
Grebes				
Least grebe			O	
Pied-billed grebe*	U	U	U	U
Horned grebe	O			O
Shearwaters and Petrels				
Greater shearwater		O		
Sooty shearwater	O			O
Audubon's shearwater			O	O
Wilson's storm-petrel		O		
Band-rumpled storm petrel (*Key West specimen*)			O	
Tropicbirds				
White-tailed tropicbird	O			
Boobies and Gannets				
Masked booby	O		O	O
Brown booby	r	r	r	r
Northern gannet	r		r	U
Pelicans				
American white pelican		r	r	r
Brown pelican	C	C	C	C
Darters and Cormorants				
Double-crested cormorant*	C	C	C	C
Anhinga	U	r	U	U
Frigatebirds				
Magnificent frigate bird	C	C	C	C
Bitterns, Herons, Egrets, and Their Allies				
American bittern	O			
Least bittern*	r	r	r	r
Great blue heron (dk morph)*	C	C	C	C

	SP	S	F	W
Great blue heron (lt morph)*	C	C	C	C
Great egret*	C	C	C	C
Snowy egret*	U	U	U	U
Little blue heron*	U	U	U	U
Tricolored heron*	C	U	C	U
Reddish egret*	C	C	C	C
Cattle egret	C	C	C	C
Green-backed heron*	C	C	C	C
Black-crowned night heron	r		r	r
Yellow-crowned night heron*	C	C	C	C

Ibises and Spoonbills

	SP	S	F	W
White ibis*	C	C	C	C
Glossy ibis	O	O	O	O
Roseate spoonbill	U	U	r	r

Storks

	SP	S	F	W
Wood stork			O	O

Flamingos

	SP	S	F	W
Greater flamingo	O		O	O

Ducks, Geese, Swans

	SP	S	F	W
Fulvous whistling duck	O		O	O
Canada goose				O
Snow goose			O	O
Wood duck			O	
Green-winged teal	r		r	r
White-cheeked pintail	O			O
Northern pintail	U		U	U
Blue-winged teal	C		C	C
Northern shoveler	U		U	U
Gadwall				O
American wigeon	C		C	C
Ring-necked duck	U		U	U
Lesser scaup	U		U	U
Oldsquaw			O	
Black scoter			O	O
Hooded merganser				O

	SP	S	F	W
Common merganser			O	O
Red-breasted merganser	U	r	C	C
Masked duck	O			

Vultures

	SP	S	F	W
Black vulture		O	O	O
Turkey vulture*	C	C	C	C

Ospreys, Kites, Eagles, and Harriers

	SP	S	F	W
Osprey*	C	C	C	C
Swallow-tailed kite	r	r	r	r
Mississippi kite			O	O
Bald eagle*	U	U	U	U
Northern harrier	U		U	U
Sharp-shinned hawk	C		C	C
Cooper's hawk	r		r	r
Red-shouldered hawk*	U	U	U	U
Broad-winged hawk	C		C	C
Short-tailed hawk	r		C	r
Swainson's hawk	r		C	r
Red-tailed hawk	r		r	r

Falcons

	SP	S	F	W
American kestrel	C		C	C
Merlin	U		C	U
Peregrine falcon	U		C	U

Rails, Gallinules, Coots

	SP	S	F	W
Black rail	U	U	U	U
Clapper rail*	U	U	U	U
Virginia rail	O		O	O
Sora rail	r		r	r
Purple gallinule*	r	r	r	r
Common moorhen*	U	U	U	U
American coot*	C	r	C	C

Limpkins

	SP	S	F	W
Limpkin	O	O	O	O

	SP	S	F	W
Plovers				
Black-bellied plover	C	U	C	C
Lesser golden plover	r		r	r
Snowy plover	O			O
Wilson's plover*	C	C	C	C
Semipalmated plover	C		C	C
Piping plover	r		r	r
Killdeer*	U	r	U	U
Mountain plover				O
Oystercatchers				
American oystercatcher	O		O	
Stilts and Avocets				
Black-necked stilt*	U	U	U	
American avocet	O		O	O
Sandpipers and Phalaropes				
Greater yellowlegs	U		U	U
Lesser yellowlegs	U		U	U
Solitary sandpiper	U		r	
Willet*	C		C	C
Spotted sandpiper	U		U	U
Upland sandpiper	r		r	
Whimbrel	r		r	C
Ruddy turnstone	C	U	C	C
Red knot	U	r	U	U
Sanderling	C	r	C	C
Semipalmated sandpiper	r	r	r	r
Western sandpiper	C	r	C	C
Least sandpiper	C	r	C	C
White-rumped sandpiper	U			
Pectoral sandpiper	r	r	r	
Purple sandpiper				r
Dunlin	U		C	U
Stilt sandpiper	r		r	r
Short-billed dowitcher	C	U	C	C
Common snipe			r	r

	SP	S	F	W
Wilson's phalarope	O		O	O
Red-necked phalarope			O	

Jaegers, Gulls, Terns, and Skimmers

	SP	S	F	W
Pomarine jaeger	O		O	O
Parasitic jaeger	O		O	O
Laughing gull*	C	C	C	C
Bonaparte's gull	r		r	r
Ringed-billed gull	C	r	C	C
Herring gull	U	r	C	C
Lesser black-backed gull			r	r
Great black-backed gull	r		r	r
Black-legged kittiwake (specimen)				O
Gull-billed tern	O			
Caspian tern	U		U	C
Royal tern	C	C	C	C
Roseate tern*		U		
Sandwich tern*	C		C	C
Common tern	U		U	U
Forster's tern	U		C	C
Least tern*	U	C	C	
Bridled tern	r	r	r	
Sooty tern	r	r	r	
Black tern	r	r		
Brown noddy	O	O		
Black skimmer				C

Alcids

	SP	S	F	W
Dovekie				O

Pigeons and Doves

	SP	S	F	W
Rock dove*	C	C	C	C
White-crowned pigeon*	U	C	U	U
White-winged dove*	U	U	U	U
Mourning dove*	C	C	C	C
Common ground dove*	C	C	C	C

Inca dove *(nested 1963–80 in Key West, probably extirpated)*

	SP	S	F	W
Ruddy quail dove	O			
Key West quail dove			O	
(1 captured, Key West)				
Scaly-naped pigeon	O		O	
(2 specimens)				

Cuckoos and Anis

	SP	S	F	W
Black-billed cuckoo	r		r	
Yellow-billed cuckoo*	U	U	U	
Mangrove cuckoo*	U	U	r	r
Smooth-billed ani	r	r	r	r

Owls

	SP	S	F	W
Barn owl			O	O
Screech owl	O			
Burrowing owl*	O		O	O
Barred owl		O		
Long-eared owl			O	
Short-eared owl		O	U	

Goatsuckers

	SP	S	F	W
Common nighthawk*	C	C	C	
Antillean nighthawk*	C	C	C	
Chuck-will's widow	U	U	U	r
Whip-poor-will	r			r

Swifts

	SP	S	F	W
Chimney swift	r		U	
Antillean palm swift	O			

Hummingbirds

	SP	S	F	W
Black-chinned hummingbird	O			
Ruby-throated hummingbird	U	r	U	U

Kingfishers

	SP	S	F	W
Belted kingfisher	C	U	C	C

Woodpeckers

	SP	S	F	W
Red-bellied woodpecker*	C	C	C	C

	SP	S	F	W
Yellow-bellied sapsucker	U		U	U
Northern flicker			O	O

Tyrant Flycatchers

	SP	S	F	W
Olive-sided flycatcher				O
Eastern wood pewee	r	U	U	
Eastern phoebe	r	r	r	r
Great-crested flycatcher*	U	U	U	U
LaSagra's flycatcher		O		
Brown-crested flycatcher	O			O
Loggerhead kingbird	O			
Western kingbird	U		U	U
Eastern kingbird	C	C	C	
Gray kingbird*	C	C	C	C
Scissor-tailed flycatcher	U		U	U

Swallows

	SP	S	F	W
Purple martin	C	C	C	
Cuban martin	O			
Southern martin		O		
Tree swallow	C		C	U
Rough-winged swallow	r		r	r
Bahama swallow	O	O		O
Bank swallow	r		r	r
Cave swallow	O			
Barn swallow	C	C	C	r
Cliff swallow				O

Jays and Crows

	SP	S	F	W
Blue jay	O	O		
American crow	O	O	O	O
Fish crow	r		r	r

Wrens

	SP	S	F	W
Carolina wren			O	
House wren	r		r	r

Old World Warblers & Thrushes

	SP	S	F	W
Ruby-crowned kinglet				O

	SP	S	F	W
Blue-gray gnatcatcher	C	U	C	C
Veery	r	U		
Gray-cheeked thrush	r	r		
Swainson's thrush	r	U		
Hermit thrush				O
Wood thrush	r		r	
American robin	r		r	r

Mockingbirds & Thrashers

	SP	S	F	W
Gray catbird	C		C	C
Northern mockingbird*	C	C	C	C
Bahama mockingbird	O	O	O	
Brown thrasher*	U	U	U	U

Pipits

	SP	S	F	W
American pipit	O			O

Waxwings

	SP	S	F	W
Cedar waxwing	C		C	C

Shrikes

	SP	S	F	W
Loggerhead shrike				O

Starlings

	SP	S	F	W
European starling*	C	C	C	C

Vireos

	SP	S	F	W
White-eyed vireo*	C	C	C	C
Bell's vireo			O	
Solitary vireo	U		r	r
Philadelphia vireo	O		O	
Yellow-throated vireo	U		U	U
Red-eyed vireo	C		C	
Black-whiskered vireo*	C	C	r	

Wood Warblers

	SP	S	F	W
Blue-winged warbler	r		r	r
Golden-winged warbler	O		O	
Tennessee warbler	U		U	r
Orange-crowned warbler	U	r	U	

	SP	S	F	W
Nashville warbler	O		O	
Northern parula warbler	C		C	C
Yellow warbler (Cuban race)*	U	U	U	U
Chestnut-sided warbler	O		O	
Magnolia warbler	U		U	r
Cape May warbler	U		U	U
Black-throated blue warbler	C		C	
Yellow-rumped warbler	C		C	C
Black-throated green warbler	U		C	U
Blackburnian warbler	U		U	
Yellow-throated warbler	C		C	C
Pine warbler	O		O	O
Prairie warbler*	C	C	C	C
Palm warbler	C		C	C
Bay-breasted warbler	O		O	
Blackpoll warbler	C		r	
Cerulean warbler		r	r	
Black-and-white warbler	C		C	C
American redstart	C		C	U
Prothonotary warbler	U		U	
Worm-eating warbler	U		U	r
Swainson's warbler	O		O	O
Ovenbird	C		C	U
Northern waterthrush	C		C	U
Louisiana waterthrush		r		r
Kentucky warbler	U		U	
Connecticut warbler	r		r	
Common yellowthroat	C		C	C
Hooded warbler	U		U	
Wilson's warbler	r		r	
Yellow-breasted chat				O

Tanagers

	SP	S	F	W
Summer tanager	U	U	r	
Scarlet tanager	U		U	

Cardinals and Buntings

	SP	S	F	W
Northern cardinal*	C	C	C	C

	SP	S	F	W
Rose-breasted grosbeak	U		U	
Blue grosbeak	U		U	
Indigo bunting	U		C	r
Painted bunting	U		U	U
Dickcissel	O		O	O

Sparrows

	SP	S	F	W
Rufus-sided rowhee				O
Chipping sparrow			O	O
Clay-colored sparrow			O	O
Vesper sparrow	O			O
Lark sparrow			O	O
Savannah sparrow	U		U	U
Grasshopper sparrow	r		r	r
LeConte's sparrow				O
Sharp-tailed sparrow				O
Swamp sparrow			r	r
White-crowned sparrow				O
Dark-eyed Junco	O			O

Blackbirds and Orioles

	SP	S	F	W
Bobolink	C		C	
Red-winged blackbird*	C	C	C	C
Tawny-shouldered slackbird				O
Yellow-headed blackbird			O	O
Brewer's blackbird			O	
Common grackle*	C	C	r	r
Shiny cowbird	U			
Brown-headed cowbird		O	O	O
Orchard oriole	C		C	
Northern oriole	C		C	U

Finches

	SP	S	F	W
Pine siskin	r		r	r
American goldfinch			C	U

Weavers

	SP	S	F	W
House sparrow*	C	C	C	C

VI. Tide Stations for the Florida Keys Sites (2003)

Tidal Differences and Other Constants

Explanation of Table

Caution—The time and height differences listed in the following table are the average differences derived from comparisons of simultaneous tide observations at the subordinate location and its reference station.

Because these figures are constant, they may not always provide for the daily variations of the actual tide, especially if the subordinate station is some distance from the reference station. Therefore, although the application of the time and height differences will generally provide reasonably accurate approximations, they cannot result in predictions as accurate as those listed for the reference stations which are based upon much larger periods of analysis and which do provide for daily variations.

Time differences—To determine the time of high water or low water at any station listed in this table, there is given in the columns headed "Differences, Time" the hours and minutes to be added to or subtracted from the time of high or low water at some reference station. A plus (+) sign indicates that the tide at the subordinate station is later than at the reference station, and the difference should be added; a minus (–) sign indicates that it is earlier and should be subtracted.

Summer or daylight saving time is not used in the tide tables.

Height differences—The height of the tide, referred to in the datum of charts, is obtained by means of the height differences or ratios. A plus (+) sign indicates that the difference should be added to the height at the reference station, and a minus (–) sign indicates that it should be subtracted. All height differences, ranges, and levels are in feet.

Ratio—For some stations, use of predicted height difference would give unsatisfactory predictions. In such cases they have been omitted and one or two ratios are given (*). Where two ratios are given, one in the "height of high water" column and one in the "height of low water" column, the high waters and low waters at the reference station should be multiplied by these respective ratios. Where only one is given, the omitted ratio is either unreliable or unknown.

For some subordinate stations there is given in parentheses a ratio as well as a correction in feet.

In those instances, each predicted high and low water at the reference station should first be multiplied by the ratio, and then the correction in feet added to or subtracted from each product as indicated.

Range—The *mean range* is the difference in height between mean high water (MHW) and mean low water (MLW). The *spring range* is the average semidiurnal range occurring semimonthly as a result of the moon being new or full. It is larger than the mean range where the type of tide is either semidiurnal or mixed, and is of no practical significance where the type of tide is diurnal. Where the tide is chiefly of the diurnal type, the table gives the *diurnal range,* which is the difference in height between mean higher high water and mean lower low water.

Datum—The datum of the predictions obtained through the height differences or ratios is also the datum of the largest-scale chart for the locality. To obtain the depth at the time of high or low water, the predicted height should be added to the depth on the chart unless such height is negative (−), when it should be subtracted. For the area covered by these tables the datums generally used are approximately *mean low water springs, Indian spring low water,* or the *lowest possible low water.*

Mean Tide Level (Half-Tide Level)—The mean tide level is a plane midway between mean low water and mean high water. Tabular values are reckoned from chart depth.

Observations Supporting Predictions—All tidal predictions made by the National Ocean Service are based upon observations taken at the location in question. For most reference stations these observations often are of a continuing nature. As such, they are used to quality-control the predictions and to update the harmonic constants used in generating annual predictions. For subordinate stations, the age and duration of their observations vary from a few days of observation taken decades ago to the most recent survey data.

Tidal Differences and Other Constants that are reported to the nearest tenth minute but whose ranges and mean tide level are reported to the nearest tenth foot are typically supported by observations taken in the 1960s and 1970s with analysis based upon the 1941–59 National Tidal Datum Epoch. Finally, stations whose positions are reported to the nearest minute and whose ranges and mean tide level are reported to the nearest tenth foot indicated either older supporting observations or simply data not yet reviewed and entered into the tables with full published precision. NOS is in the continuous process of updating the tables with all available data. Old observations are not, in and of themselves, an indication of poor present predictions. Certain coastal areas do not undergo much human or natural modification while other coastal areas are subject to nearly constant modification by both agents. Local knowledge of conditions is still very important to the wise use of these astronomical predictions.

Note—Dashes are entered in the place of data that are unknown, unreliable, or not applicable.

No.	PLACE	POSITION Latitude North	POSITION Longitude West	DIFFERENCES Time High Water h m	DIFFERENCES Time Low Water h m	DIFFERENCES Height High Water ft	DIFFERENCES Height Low Water ft	RANGES Mean ft	RANGES Spring ft	Mean Tide Level ft
				on Miami Harbor						
3891	Bear Cut, Virginia Key	25° 43.9'	80° 09.7'	+0 49	+0 52	*0.82	*0.82	2.05	2.46	1.16
3893	Key Biscayne Yacht Club, Biscayne Bay	25° 41.9'	80° 10.2'	+1 07	+1 35	*0.80	*0.81	2.00	2.40	1.13
3895	Coral Shoal, Biscayne Channel	25° 39.1'	80° 09.4'	+0 34	+0 41	*0.82	*0.81	2.05	2.46	1.15
3897	Cutler, Biscayne Bay	25° 37.0'	80° 18.3'	+1 23	+2 00	*0.79	*0.88	1.98	2.38	1.13
3899	Soldier Key	25° 35'	80° 10'	+0 53	+1 20	*0.74	*0.75	1.9	2.3	1.0
3901	Fowey Rocks	25° 35'	80° 06'	+0 01	+0 03	*0.97	*0.94	2.4	2.9	1.4
3903	Ragged Keys, Biscayne Bay	25° 32.0'	80° 10.3'	+1 07	+1 25	*0.66	*0.66	1.65	1.90	0.95
3905	Boca Chita Key, Biscayne Bay	25° 31.4'	80° 10.6'	+1 24	+1 43	*0.63	*0.63	1.57	1.88	0.94
3907	Sands Key, northwest point, Biscayne Bay	25° 30.3'	80° 11.3'	+1 48	+2 30	*0.58	*0.56	1.46	1.64	0.82
3909	Coon Point, Elliott Key, Biscayne Bay	25° 28.7'	80° 11.4'	+2 18	+3 00	*0.57	*0.57	1.44	1.63	0.82
3911	Elliott Key Harbor, Elliott Key, Biscayne Bay	25° 27.2'	80° 11.8'	+2 19	+3 04	*0.59	*0.59	1.48	1.67	0.83
3913	Turkey Point, Biscayne Bay	25° 26.2'	80° 19.7'	+2 33	+3 25	*0.65	*0.65	1.64	1.85	0.94
3915	Billys Point, south of Elliott Key, Biscayne Bay	25° 24.9'	80° 12.6'	+2 31	+3 24	*0.58	*0.56	1.46	1.65	0.82
3917	Sea Grape Point, Elliott Key	25° 28.6'	80° 10.8'	-0 02	-0 01	*0.92	*0.92	2.30	2.74	1.39
3919	Christmas Point, Elliott Key	25° 23.5'	80° 13.8'	+0 36	+0 41	*0.73	*0.73	1.82	2.13	1.06
3921	Adams Key, south end, Biscayne Bay	25° 23.8'	80° 14.0'	+1 24	+1 12	*0.61	*0.61	1.52	1.75	0.90
3923	Totten Key, west side, Biscayne Bay	25° 22.7'	80° 15.4'	+2 42	+3 25	*0.50	*0.50	1.26	1.41	0.71
3925	East Arsenicker, Card Sound	25° 22.4'	80° 17.5'	+2 49	+3 13	*0.36	*0.36	0.91	1.04	0.54
3927	Card Sound, western side	25° 20.7'	80° 19.9'	+3 14	+3 44	*0.27	*0.27	0.68	0.77	0.40
3929	Pumpkin Key, south end, Card Sound	25° 19.5'	80° 17.6'	+2 58	+2 56	*0.25	*0.25	0.63	0.71	0.43
3931	Wednesday Point, Key Largo, Card Sound	25° 18.6'	80° 17.9'	+3 01	+3 34	*0.31	*0.31	0.77	0.88	0.46
3933	Cormorant Point, Key Largo, Card Sound	25° 17.4'	80° 20.3'	+3 08	+3 05	*0.29	*0.29	0.73	0.82	0.43
3935	Little Card Sound bridge	25° 17.2'	80° 22.2'	+3 51	+4 16	*0.21	*0.21	0.53	0.59	0.32
3937	Ocean Reef Harbor, Key Largo	25° 18.6'	80° 16.8'	+0 13	+0 18	*0.93	*0.93	2.33	2.84	1.37
3939	Main Key, Barnes Sound	25° 14.4'	80° 24.0'	+5 27	+6 20	*0.16	*0.16	0.41	0.46	0.26
3941	Manatee Creek, Manatee Bay, Barnes Sound	25° 14.1'	80° 25.8'	+5 37	+6 24	*0.16	*0.16	0.39	0.44	0.25
3943	Manatee Creek, Hwy. 1 bridge, Long Sound <26>	25° 14.1'	80° 26.1'	—	—	—	—	—	—	—
3945	Carysfort Reef	25° 13.3'	80° 12.7'	+0 42	+0 43	*0.93	*0.93	2.34	2.60	1.36
3947	Jewfish Creek entrance, Blackwater Sound <26>	25° 11.0'	80° 23.2'	—	—	—	—	—	—	—
3949	Deep Six Marina, Blackwater Sound <26>	25° 08.4'	80° 24.2'	—	—	—	—	—	—	—
3951	Garden Cove, Key Largo	25° 10.3'	80° 22.0'	+0 22	+0 29	*0.86	*0.86	2.16	2.53	1.24
3953	Largo Sound, Key Largo	25° 08.4'	80° 23.7'	+2 36	+3 07	*0.32	*0.32	0.80	0.96	0.47
3955	Key Largo, South Sound, Key Largo	25° 06.8'	80° 25.0'	+0 46	+1 53	*0.61	*0.56	1.55	1.86	0.85
3957	Point Charles, Key Largo	25° 04.5'	80° 26.6'	+0 33	+0 41	*0.84	*0.84	2.10	2.52	1.23
3959	Rock Harbor, Key Largo	25° 04.9'	80° 26.7'	+0 43	+0 40	*0.85	*0.85	2.14	2.57	1.24
3961	Rock Harbor, Key Largo	25° 04.9'	80° 26.8'	+0 45	+0 31	*0.85	*0.88	2.2	2.6	1.2
3963	Mosquito Bank	25° 01'	80° 24'	+0 22	+0 31	*0.88	*0.88	2.2	2.6	1.2
3965	Molasses Reef	25° 05.7'	80° 23'	+0 14	+0 12	*0.88	*0.88	2.2	2.6	1.2
3967	Sunset Cove, Key Largo, Buttonwood Sound <26>	25° 02.1'	80° 30.3'	—	—	—	—	—	—	—
3969	Hammer Point, Key Largo, Florida Bay <26>	25° 00.9'	80° 30.6'	—	—	—	—	—	—	—
3971	Tavernier, Key Largo, Florida Bay <26>	25° 00.9'	80° 30.9'	—	—	—	—	—	—	—
3973	Tavernier Harbor, Hawk Channel	25° 00.2'	80° 31.0'	+0 31	+0 29	*0.83	*0.83	2.09	2.55	1.23
3975	Tavernier Creek, Hwy. 1 bridge, Hawk Channel	25° 00.2'	80° 31.8'	+0 48	+0 56	*0.53	*0.53	1.32	1.58	0.81
3977	Plantation Key, northern end, Florida Bay <26>	25° 00.1'	80° 32.6'	—	—	—	—	—	—	—

No.	PLACE	POSITION		DIFFERENCES				RANGES		Mean Tide Level
		Latitude North	Longitude West	Time High Water	Low Water	Height High Water	Low Water	Mean	Spring	
				on Miami Harbor						
				h m	h m	ft	ft	ft	ft	ft
3979	Crane Keys, north side, Florida Bay	25° 00.3'	80° 37.1'	+3 19	+4 40	*0.16	*0.16	0.40	0.48	0.24
3981	East Key, southern end, Florida Bay	24° 59.8'	80° 36.6'	+3 06	+4 10	*0.21	*0.21	0.52	0.62	0.28
3983	Plantation Key, Hawk Channel	24° 58.4'	80° 33.0'	+0 28	+0 16	*0.88	*0.88	2.20	2.64	1.27
3985	Yacht Harbor, Cowpens Anchorage, Plantation Key	24° 57.9'	80° 34.1'	+3 08	+4 04	*0.21	*0.21	0.53	0.64	0.31
3987	Snake Creek, Hwy. 1 bridge, Windley Key	24° 57.1'	80° 35.3'	+1 12	+1 00	*0.43	*0.43	1.07	1.28	0.61
3989	Snake Creek, USCG Station, Plantation Key	24° 57.2'	80° 35.2'	+1 31	+2 00	*0.33	*0.33	0.82	0.98	0.48
3991	Whale Harbor, Windley Key, Hawk Channel	24° 56.4'	80° 36.5'	+0 30	+0 55	*0.62	*0.62	1.56	1.87	0.83
3993	Whale Harbor Channel, Hwy. 1 bridge, Windley Key	24° 56.3'	80° 36.6'	+0 39	+1 04	*0.54	*0.54	1.36	1.63	0.78
3995	Upper Matecumbe Key, Hawk Channel	24° 54.9'	80° 37.9'	+0 57	+0 53	*0.79	*0.79	1.98	2.38	1.16
3997	Alligator Reef, Hawk Channel	24° 51.0'	80° 37.1'	+0 31	+0 28	*0.77	*0.77	1.93	2.37	1.15
3999	Flamingo, Florida Bay	25° 08.5'	80° 55.4'	+5 28	+7 20	*1.47	*1.08	2.02	2.52	1.27
4001	Upper Matecumbe Key, west end, Hawk Channel	24° 53.8'	80° 39.5'	-1 00	+0 14	*0.98	*0.33	1.44	1.80	0.80
4003	Indian Key, Hawk Channel	24° 52.6'	80° 40.6'	-0 58	-0 35	*1.30	*0.71	1.84	2.30	1.09
4005	Shell Key Channel, Florida Bay	24° 54.8'	80° 39.6'	-0 20	+0 45	*0.78	*0.78	1.02	1.28	0.58
4007	Lignumvitae Key, NE side, Florida Bay	24° 54.2'	80° 41.7'	+0 09	+1 31	*0.52	*0.52	0.68	0.85	0.37
4009	Lignumvitae Key, west side, Florida Bay	24° 54.0'	80° 42.3'	+0 32	+1 54	*0.47	*0.47	0.62	0.74	0.35
4011	Little Basin, Upper Matecumbe Key, Florida Bay	24° 55.4'	80° 38.4'	+0 08	+1 15	*0.61	*0.61	0.80	1.00	0.40
4013	Shell Key, northwest side, Lignumvitae Basin	24° 55.4'	80° 40.3'	+0 31	+1 57	*0.46	*0.46	0.60	0.75	0.33
4015	Islamorada, Upper Matecumbe Key, Florida Bay	24° 55.5'	80° 37.9'	+0 39	+2 07	*0.37	*0.37	0.49	0.57	0.30
4017	Indian Key Anchorage, Lower Matecumbe Key	24° 52.1'	80° 42.2'	-1 27	-0 55	*1.40	*0.96	1.94	2.39	1.20
4019	Matecumbe Bight, Lower Matecumbe Key, Fla. Bay	24° 51.9'	80° 43.0'	-0 15	+0 35	*0.55	*0.38	0.77	0.96	0.48
4021	Matecumbe Harbor, Lower Matecumbe Key, Fla. Bay	24° 51.1'	80° 44.4'	-0 25	+0 23	*0.59	*0.33	0.83	1.04	0.50
4023	Channel Two, east, Lower Matecumbe Key, Fla. Bay	24° 50.7'	80° 44.9'	-0 49	-0 42	*0.85	*0.54	1.18	1.48	0.72
4025	Channel Two, west side, Hawk Channel	24° 50.5'	80° 45.2'	-1 06	-0 54	*1.12	*0.75	1.55	1.94	0.96
4027	Channel Five, east side, Hawk Channel	24° 50.2'	80° 46.0'	-0 54	-0 42	*0.90	*0.58	1.25	1.56	0.77
4029	Channel Five, west side, Hawk Channel	24° 50.4'	80° 46.8'	-0 58	-0 41	*1.00	*0.67	1.39	1.74	0.85
4031	Jewish Hole, Long Key, Florida Bay	24° 50.3'	80° 47.9'	-0 11	+1 32	*0.42	*0.38	0.56	0.70	0.37
4033	Long Key Bight, Long Key	24° 49.7'	80° 48.5'	-0 59	-0 43	*1.03	*0.62	1.44	1.80	0.87
4035	Long Key Lake, Long Key	24° 49.2'	80° 49.0'	+0 33	+0 57	*0.62	*0.46	0.85	1.06	0.53
4037	Long Key, western end	24° 48.1'	80° 51.0'	-1 01	-0 54	*0.82	*0.33	1.18	1.49	0.67
4039	Conch Key, eastern end	24° 47.5'	80° 53.0'	-1 09	-0 45	*0.85	*0.54	1.18	1.48	0.72
4041	Toms Harbor Cut	24° 47.0'	80° 54.4'	-1 19	-0 30	*0.37	*0.38	0.48	0.60	0.33
4043	Toms Harbor, Duck Key <26>	24° 46.4'	80° 54.9'	—	—	—	—	—	—	—
4045	Duck Key, Hawk Channel	24° 46.0'	80° 54.8'	-1 11	-0 40	*0.96	*0.50	1.37	1.70	0.81
4047	Toms Harbor Channel, Hwy. 1 bridge	24° 46.6'	80° 55.4'	+5 07	+4 49	*0.38	*0.38	0.50	0.62	0.45
4049	Grassy Key, north side, Florida Bay	24° 46.4'	80° 56.5'	+5 41	+6 49	*0.66	*0.66	0.87	1.00	0.70
4051	Grassy Key, south side, Hawk Channel	24° 45.3'	80° 57.5'	-0 52	-0 26	*1.22	*0.71	1.72	2.15	1.03
4053	Fat Deer Key, Florida Bay	24° 44.0'	81° 01.8'	+5 09	+6 26	*0.87	*0.87	1.14	1.42	0.82
4055	Vaca Key—Fat Deer Key bridge	24° 43.8'	81° 01.8'	-1 11	-0 36	*0.95	*0.71	1.31	1.64	0.83
4057	Key Colony Beach	24° 43.1'	81° 01.1'	-1 17	-0 53	*1.22	*0.83	1.69	2.10	1.05
4059	VACA KEY, USCG STATION, FLORIDA BAY	24° 42.6'	81° 06.4'	—	—	—	—	0.75	0.86	0.52
4061	Boot Key Harbor bridge, Boot Key	24° 42.2'	81° 06.3'	-1 03	-0 37	*1.13	*0.75	1.57	1.96	0.96
4063	Sombrero Key, Hawk Channel	24° 37.6'	81° 06.7'	-1 03	-0 39	*1.18	*0.79	1.64	2.02	1.01

No.	Place	Latitude	Longitude							
4065	Knight Key Channel, Knight Key, Florida Bay	24° 42.4'	81° 07.5'	-0 02	-0 18	*0.54	*0.50	0.72	0.90	0.48
4067	Pigeon Key, south side, Hawk Channel	24° 42.2'	81° 09.3'	-0 55	-0 26	*0.81	*0.50	1.14	1.42	0.69
4069	Pigeon Key, north side, Florida Bay	24° 42.3'	81° 09.4'	-0 10	+0 45	*0.46	*0.46	0.60	0.75	0.44
4071	Molasses Key Channel, Molasses Keys	24° 41.0'	81° 11.5'	-0 56	-0 16	*0.79	*0.50	1.10	1.38	0.67
4073	Money Key	24° 41.0'	81° 12.9'	+0 03	+1 17	*0.58	*0.67	0.76	0.95	0.54
4075	Little Duck Key, east end, Hawk Channel	24° 40.9'	81° 13.7'	-0 49	+0 05	*0.67	*0.69	0.88	1.10	0.60
4077	East Bahia Honda Key, south end, Florida Bay	24° 46.5'	81° 13.6'	+4 04	+2 49	*0.69	*0.55	0.90	1.12	0.77
4079	Cocoanut Key, Florida Bay	24° 44.7'	81° 14.2'	+3 52	+2 50	*0.55	*1.00	0.72	0.90	0.66
4081	West Bahia Honda Key	24° 46.8'	81° 16.3'	+3 59	+4 01	*0.97	*1.00	1.27	1.59	0.88
4083	Horseshoe Keys, south end	24° 46.0'	81° 17.0'	+3 54	+3 54	*0.86	*0.96	1.09	1.36	0.79
4085	Johnson Keys, south end	24° 44.6'	81° 18.0'	+3 36	+2 33	*0.72	*1.38	0.88	1.10	0.67
4087	Johnson Keys, north end	24° 46.0'	81° 19.4'	+3 35	+4 22	*1.31	*0.46	1.70	2.12	1.18
4089	Missouri Key–Little Duck Key Channel	24° 40.8'	81° 14.1'	-0 52	-0 36	*0.70	*0.50	1.08	1.22	0.60
4091	Missouri Key–Ohio Key Channel, west side	24° 40.4'	81° 14.6'	-0 22	-0 22	*0.77	*0.62	1.08	1.35	0.66
4093	Ohio Key–Bahia Honda Key Channel, west side	24° 39.3'	81° 15.1'	-0 57	-0 14	*0.81	*0.42	1.10	1.38	0.70
4095	Bahia Honda Key, Bahia Honda Channel	24° 40.2'	81° 16.9'	-0 45	-0 27	*0.86	*0.71	1.19	1.49	0.74
4097	Big Pine Key, Spanish Harbor	24° 38.9'	81° 19.8'	-0 44	-0 03	*0.75	*0.83	1.07	1.34	0.64
4099	Big Pine Key, Doctors Arm, Bogie Channel	24° 41.4'	81° 21.4'	+0 41	+1 47	*0.63	*0.83	0.80	1.00	0.57
4101	Big Pine Key, Bogie Channel Bridge	24° 41.9'	81° 20.9'	+2 10	+2 11	*0.65	*0.79	0.80	1.00	0.60
4103	No Name Key, east side, Bahia Honda Channel	24° 41.9'	81° 19.1'	+1 35	+1 33	*0.58	*1.00	0.70	0.88	0.60
4105	Little Pine Key, south end	24° 42.8'	81° 18.2'	+1 07	+1 07	*0.56	*1.04	0.68	0.85	0.55
4107	Porpoise Key, Big Spanish Channel	24° 43.1'	81° 21.1'	+3 23	+2 29	*0.72	*1.08	0.88	1.10	0.53
4109	Water Key, west end, Big Spanish Channel	24° 44.4'	81° 20.5'	+3 35	+2 37	*0.81	*1.21	1.00	1.00	0.68
4111	Mayo Key, Big Spanish Channel	24° 44.0'	81° 21.7'	+3 38	+3 01	*0.92	*1.08	1.17	1.25	0.75
4113	Little Pine Key, north end	24° 45.0'	81° 19.7'	+3 01	+3 28	*1.05	*1.08	1.33	1.46	0.85
4115	Big Pine Key, northeast shore	24° 43.7'	81° 23.2'	+3 19	+2 30	*0.86	*1.33	1.08	1.35	0.96
4117	Crawl Key, Big Spanish Channel	24° 45.4'	81° 21.5'	+3 34	+4 13	*1.33	*0.83	1.08	1.35	0.80
4119	Big Pine Key, north end, Big Spanish Channel	24° 44.7'	81° 23.4'	+4 24	+5 56	*0.96	*1.29	1.74	2.18	1.19
4121	Annette Key, north end, Big Spanish Channel	24° 45.5'	81° 22.2'	+3 30	+4 33	*1.44	*1.62	1.29	1.61	0.85
4123	Little Spanish Key, Spanish Banks	24° 46.5'	81° 24.7'	+3 25	+4 30	*1.74	*1.50	1.92	2.40	1.27
4125	Big Spanish Key	24° 47.3'	81° 24.2'	+3 19	+4 29	*1.97	*1.62	2.30	2.88	1.54
4127	Munson Island, Newfound Harbor Channel	24° 37.4'	81° 24.1'	-0 40	-0 12	*0.98	*0.67	2.69	3.36	1.71
4129	Ramrod Key, Newfound Harbor	24° 39.0'	81° 23.7'	-0 41	-0 05	*0.90	*0.50	1.36	1.70	0.84
4131	Middle Torch Key, Torch Ramrod Channel	24° 39.7'	81° 22.5'	-0 16	+1 29	*0.69	*0.38	1.28	1.60	0.76
4133	Little Torch Key, Torch Channel	24° 39.9'	81° 21.0'	+0 11	+1 45	*0.57	*0.46	0.98	1.22	0.58
4135	Big Pine Key, Newfound Harbor Channel	24° 39.1'	81° 23.3'	-0 09	+0 44	*0.82	*0.54	0.80	1.00	0.48
4137	Big Pine Key, Coupon Bight	24° 39.9'	81° 23.2'	-0 20	+0 49	*0.87	*0.33	1.16	1.45	0.69
4139	Little Torch Key, Pine Channel Bridge, south side	24° 39.1'	81° 22.3'	-0 15	+0 57	*0.68	*0.38	1.22	1.52	0.74
4141	Little Torch Key, Pine Channel Bridge, south side	24° 39.9'	81° 22.1'	-0 13	+0 54	*0.69	*0.33	0.97	1.21	0.56
4143	Big Pine Key, Pine Channel Bridge, south side	24° 40.1'	81° 23.0'	-0 10	+1 03	*0.67	*0.42	0.98	1.22	0.58
4145	Big Pine Key, Pine Channel Bridge, north side	24° 40.2'	81° 23.0'	+0 03	+1 44	*0.57	*0.62	0.96	1.20	0.56
4147	Big Pine Key, west side, Pine Channel	24° 41.4'	81° 24.4'	+0 21	+1 52	*0.52	*1.29	0.81	1.01	0.49
4149	Howe Key, south end, Harbor Channel	24° 43.5'	81° 26.6'	+4 43	+4 49	*0.72	*1.33	0.71	0.89	0.45
4151	Big Torch Key, Harbor Channel	24° 44.3'	81° 27.0'	+3 47	+5 51	*1.58	*0.71	0.96	1.20	0.63
4153	Water Keys, south end, Harbor Channel	24° 44.8'	81° 25.7'	+3 42	+5 41	*1.52	*0.58	2.14	2.68	1.38
4155	Howe Key, northwest end	24° 45.5'	81° 26.1'	+3 29	+5 22	*1.68	*0.46	2.11	2.64	1.29
4157	Summerland Key, Niles Channel South	24° 39.1'	81° 26.2'	-0 36	+0 11	*0.71	*0.71	2.28	2.85	1.46
4159	Summerland Key, Niles Channel Bridge	24° 39.6'	81° 25.4'	-0 10	+0 56	*0.85	*1.21	1.14	1.42	0.74
4161	Ramrod Key, Niles Channel Bridge	24° 39.6'	81° 26.0'	-0 13	+1 12	*0.67	*1.21	0.90	1.12	0.59
4163	Big Torch Key, Niles Channel	24° 42.3'	81° 28.7'	+3 15	+2 05	*0.61	*1.83	0.77	0.96	0.58
4165	Knockemdown Key, north end	24° 42.9'	81° 26.0'	+3 30	+4 54	*1.35	*0.75	1.80	2.25	0.56
4167	Raccoon Key, east side	24° 44.5'	81° 29.0'	+3 20	+5 09	*1.50		2.04	2.55	1.31
4169	Content Keys, Content Passage	24° 47.4'	81° 29.0'	+2 47	+3 50	*2.13		2.86	3.58	1.87
4171	Key Lois, southeast end	24° 36.4'	81° 28.2'	-1 15	-0 45	*1.06		1.46	1.82	0.91

No.	PLACE	POSITION Latitude North	POSITION Longitude West	DIFFERENCES Time High Water (h m)	DIFFERENCES Time Low Water (h m)	DIFFERENCES Height High Water (ft)	DIFFERENCES Height Low Water (ft)	RANGES Mean (ft)	RANGES Spring (ft)	Mean Tide Level (ft)
	Florida Keys—cont. Time meridian, 75° W			**on Key West**						
4173	Sugarloaf Key, east side, Tarpon Creek	24° 37.7'	81° 30.6'	−0 41	+0 15	*0.89	*0.58	1.24	1.55	0.76
4175	Gopher Key, Cudjoe Bay	24° 38.5'	81° 29.1'	−0 46	+0 17	*0.90	*0.71	1.22	1.52	0.78
4177	Sugarloaf Key, Pirates Cove	24° 39.2'	81° 30.9'	−0 48	+1 41	*0.59	*0.75	0.74	0.92	0.55
4179	Cudjoe Key, Cudjoe Bay	24° 39.6'	81° 29.5'	−0 38	+0 41	*0.87	*0.71	1.18	1.48	0.76
4181	Summerland Key, southwest side, Kemp Channel	24° 39.0'	81° 26.8'	−0 26	+0 50	*0.81	*0.54	1.12	1.40	0.69
4183	Cudjoe Key, Kemp Channel Bridge	24° 39.7'	81° 28.1'	— —	— —	*0.59	*0.50	0.79	0.99	0.52
4185	Cudjoe Key, northeast side, Kemp Channel	24° 41.2'	81° 29.0'	+3 45	+4 40	*1.63	*1.46	2.17	2.71	1.43
4187	Cudjoe Key, north end, Kemp Channel	24° 42.0'	81° 30.6'	+3 32	+3 24	*1.01	*0.71	1.40	1.75	0.87
4189	Sugarloaf Key, northeast side, Bow Channel	24° 40.3'	81° 32.0'	+3 47	+2 55	*0.77	*0.71	1.01	1.26	0.69
4191	Cudjoe Key, Pirates Cove	24° 39.8'	81° 30.8'	+3 50	+5 20	*1.29	*0.79	1.82	2.28	1.09
4193	Sugarloaf Key, north end, Bow Channel	24° 41.6'	81° 33.3'	+3 37	+4 39	*1.56	*1.17	2.14	2.68	1.35
4195	Pumpkin Key, Bow Channel	24° 43.0'	81° 33.7'	+3 17	+5 24	*1.57	*0.50	2.32	2.90	1.28
4197	Sawyer Key, outside, Cudjoe Channel	24° 45.5'	81° 33.7'	+2 45	+5 19	*1.43	*0.50	2.10	2.62	1.17
4199	Sawyer Key, inside, Cudjoe Channel	24° 45.5'	81° 33.7'	+2 37	+5 19	*1.43	*0.50	2.10	2.62	1.17
4201	Johnston Key, southwest end, Turkey Basin	24° 42.6'	81° 35.6'	+3 26	+5 38	*1.10	*0.38	1.59	1.99	0.92
	Upper Sugarloaf Sound									
4203	Perky	24° 38.9'	81° 34.2'	+5 37	+8 25	*0.28	*0.08	0.42	0.52	0.23
4205	Park Channel Bridge	24° 39.3'	81° 32.4'	+5 47	+8 33	*0.26	*0.29	0.34	0.42	0.24
4207	North Harris Channel	24° 39.0'	81° 33.2'	+5 32	+8 04	*0.25	*0.25	0.33	0.41	0.22
4209	Sugarloaf Shores East <26>	24° 38.6'	81° 33.6'	— —	— —	—	—	—	—	—
4211	Tarpon Creek	24° 37.8'	81° 31.0'	−0 29	+0 17	*0.35	*0.38	0.46	0.58	0.32
	Lower Sugarloaf Sound <27>									
4213	Sugarloaf Shores <27>	24° 38.0'	81° 33.1'	— —	— —	—	—	—	—	—
4215	Sugarloaf Beach <27>	24° 36.4'	81° 34.0'	— —	— —	—	—	—	—	—
4217	Sugarloaf Shores North <27>	24° 38.4'	81° 34.9'	— —	— —	—	—	—	—	—
4219	Saddlebunch Keys, south end <27>	24° 36.1'	81° 35.2'	— —	— —	—	—	—	—	—
4221	Lower Sugarloaf Channel Bridge <27>	24° 36.1'	81° 35.9'	— —	— —	—	—	—	—	—
4223	Saddlebunch Keys, Channel No. 2 <27>	24° 36.9'	81° 36.1'	— —	— —	—	—	—	—	—
4225	Saddlebunch Keys <27>	24° 37.1'	81° 36.1'	— —	— —	—	—	—	—	—
4227	Snipe Keys, southeast end, Inner Narrows	24° 39.5'	81° 36.5'	+3 25	+5 39	*1.28	*0.83	1.79	2.24	1.10
4229	Snipe Keys, Middle Narrows	24° 40.0'	81° 37.8'	+3 44	+5 54	*1.02	*0.67	1.42	1.78	0.87
4231	Snipe Keys, Snipe Point	24° 41.5'	81° 40.4'	+2 15	+3 33	*1.69	*1.29	2.31	2.89	1.47
4233	Waltz Key, Waltz Key Basin	24° 38.8'	81° 39.2'	+3 53	+4 57	*1.03	*0.96	1.36	1.70	0.91
4235	Duck Key Point, Duck Key, Waltz Key Basin	24° 37.4'	81° 41.1'	+3 27	+5 39	*1.19	*0.96	1.61	2.01	1.03
4237	O'Hara Key, north end, Waltz Key Basin	24° 37.0'	81° 37.5'	+3 53	+5 39	*1.03	*0.83	1.40	1.75	0.90
4239	Saddlebunch Keys, Channel No. 5	24° 36.7'	81° 37.0'	+4 32	+6 58	*0.66	*1.12	0.76	0.95	0.65
4241	Saddlebunch Keys, Channel No. 4	24° 36.9'	81° 36.2'	+4 35	+5 36	*0.54	*0.29	0.76	0.95	0.45
4243	Saddlebunch Keys, Channel No. 3	24° 37.4'	81° 38.3'	+1 44	−0 10	*0.43	*0.21	0.62	0.78	0.36
4245	Bird Key, Similar Sound	24° 35.3'	81° 38.7'	−0 21	+1 03	*0.59	*0.42	0.82	1.02	0.51
4247	Shark Key, southeast end, Similar Sound	24° 36.2'	81° 37.3'	+0 18	+1 51	*0.52	*0.46	0.70	0.88	0.46
4249	Saddlebunch Keys, Similar Sound	24° 36.0'	81° 39.3'	+0 39	+2 41	*0.37	*0.21	0.52	0.65	0.31
4251	Geiger Key, inside <26>	24° 35.0'	81° 39.3'	+4 21	+6 54	*0.84	*0.33	1.22	1.52	0.69
4253	Big Coppitt Key, northeast side, Waltz Key Basin	24° 36.1'	81° 40.1'	+5 02	+6 06	*0.76	*0.88	0.97	1.21	0.69
4255	Rockland Key, Rockland Channel Bridge	24° 35.5'	81° 41.9'	+3 54	+5 22	*0.94	*0.71	1.28	1.60	0.81
4257	Boca Chica Key, Long Point	24° 36.2'	81° 43.5'	+3 09	+3 07	*0.70	*0.67	0.91	1.14	0.62
4259	Channel Key, west side	24° 34.6'	81° 43.2'	+1 23	+1 29	*0.57	*0.79	0.72	0.90	0.52
4261	Boca Chica Channel Bridge	24° 34.8'	81° 44.3'	+2 25	+2 57	*0.73	*0.88	0.94	1.18	0.66
4263	Key Haven – Stock Island Channel	24° 35.1'	81° 46.5'	+1 59	+2 06	*0.81	*0.79	1.04	1.30	0.73
4265	Sigsbee Park, Garrison Bight Channel	24° 35.1'	81° 47.0'	−0 52		*1.07	*0.92	1.44	1.80	0.94
4267	KEY WEST, south side, Hawk Channel	24° 32.7'	81° 48.5'	*0.94		*0.94		1.31	1.64	0.90
4269	**KEY WEST**	24° 33.2'	81° 48.5'	*Daily predictions*						
4271	Sand Key Lighthouse, Sand Key Channel	24° 27.2'	81° 52.6'	−1 03	−0 39	*0.94	*0.79	1.26	1.58	0.82
4273	Garden Key, Dry Tortugas	24° 37.6'	82° 52.3'	+0 29	+0 33	*0.94	*1.33	1.14	1.42	0.89

Index

Orange lumpy encrusting sponge (*Ulosa ruetzleri*), 83–84
Orthinological Biography (Audubon), 58
Osprey (*Pandion haliaetus*), 59
Overseas Highway, mile markers, 12

P

Paddling techniques, 20–21
Painted tunicate (*Clavelina picta*), 101
Pale anemone (*Aiptassia pallida*), 88
Palm warbler (*Dendroica palmarum*), 72
Paradise Paddlers Club, 128
Parrotfish, 85
Pea crab (*Dissodactlyus*), 96
Pearl fish, 100
Pelican Key, 143
Peregrine falcons (*Falco peregrinus*), 60
Perky Creek trip
    launch site, 116, 151
    overview, 151–152
    suggested route, 152
Permit fish (*Trachinotus falcatus*), 47, 48
Peterson cleaner shrimp (*Periclemenes yucatansis*), 87
Petticoat algae (*Padina* species), 104
Pigeon Key, 203, 221
Pilchard, 43
Pine Point, 214
Pinfish (*Lagodon rhomboids*), 46
Pink mangrove sponge (*Acervochalina molitba*), 84
Pink shrimp (*Penaeus* species), 96–97
Pink-tipped anemone (*Condylactis gigantea*), 87
Piper Tripacer, 196
Portuguese man-o'-war (*Physalia physalia*), 84
Prairie warbler (*Dendroica discolor*), 72
Prickly pear cactus (*Opuntia* species), 34
Public Ramp Mile Marker 5.3, launch site, 113
Purple bleeding sponge (*Iotrochota birotula*), 82

Q

Queen conch (*Strombus gigus*), 90

R

Racer snake (*Coluber constrictor*), 55
Radabob Key, 207
Ramroad Key Swimming Hole, launch site, 119
Ramrod Key, 163–164
Rattlesnake Key, 207
Red coralline algae (*Goniolithon* stricta), 105
Red mangrove (*Rhizophora mangle*), 30–32, 171
Red rat snake (*Elphae guttata*), 55
Redbeard algae (*Gracilaria tikvahiae*), 104
Red-bellied woodpecker (*Melanerpes carolinus*), 70–71
Red-breasted merganser (*Mergus serrator*), 62
Reddish egret (*Egretta rufescens*), 64
Redfish (*Sciaenops ocellatus*), 48–49
Red-shouldered hawk (*Buteo lineatus*), 60
Red-winged blackbird (*Agelaius phoeniceus*), 72
Remora, 37
Ribbon snake (*Thamnophis sauritus*), 55
Riding Key, 218, 219
Rimrock crowned snake (*Tantilla oolitica*), 56
Ringed anemone (*Bartholemea annulata*), 88
Ringneck snake (*Diadophis punctatus*), 56
Riviera Canal, launch site, 112, 135
Rock dove (*Columba livia*), 69
Rock-boring urchin (*Echinometra lucunter*), 99
Rose coral (*Manicina areolata*), 86
Roseate spoonbill (*Ajaia ajaia*), 66
Round Key, 140, 146
Royal tern (*Sterna maxima*), 68
Ruddy turnstone (*Arenaria interpres*), 68

S

Saddlebunch #3, launch site, 115, 144
Saddlebunch #5, launch site, 115
Saddlehill Key, 143
Sailfin molly (*Poecilia latipinna*), 42
Salt Creek Run trip
    launch sites, 112–113, 135
    overview, 135
    suggested route, 135–137
Salt Ponds, 135, 136
Saltwort (*Batis maritime*), 33